JOHN HAGGAI

LEAD ON !

Leadership That Endures

in a Changing World

WORD PUBLISHING

Word (UK) Ltd
Milton Keynes, England

WORD BOOKS AUSTRALIA
Heathmont, Victoria, Australia
SUNDAY SCHOOL CENTRE WHOLESALE
Salt River, South Africa
ALBY COMMERCIAL ENTERPRISES PTE LTD
Scotts Road, Singapore
CHRISTIAN MARK
Auckland, New
CROSS (H
Hong K
EUNSUN
Seoul, K
PRAISE IN
Quezon City, Philippines

LEAD ON!

First published in the USA by Word Incorporated, Waco, Texas.

First UK Edition 1987.

ISBN 0–85009–102–0

Unless otherwise noted, all Scripture quotations are from The New King James Version, copyright © 1979, 1980, 1982, by Thomas Nelson, Inc, Publishers. Those marked KJV are from the King James Version.

Reproduced, Printed and Bound in Great Britain for Word (UK) Ltd, by Cox & Wyman Ltd, Reading.

To
Dr. Kyung Chik Han (Han Kyung Chik)
of Korea, whom I consider to be
the outstanding leader of my lifetime.

Contents

Foreword

Too often "attempts to analyze leadership tend to fail because the would-be analyst misconceives his task. He usually does not study leadership at all. Instead, he studies popularity, power, showmanship, or wisdom in long-range planning." So said W. C. H. Prentice, writing for the *Harvard Business Review* twenty-five years ago.[1] Prentice was right then; he's still right.

To Prentice's list of misconceptions, I could add many more from present-day analysts of Christian leadership: the servant spirit, organizational acumen, administrative expertise, and fervency in prayer. All of these, important as they are, fail to address the subject of leadership.

It is the identification of twelve principles of leadership that sets this book apart from others. These principles are not skills—although skills may be used to enhance them—but they are characteristics. They are those factors that make a leader different from other people. Developing these principles will help you to fulfill the responsibilities of your leadership position in the most effective way possible.

You will notice that this book centers on leaders, not simply on achievers. We thank God for those achievers who enrich our culture and who inspire by their example. However, I make a distinction between achievers and leaders. Not all achievers are leaders, although the kind of leader I'm talking about is also an achiever.

For more than twenty years I have been observing leaders from Asia, Africa, Latin America, and Oceania. I have been with heads of state and heads of corporations, with international bankers and South

Sea islanders. It was this observation that began my concentrated study of what constituted leadership.

Sixteen years ago, the Haggai Institute for Advanced Leadership Training began in Singapore. This Institute has presented the principles of leadership found in this book to influential Third World leaders. They have examined the characteristics of a true leader. They have seen how the skills they sometimes practiced by intuition could be sharpened and made more effective. These highly credentialed leaders equal and in some cases excel my Western colleagues in leadership skill. I've learned from them. This volume encompasses the principles I've heard discussed and seen expressed in the lives of these leaders.

Among the nearly 4,000 people who have been through this training are the Arab world's premier Christian author, a pastor of one of the two largest churches in the world (60,000 members and growing!), a general of the second largest army in Asia, university presidents, a former secretary of state, a former strategy chief for the Mau Maus, archbishops, celebrated doctors, media leaders, and others.

I have written this book because our world needs leaders and because I believe the cultivation of the twelve principles discussed here will make better leaders. I have also written this because of the need for such a book that bypasses Western ethnocentricity—the prejudices of race and culture.

Cultural differences do exist. What would a Westerner think if, in response to a request for directions to a certain town, a man responded in total silence . . . only pursing his lips and pointing with his chin in a certain direction? If you're from a certain area in Africa, you'd understand that your request had been answered politely.

In many areas of Asia, crossing the legs in public is rude and insulting. When I mentioned this in an address a few years ago, my father, who was born in Damascus, Syria, said, "I had a flashback while you were speaking.

"As I prepared to flee Damascus in 1912, a godly Syrian told me to watch out for modernists in some American churches. 'Modernists deny the inspiration of Scriptures and the great Bible truths like Christ's virgin birth, atoning death and resurrection from the dead.' I determined to avoid these heretics and stay true to the Bible."

Shortly after his arrival in America, my father attended the First Presbyterian Church in Bridgeport, Ohio. To his great astonishment, he saw the pastor cross his legs . . . and on the platform of all places! *Oh, oh,* he thought, *the minister must be a modernist; he has his legs crossed!* Later my father learned that crossing the legs in American society carried no stigma.

In parts of the Third World, presenting a gift with the left hand is the pinnacle of rudeness, an insult as monstrous as spitting in someone's face in the West. Why? Because the left hand is the profane hand—the one which takes care of toiletries, for example.

In the West, there's an unwritten rule that you put your face no closer than eighteen inches (4.57 centimeters) to another person. In some areas of Latin America, friends will talk almost nose to nose.

In parts of India, the leader shows his importance by tardiness. You go to a government office. They open the door and invite you in. The top man may go to his desk, take thirty minutes to read a paper while you wait; he's showing his importance.

Biblical truths span *all* cultures; however, their specific application must be tailored to each culture. Because this is not done, many good books create confusion when leaders of other cultures read them. Still, certain principles remain constant. Laws are constant. The law of gravity never changes. The laws of physics remain the same. And since God is the lawmaker, He is the architect of these constants. The aim of this book is to discover and spotlight these constants as far as leadership is concerned.

My major sources have been the Bible and the analysis of men and women who have deliberately and successfully exerted a special influence of beneficial permanence on the many whom they have led toward goals of fulfilled needs. I have asked myself, "What has worked, where, and under what conditions?"

In addition to the Bible, I have read biographies, memoirs, news stories, and journals. During my 61 trips around the world and 145 intercontinental journeys, I've visited schools, farms, businesses, government headquarters, churches, publication houses, and athletic events. I've met, studied, and worked with leaders such as Dr. Han Kyung Chik of Korea—a leader whom I consider to be without peer in our world today.

Keep in mind that in this book I deal with principles, not with detailed action steps. For instance, while I discuss the principle of vision, I cannot delineate the vision God gives you. Nor can I define your personal mission. While I discuss goals, I can't spell out the steps that you must take to accomplish them. This you must do. And while I deal with the principle of love, you will have to determine how to express love. While I discuss the principle of communication, I can't put words in your mouth or at the end of your pen.

The twelve principles in this book are important not only for those who lead thousands but for those who lead small groups as well. The size of the group does not reflect the quality of the leadership.

The family is the small group that most needs leadership. The Western press screams out the news of today's revolt against leadership in the home. Worse still, in many homes there's no leadership against which to revolt!

Where normal conditions prevail, fathers, leading by love, will find in the principles of this book the insight and inspiration for leading their wives and children to undreamed of heights of abundant living.

Thomas Dixon, a self-taught and powerful clergyman, gave such leadership to his family that each of his five children matured into world Christians. Theirs is the only family in which all five children were listed in "Who's Who in America" at the same time. Each one made an impact because of the leadership of the father.

The ultimate example of leadership is Jesus. His group consisted of twelve, including one who doubted, one who denied knowing Him, and one who betrayed Him to murderers. Yet, with this small group, He changed the world.

May this book, while making clear the essential principles of leadership, help to demystify the practice of leadership. I hope it will encourage those who should be leading to overcome the fear of risk. I pray that it will help you to rise to your full potential.

Look over the table of contents. Then read the book through at a relaxed pace. After that, I suggest you study it, principle by principle. Determine which principles you need to master. Underline what you consider important to you. Note in the margin what you think should be added to, altered, or eliminated. Disagree, and write out why you disagree. Think! Then reread; rethink! Through repetition, internalize the parts of this book you deem important.

Leadership is an awesome responsibility. Develop these principles of leadership and you will see your effectiveness soar. God wants you to develop the potential He has given you. The extent to which your performance fails to live up to your potential is the extent to which you are failing God. The extent to which you are fulfilling your potential is the extent to which you are serving God.

As many writers have done, I have struggled with the shortcoming of the English language that requires a choice of "he" or "she" when referring to a word such as *leader* that has no gender. Leaders can, of course, be male or female. For expediency's sake, I have taken the traditional approach and used "he," "his," and "him" to refer to all people. I trust this will not be a stumblingblock to women leaders reading this book.

Acknowledgments

Because of her interest in my writing from my prenatal days, my mother must head the list of those I wish to acknowledge. She had been told that an unborn child is influenced by the dominating thoughts of its mother's mind during pregnancy. While she wasn't sure it was a fact, she was certain that positive, productive thoughts would have no damaging effect, and so she concentrated on my being a person of words, of letters.

Because I was a sickly child, I spent most of my boyhood days in the house. My mother used many of these hours to discuss her favorite authors and play games that revolved around famous writers. She encouraged me to keep a written diary. Aware of the great need for good writers of Christian fiction and nonfiction, she gave me books that she thought represented good writing; some of them related to leadership. One book she highly regarded was *The Investment of Influence* by Newell Dwight Hillis. Not once did she belittle my dreams.

My father, from whom I developed a great love for the Bible.

My brother Tom, with whom I have interacted for more than thirty years on the subject of leadership.

Three missionaries, all deceased, who made a profound impact on my early days, from four years of age to eighteen years of age: Paul Metzler, Carl Tanis, and Paul Fleming.

Ernest H. Watson of Australia, of whom you will read in this book.

Sir Cyril Black of Wimbledon, England.

Paul M. Cell, who first opened my eyes to the importance and teaching of the stewardship of money.

Two speech professors who taught me communications: Professor J. Manley Phelps of DePaul University and T. J. Bittikofer of Moody Bible Institute.

Matthijs Van den Heuvel of the Netherlands, Portugal, and now Switzerland, who, in the 1960s and 1970, demonstrated a leadership in Portugal that God used to bring blessings of beneficial permanence to thousands of Portugese, both Catholics and Protestants.

J. C. Massee, who influenced my life from 1928 until he passed away a few years ago at the age of 94.

Paul J. Meyer, progenitor of Success Motivation Institute of Waco, Texas. The elements of the SMART goals which I mention in chapter 3 I learned from him. Leaders in seventy-five nations concur he has produced the best motivation materials available. I have meticulously gone through more than twenty of his fifty courses during the past twenty-five years, and I recommend them without reservation. What makes them especially valuable is that Paul is a supernaturalist rather than a humanist, and everything he writes and says is predicated on his personal commitment to the Lord Jesus Christ. He understands "beneficial permanence."

Anthony D'Souza of Francis Xavier University in Bombay and faculty member of Haggai Institute in Singapore.

My younger colleague Michael Youssef, much of whose Ph.D. work focused on the father of contemporary leadership studies, Max Weber of Germany.

Benjamin Moraes of Brazil.

The late Chandu Ray of Pakistan and Australia.

George Samuel of India.

The men and women who have served on the various Haggai Institute boards of directors and trustees around the world.

Larry Stone, whose superb editing and counsel brought this book to a final conclusion and publication. Larry is one of those rare persons who can accept candor as well as express it. This made for a good relationship and an immeasurable improvement of the manuscript.

Norma Byrd, my research and literary assistant, whose expertise in checking out syntax, grammar, and structure made for greater clarity. She demonstrated dedication and attention to detail in typing and retyping the manuscript, from its inception, through its metamorphic stages, to completion.

Harold Keown, Jr., who reviewed the manuscript carefully.

S. H. Adamson, a young man who, in his twenties, presented me with a copy of *Leaders and Leadership* by Henry S. Bogardus. In the flyleaf he wrote, "To a Christian leader with the prayer that he might become an even greater leader for Christ. S. H. Adamson, 2/24/53."

Won Sul Lee of Korea, who urged me for ten years to write a book on leadership.

Paul Hiebert, who kept pressuring me to finish it as quickly as possible.

A special thanks to my wife, Christine, for patiently enduring my long stretches of preoccupation during the writing of the book.

And to a host of others whose contribution to my life and understanding have influenced this volume.

LEAD
ON!

1

A Call to

LEADERSHIP

God is calling leaders. Not power holders. Not Madison Avenue hype artists. Not mutual congratulation experts. Not influence peddlers. Not crowd-manipulating, exhibitionistic demagogues. God is calling leaders!

THE LEADERSHIP CRISIS

The call for leaders is necessary because we are experiencing a crisis of leadership in our world. It is similar to the crisis of spiritual leadership eighteenth-century Europe experienced. Agnostics had been on a rampage. The books of Morgan and Hume, with their denials of all that was spiritually right and noble, were published and distributed with reckless abandon. The populace in general regarded Christianity as a pipe dream and its teachings as fit only for ridicule. Voltaire, who criticized supernaturalism, religion, and Christianity, was Europe's most popular writer. Frederick the Great of Prussia was a practical atheist. Across Europe, men were hailing the disappearance of Christianity. The deterministic, fatalistic, and materialistic teachings of these agnostics saturated the thinking of the people and snapped the fetters of moral restraint.

Revolution was raging in France. In England, every sixth house became a grog shop. In the streets of London, gin shops offered to sell "enough gin for one pence to make one drunk, or enough for two pence to give a dead drunk." Free-thinking clubs were everywhere. Europe needed spiritual leaders.

A few young men knew that the only way to save the world from impending doom was a return to the message of the Bible. Men like John and Charles Wesley and George Whitfield became flaming evangels and carried the message of the Bible throughout Britain and America.

This evangelical leadership made a positive impact worldwide. John Howard instituted prison reforms in Europe. In the next century, J. Hudson Taylor founded the China Inland Mission, which by 1910 had sent out 968 missionaries. John Barnardo began his mission work in London which rescued and trained 70,000 homeless children. William Booth organized the Salvation Army which was to encircle the globe.

God used these leaders to save a civilization and to give it spiritual direction.

Just as eighteenth-century Europe needed leaders, our changing world needs leaders today. By next year at this time, there will be ninety million more people on this planet than there are today. Who will lead them? Will their leaders develop them or destroy them? Will these leaders improve our world or imperil our global village? India's annual net increase (births over deaths) exceeds the total population of Australia. What kind of leadership will these millions of people have?

Will the leaders of these new citizens of the world be honorable or corrupt? Self-sacrificing or self-aggrandizing? Humble or haughty? Will the new leaders be like Adolph Hitler, the dictator of Germany, or like Han Kyung Chik, the Christian statesman of Korea? Will they be like Al Capone, the gangster of Chicago, or John Calvin, the theologian of Geneva? Will they be like Nero, the oppressor, or Paul, the apostle?

The population explosion is frightening and real and is one cause of the crisis of leadership. Another cause of this crisis is that many in leadership positions have abdicated their responsibility.

Recently a highly placed woman educator told me, "My husband and I are weary of going to our church every Sunday and hearing our minister air his own personal problems and apprehensions. We want a word of authority, a word from God, a word to help us with our problems." Such a minister forfeits leadership and thus compounds the problems of the people in the pews. This minister demonstrates the crisis in leadership.

A top multinational executive friend of mine, who had massive personal problems, sought the help of a psychologist. Before the third session, the psychologist was seeking counsel from my friend, the patient. The psychologist demonstrated the crisis in leadership.

One celebrated head of state is known to leave his country when an emergency arises he cannot handle. On the one hand, that might be the wisdom of benign neglect; on the other hand, that may be a demonstration of the crisis in leadership.

The editor of one of the world's most prestigious multinational business journals wrote sometime ago, "What we hear in the pulpit on Sunday is what we ourselves wrote during the week. What we want to hear is a new voice, a voice from beyond . . . the voice of God." What an indictment of leaderlessness—at least in one pulpit!

This crisis of leadership trickles down from the presidency of corporations, the governorship of states, and the pulpits of churches to local leaders. There is today a crisis of leadership in the family. This is more pronounced in the West, but evidence of increased family breakdown mounts in the Third World as well. Divorce, with its growing threat, is frequently the ultimate abdication of leadership in the family. In the West, self-centeredness prevents parents from taking the time and effort to lead—not just manage—their children.

At all levels, our world's societies plead for leadership—in our educational system, in international politics, in our Christian churches. The masses look for true leadership. The world does not need a coterie of elitists who talk love and compassion while isolating themselves from *real* people. It does not need a retinue of cliché-spouting, self-avowed "quick fix" magicians. The world is looking for men and women—leaders—committed to God and compassionately concerned for people. The world needs leaders who will exert that special influence over aching people looking for a way to resolve their personal crises. This influence carries the stamp of beneficial permanence.

Through the prophet Ezekiel, God described the crisis in leadership in Ezekiel's day: "So I sought for a man among them who would make a wall, and stand in the gap before Me on behalf of the land, that I should not destroy it; but I found no one" (Ezekiel 22:30).

There are examples today of strong leadership, but they are rare. On 26 June 1983, for instance, I read William Pfaff's editorial in the *International Herald Tribune* in tribute to Pope John Paul II:

The pope has undertaken the liberation of Eastern Europe.

His program involves serious risks, but it also displays an intelligence, an understanding of history, and a power of will that is all but invisible among Western statesmen, and certainly nonexistent in today's Washington. . . .

The pope obviously does not expect a retreat of armies, collapse of alliances, unbarring of the Iron Curtain. He nonetheless means to change the terms on which the Poles and others in Eastern Europe are ruled, and to force concessions from the Communist authorities.

He seems largely indifferent to what Western governments . . . may think of this. . . . He simply does not think that Soviet Russia is all powerful and unchallengeable.[2]

We are glad when we see the kind of leadership Pope John Paul II displayed. But the crisis in leadership still exists. Who will stem the tide? Perhaps you will be the one. Will you face up to the danger and act upon the opportunity?

WHAT IS LEADERSHIP?

Before discussing leadership further, let's define the word *leadership*. If those who attempt to analyze leadership misconceive their task, as W. C. H. Prentice said, it is in part caused by a misunderstanding of what leadership is.

Leadership is the discipline of deliberately exerting special influence within a group to move it toward goals of beneficial permanence that fulfill the group's real needs.

Each word in this definition is important. *Discipline* was chosen to indicate that leaders are made, not born. There are some who intuitively exercise some of the characteristics of a leader, but true leadership is a discipline.

Deliberately indicates a commitment on the part of the leader to his calling as a leader. For all leaders, and for the Christlike leader especially, this should be a spiritual commitment. I believe that spiritual commitment strengthens the so-called secular enterprise rather than weakens it. Godly leadership carries the stamp of unique superiority anywhere in the world. In times of painful reverses, strength and wisdom are found. In times of enormous achievement, gratitude and humility are revealed.

Around the world an increasing number of leaders in all vocations unashamedly display a personal Bible on their desks, begin board meetings with prayer, and relate their activities to the principles of Scripture. I have encountered this in Japan and Fiji, in Germany and Lebanon, in Brazil and Canada, on the subcontinent of India, and the great continent of Africa.

The true leader exerts *special influence*. That influence is not forced on others. Many who think of themselves as leaders are really power-holders, exerting force on people. People follow them out of fear. A true leader's power, however, is the result of a profound trust among his followers. They are convinced that through him and with him they can realize self-enriching, humanitarian, ennobling, and God-glorifying results which would otherwise seem unlikely or impossible. True leaders are followed out of respect and love because they display love, humility, and self-control. Jesus Christ, of course, was our greatest example in this regard. He told His disciples, "If you love Me, keep My commandments" (John 14:15).

People who are in some way homogeneous are usually thought of as a *group*. In some way they are similar. Perhaps they are members of the same family or tribe with the same grandparents or ancestors. Perhaps they are members of the same church. Perhaps they are all alumni of the same school and, therefore, have all experienced a similar educational background. Or perhaps they are citizens of the same country. It is essential that the leader understand the group's sameness and all its implications.

More important than the sameness of origin, education, or nationality, however, is sameness of purpose. People feel most like a group when they are unified in purpose. Perhaps the purpose is to increase the membership of a church or to stop a law from being passed. An example of unity of purpose was President Roosevelt's mobilization of the United States to fight World War II while just a few months earlier it had been an isolationist country. An example of unity of purpose for evil was Hitler's unification of the Nazis with the purpose of exterminating the Jews and the establishment of world control.

The most important factor in forming a cohesive group is a unity of purpose. The leader's ability at fostering such unity is an important factor in his success as a leader.

The word *goals* has two meanings. Broadly, it refers to the leader's vision, his dream of what he sees his group being or doing. This concept is developed in chapter 2. It is the leader's vision that sets him apart and makes him a leader. The commitment to act upon the leader's vision becomes his mission. *Goals* also refers to a set of specific, measurable achievements designed to implement the mission. The development of effective goals is discussed in chapter 3.

Permanence refers to the fact that the vision of a leader should be for changes that are continuing, enduring, and lasting—for time and eternity. The term *beneficial permanence* contrasts with *malevolent permanence*. There have been many who have exhibited all of the characteristics or principles of a leader but who have sought goals detrimental to the group rather than for the group's benefit.

The twelve principles of leadership found in this book can be used for good or for evil. Amin, Hitler, and Nero all demonstrated powerful leadership characteristics, but their leadership corrupted, destroyed, and damned. Their leadership resulted in malevolent permanence. When parents shut off children from all access to the knowledge of God, they create a malevolent permanence.

I have written this book for those who desire to develop leadership with the dimension of beneficial permanence. The ultimate criterion is Christlike leadership. This is the leadership that most honors God and benefits all humankind.

The leader must have an understanding of the *real needs* of others. He maintains a sensitivity, a keen awareness, to the people for whom God has given him responsibility. He is attuned to his surroundings, thoroughly assesses the situation, and prepares to take action. But his sensitivity to others is always focused through the vision God has given him. He seeks to move the group toward goals that will fulfill the group's real needs—whether the group understands those needs or not. Such leadership demands foresight, wisdom, determination, and knowledge of God's will. History is full of instances when the group wanted what was *not* in its best interest. Samuel, for instance, was given permission by God to let the children of Israel choose a king so that they could be like their ungodly neighbors—even though it was not meeting their real needs. On the other hand, Abraham Lincoln moved the United States toward goals that fulfilled the real needs of the people—unity with freedom for all citizens—even though many people did not understand the beneficial permanence that would result.

Leadership, then, is the discipline of deliberately exerting special influence within a group to move it toward goals of beneficial permanence that fulfill the group's real needs.

LEADERSHIP AND CHANGE

Is this discussion of a "leadership crisis" a bit alarmist? Surely we would also have crises where there are shortages of doctors and teachers and scientists. The difference is that the leader induces and directs the change that most benefits the group. Change will occur whether there is effective leadership or not. But without positive leadership, the change will tend to be that of deterioration and destruction rather than improvement.

The crisis of leadership, therefore, occurs because constant change will not wait for a leader to appear. Our world is not like an automobile in a driveway waiting for a driver. It is rather like an automobile moving down a highway at fifty-five miles per hour. Without a driver, it will surely crash. With a driver, it will go where we want it to go.

Everything changes. There is no living thing that does not change and move. Constant change is the essence of all existence. The present becomes the past, and both determine the future. The future becomes the present. New life arises from the old.

Oscar Wilde said in his book *Soul of Man Under Socialism,* "The only thing that one really knows about human nature is that it changes. Change is the one quality we can predicate of it. The systems that fail are those that rely on the permanency of human nature, and not its growth and development." The only changeless thing about human nature is change itself! The Greek philosopher Heraclitus said that you cannot step into the same stream twice.

Financier John Templeton once told me that "a leader must encourage change." He must not simply tolerate or accept it, but a leader must actually *encourage* it. The ultraconservative thought pattern that insists on a 1950 mindset would find no ally in this seventy-year-old man's philosophy. I found it refreshing to spend time with a person who acts rather than reacts and who uses the past only to give insight into the present and direction for planning the future.

The current crisis requires millions of leaders now. The need grows every day. You can make a difference, but you will have to face up to the dangers, seize the opportunity, and pay the price.

ARE LEADERS BORN OR MADE?

Surely there are some who constitutionally will be better leaders than others. They will be better in their ability to utilize that combination of gifts that secures willing and intelligent "followership." However, through training, anyone who guides the action of others in a purposeful way can be made more influential and effective.

All things being equal, it would appear that those who lead effectively have a generous endowment of physical and emotional energy. They have a compelling drive toward a specific purpose or goal. They have a mastery of the methods of achieving the aim they profess. They are capable of sustaining the confidence, loyalty, and frequently the affection of those whom they lead. They are persuasive in enlisting followers to support the cause that demonstrably leads to the followers' own best interests.

In 1980, the *Harvard Business Review* collected fifteen articles on leadership under the title *Paths Toward Personal Progress: Leaders Are Made, Not Born.* These articles explain that like a surgeon, an astronaut, or a pulpit orator, a leader is made, not born. God may give special gifts, but these gifts will never surface if no effort is made to develop and exercise them.

A leader works toward a goal through the cooperation of people. The process of gaining their cooperation can be learned and developed. The leader motivates people's participation by insuring their personal fulfillment through involvement in the common venture.

Aptitude for leadership cannot be dismissed. Aptitude is inherited potential ability in a special field. It possesses driving power, but it is dependent upon personal discipline and social environment for ultimate expression and development.

On the other hand, since leaders are made, not born, lack of aptitude does not disqualify one from being a leader. God designed leadership roles for Moses, Jeremiah, and Paul the apostle, but they had to learn leadership skills just as a man called to the gospel ministry must learn how to preach.

A vocal teacher once told Mary Martin that she should abandon her goal to become a singer; she had an inferior voice and would never make it in the field of music. Mary Martin determined otherwise and for half a century reigned as one of America's most respected and popular singers. She overcame her aptitude deficiency by determination and exacting self-discipline.

My late brother, Ted, decided to become an electrical engineer, but his college aptitude tests put him at the bottom of the class in math. His teachers told him to forget his chosen field and select another. He refused. Day after day he worked on developing skill in math. He lost thirty pounds, and his adviser feared for his health; but by his third year in college, Ted was tutoring in math and graduated with honors. Later, he was given the L. A. Hyland award for scientific achievement.

Demosthenes suffered such speech impediments that he was embarrassed to speak to a group. He shaved one side of his head so he wouldn't be tempted to waste time by seeing anybody. He then invested agonizing hours by the sea in his unrelenting practice to overcome his speech problems. Demosthenes became the most famous orator of all time.

Just as attitude can overcome lack of aptitude in other areas of life, it can overcome lack of aptitude for leadership. In *You Can Be a Powerful Leader,* Ivan W. Fitzwater says leadership is neither an inborn trait nor an inherited tendency. He says the real difference between leaders and nonleaders is attitude.

You may not have the aptitude for leadership, yet, under God, you can develop into a leader. Think now of those God has given you to lead. If you're a child of God, and if you have a burning desire to be a leader, the very desire is His guarantee that you *can* be a leader. It will take unrelenting discipline to develop the skills needed. But you can rise above aptitude.

WHAT KIND OF LEADERSHIP?

A frightened world is looking for leadership. It is looking for those who have a vision and can deliberately exert special influence to move a group or a country toward goals of beneficial permanence that will fulfill the real needs of the people.

For the Christian, a position of leadership must lead to the pursuit of world evangelism. World evangelism is not to be a hobby with Christians, but an all-consuming priority. Thus, if the Christian is in a position of leadership over non-Christians, the foremost beneficial permanence that the leader would want for his followers is their salvation through Jesus Christ. If the Christian is in a position of leadership over other Christians, he should be motivating them to pursue world evangelism themselves. The true Christian never coerces.

Christ explicitly commanded every believer to put world evangelism in a place of priority in his life. He said, for instance, "Go therefore and make disciples of all the nations, baptizing them in the name of the Father and of the Son and of the Holy Spirit" (Matthew 28:19; see also Mark 16:15 and Acts 1:8).

There are many ways to carry out Christ's command for world evangelism. On the one hand, every attitude and action of the believer should focus on this objective. But evangelism does not just mean being a missionary or pastor. I think of late leaders such as Dr. Helen Kim, a premier educator in Korea, of Thomas F. Staley, an investment banker from Wall Street, of Eliseo Pajaro, a prominent musician from the Philippines, of John Bolten, Sr., a German-American industrialist, and of Benjamin Moraes, a jurist, linguist, professor, and pastor from Brazil. Although these were all leaders in their fields, they were all also carrying out Christ's command for world evangelism.

In this day of crisis and change, who will lead? Only the leader who recognizes the authority of Jesus Christ can point the way to true values. Only such a leader can defuse the ticking time bomb of angry people in the world. The world longs for a leader with the skill and courage to enlighten with the truth that "one's life does not consist in the abundance of the things he possesses" (Luke 12:15).

If it is your desire to be that leader with the dimension of beneficial permanence, this book can help you. The twelve principles of leadership—

vision, goalsetting, love, humility, self-control, communication, invest-ment, opportunity, energy, staying power, authority, and awareness—will help you understand and practice effective leadership.

SUMMARY

God is calling leaders. This call is necessary because of the crisis of leadership, a crisis brought about by the population explosion and the fact that our so-called leaders do not want to lead. Our world's society pleads for leadership.

What is leadership? It is the discipline of deliberately exerting special influence within a group to move it toward goals of beneficial permanence that fulfill the real needs of the group.

Leadership is no option. The leadership crisis is not like a crisis of a lack of plumbers. Our society is moving quickly and changing rapidly, and we must be directed and led.

Leaders are made, not born. Admittedly, some people have more aptitude for leadership than others, but aptitude alone will not make a leader. Conversely, someone with no aptitude for leadership but with a burning desire to lead can attain leadership success.

What kind of leadership does our world need? Bible-based, Christ-centered leadership is the only kind that will defuse the ticking time bomb of angry people on the earth. Such a leadership will have world evangelism as its primary concern.

2

The Principle of

VISION

In 1863, Abraham Lincoln signed the Emancipation Proclamation that freed the slaves in America. And yet 100 years later black people in America were still the victims of segregation. In 1963, in a speech at the Lincoln Memorial, Martin Luther King, Jr., expressed his vision for America. He wanted "the riches of freedom and the security of justice" for *all* people. "*Now* is the time to open the doors of opportunity to all of God's children," he said. "*Now* is the time to lift our nation from the quicksand of racial injustice to the solid rock of brotherhood. . . .

"I say to you today, my friends, that in spite of the difficulties and frustrations of the moment I still have a dream. . . . I have a dream that one day in the red hills of Georgia the sons of former slaves and the sons of former slave owners will be able to sit down together at the table of brotherhood. I have a dream that one day even the state of Mississippi, a desert state sweltering with the heat of injustice and oppression, will be transformed into an oasis of freedom and justice. I have a dream that my four little children will one day live in a nation where they will not be judged by the color of their skin but by the content of their character. I have a dream . . . of that day when all of God's children, black men and white men, Jews and Gentiles, Protestants and Catholics, will be able to join hands and sing in the words of the old Negro spiritual, 'Free at last! Free at last! Thank God almighty, we are free at last!' "[3]

Regardless of how King's critics assess his personal character and conduct, no one can deny he had a vision and deliberately exerted special influence to move the country in which he lived toward the goals that permanently fulfilled the real needs of that country. He expressed that vision in a clearer and more moving way than most leaders. A vision such as Martin Luther King had sets a leader apart.

Leadership begins when a vision emerges. Proverbs 29:18 says, "Where there is no vision, the people perish" (KJV). The true meaning of these words is "Without a vision, the people cast off restraint." When a group is under the direction of a person who has no vision, the result is confusion, disorder, rebellion, uncontrolled license, and—at worst—anarchy.

The principle of vision is the key to understanding leadership. With a clear-cut vision to which he is wholeheartedly committed, a person has taken the first step toward leadership. Without such a commitment to a vision, a person cannot be a leader but will be an imitation, playing at what he wishes he could be.

UNDERSTAND WHAT A VISION IS

A vision is a clear picture of what the leader sees his group being or doing. A vision could be of health where there is sickness—such as Albert Schweitzer had for Africa; of knowledge where there is ignorance—which motivated Gilbert Tennent to found what is now Princeton University; of freedom where there is oppression; or of love where there is hatred. From that clear picture, the leader then plans how that vision will become a reality.

When John Sung returned to his native China in 1929, after having received his Ph.D. from Ohio State University, his preacher father said, "Good, John. Now, with your education, you can get an important teaching post and provide an education for your six brothers." Chinese children always obey the direct commands of their fathers. It was unusual, therefore, for John to tell his father that he could not take a teaching post because God had called him to evangelize China and southeast Asia. John had a vision of Chinese people becoming followers of Jesus Christ, and he felt he had only fifteen years to fulfill that vision.

Over the next fifteen years, John Sung did the work of a dozen men. And, in fact, he died at the end of those fifteen years, in 1944! John Sung was committed to the fulfillment of his vision. That explains his feverish pace in carrying it out. Asia and the South Pacific are different today because of the ministry of John Sung. It all began with a vision translated into a mission and implemented by well-defined goals.

Mahatma Gandhi had a vision of a free and independent India at a time when it was governed by the British. Henry Ford had a vision of every family in America owning its own automobile at a time when most people were frightened of the new invention. William Wilberforce had a vision of the abolition of slavery at a time when slaves were a very profitable trade item for the British. Daniel K. Ludwig had a vision for a self-supporting industrial region in the heart of the Brazilian jungle at a time when there was no industry, no electricity, and no cities of any kind for hundreds of miles. Mahatma Gandhi, Henry Ford, William Wilberforce, and Daniel Ludwig committed themselves to the clear picture they had of what their group would become or do as a result of the special influence they would exert.

The vision of the leader is different from the vision of the scientist who works alone. The solitary scientist's success will benefit others, but it doesn't require the direct involvement of others. The leader, however, works through other people.

Having a vision is not enough. There must be a commitment to act on the vision. That is called a mission. There must also be a set of specific, measurable steps to achieve the mission. Those steps are called goals. Goals design the program for achieving the mission and thus fulfilling the vision. A leader will have one vision and one mission but many goals.

God blessed me by giving me my life's vision—the evangelization of the world—when I was only ten years old. I saw clearly people in freedom and peace under the lordship of Jesus Christ, people who had formerly lived in slavery to their sin and hatred. I committed myself to the fulfillment of that vision, and I had a mission. To pursue that life mission has required a program of many goals, including finding and maintaining buildings in Singapore to house the Haggai Institute (physical goals), reading three books a week to be aware of the cultures of the world (mental goals), building friendships with people who could share my vision and mission (social goals), raising an endowment to carry on the work of the Lord through the Institute (financial goals).

A mission is simply a vision acted upon. This is clearly illustrated by America's Apollo program.

In 1960, President John Kennedy challenged the American people with his dream of an American on the moon by 1970. That was a vision. Almost immediately, the government launched a program designed to accomplish that vision—the Apollo mission. The president communicated his vision to the American people. The people, through the government, then committed to the fulfillment of that vision with a mission. The mission required an elaborate goals program consisting of millions of individual goals.

The biblical story of Nehemiah reveals that he had a vision of a rebuilt wall around Jerusalem. Nehemiah was in captivity 1500 kilometers from Jerusalem. He was a servant, a cupbearer to King Artaxerxes of Persia. The holy city of Jerusalem had been captured and much of it destroyed. But Nehemiah had a vision of a rebuilt Jerusalem with strong walls for the glory of God. His mission was to realize the vision. Then came an elaborate system of goals to carry out the mission. His first step was prayer. Next Nehemiah presented his case to King Artaxerxes. And then he set out a plan for rebuilding the walls and overcoming opposition. Nehemiah is one of history's greatest examples of leadership.

It's one thing to be consumed by a vision for world evangelism—the picture of every person on our planet hearing the gospel in an understandable, culturally relevant way. It's even a greater thing to create a mission designed to realize the vision. And it is yet a greater undertaking to create, under God, the goals program necessary to carry out the mission and fulfill the vision.

The leader cherishes his vision. He thinks on it by day and dreams of it by night. He transfers the vision to the group. He then motivates the group to commit to the mission that will realize the vision and meet their real needs.

Continuously thinking about the vision induces action. It sounds the death knell to complacency. As the psalmist said, "My heart was hot within me; while I was musing, the fire burned" (Psalm 39:3).

Understand Where a Vision Comes From

Any worthy vision comes from God, whether it deals with so-called "spiritual" matters or not—and whether the person with the vision is a Christian and realizes the source of the vision or not. Worthy visions are a gift of God. James said, "Every good gift and every perfect gift is from above, and comes down from the Father of lights, with whom there is no variation or shadow of turning" (James 1:17).

Our tendency is to compartmentalize our lives so that God is seen as having influence on and relevance to "spiritual" visions, missions, and goals, but little relationship to "secular" visions, missions, and goals. But St. Augustine said, "Let every Christian understand that wherever truth is found, it belongs to his Master." God is the God of *all* truth. And God is the source of *all* worthy visions.

In 1774 and 1775, the American colonies were contemplating

breaking away from England. Confusion, disagreement, and rancor threatened to undermine the purpose of the Continental Convention. Yet many of the participants had a clear vision and credited it to God. Benjamin Franklin told the Convention, "I believe that Providence guides the affairs of men, and never a sparrow falls to the ground that God does not attend its funeral, and that all the hairs of our heads are numbered. I don't believe that an empire or a republic can be launched without His help, and I move you, Mr. President, that this convention open with prayer and that we petition Divine guidance and help in the step we are about to take."

America's founders shared a vision of freedom for the colonies. To actualize that vision required a mission, implemented by a full goals program. They knew that their vision came from God.

A vision for the kind of change that will yield beneficial permanence for the group comes from God whether the leader acknowledges it or not. More than five hundred years ago, God gave King Sejong a vision of an improved language for his Korean people. King Sejong actualized his vision through a mission implemented by a goals program that gave the Koreans the first alphabet in the Orient. He did not know the God of the Bible and His Son Jesus Christ, but he successfully fulfilled the vision God had nevertheless given him.

God rules over the affairs of men. He gives vision and understanding.

Sometimes a vision may result in great wealth, and sometimes it results in relative poverty. But if it is a worthy vision, it originates with God. Paul J. Meyer started out without a dollar. At the age of twenty-five he was a millionaire. He had built the largest insurance agency in the world. His young pastor, Dr. Bill Hinson, challenged him: "Paul, you're happiest when you're helping others reach their full potential." Paul caught the vision of motivating others to achieve their full potential and left the insurance business. It didn't seem as if he would make as much money as he had done selling insurance, but he couldn't stifle the vision God had given him.

Today, Paul Meyer's Success Motivation Institute has helped thousands. Leaders in seventy-five countries point to the SMI program as the instrument that opened a new world of possibility to them. The SMI program has transformed some welfare recipients into corporate heads and university scholars.

It's tragic that so many times God's people seem impervious to the opportunities all about them. They settle for less when God wants them to master the highest echelons of achievement.

For the Christian, a vision of any kind must start with an

understanding of God. God is perfect, immutable, and eternal. Christlike leaders see God and recognize their dependence upon Him. No one can fully understand himself or his environment until his vision of God is clear.

After gaining an understanding of God, the Christian leader must understand himself. A proper self-evaluation precedes any achievement of beneficial permanence. The person who would be a leader God can use sees his potential as God sees it.

As the leader catches a vision of himself, he may be tempted, like Isaiah, to mourn, "Woe is me, for I am undone! Because I am a man of unclean lips. And I dwell in the midst of a people of unclean lips." He may feel, like Moses, that inadequacy disqualifies him for the job. But God will work through the sinner, through the inadequate person, if that person has faith not in his own power but in the power of God— the God who provided the vision to begin with. It requires faith to cherish the vision, convert the vision into a mission, implement it with a proper goals program, and mobilize others to fulfill their own real needs. The Christlike leader must not only have an understanding of God and of himself, but he must also have an understanding of the real needs of others. His sensitivity to others is always focused through the vision God has given him. Without a vision, awareness and sensitivity to the needs of others leads only to corrosion of the spirit and confusion of the mind.

UNDERSTAND WHY A VISION IS IMPORTANT

Without a wholehearted commitment to a vision, you cannot be a leader. You may be in a leadership position, you may be a manager, but what separates the true leaders from others is vision. A vision is important because it is a key factor in successful leadership.

Vision underlies and underpins all leadership. Without a vision, there will not be an adequate mission. Without a mission, there is no possibility of a productive goals program. Without a goals program, there is no leadership. Without leadership, the world will languish in sin and sorrow. Leadership begins with a vision.

A manager can preside over the status quo, but it takes a leader to motivate people to accomplish those changes that meet their real needs. While the world needs managers today, the world's most desperate need is for leaders. And what sets a leader apart from a manager is that a manager does not encourage change, whereas a leader demands change because he is moving a group toward goals of beneficial permanence. A leader has a vision.

A vision is important because it is the foundation of all true leadership. The significance of a person's leadership depends on the "bigness" of his vision. Prime Minister Lee Kuan Yew of Singapore had a significant vision that affected not only his own nation, but all of southeast Asia. His influence has rippled across the world. A father may have a vision for the educational or spiritual goals of his family that is less significant because it affects fewer people. For those people, however, the vision is no less important. While the significance of a leader's vision depends on the bigness, the effectiveness of a person's leadership depends on how well he moves the group toward the fulfillment of his vision—and their real needs.

UNDERSTAND WHO MUST GRASP THE VISION

Both the leader and the followers must grasp the vision. Leadership starts with a vision on the part of the leader, but for the followers to give credence to the leader's direction, they must understand the vision too. A major responsibility of the leader, therefore, is to accurately communicate his vision to his group. He must make the definition and dimension of the vision clear to the followers. How to do this is more fully developed in chapter 7 on the principle of communication.

The leader's grasp of the vision begins with a clear understanding not only of his own vision, but of his potential under God. He must know that God created him to be somebody, and then he is to fulfill the vision God gave him. Paul the apostle said, "Not that I have already attained, or am already perfected; but I press on, that I may lay hold of that for which Christ Jesus has also laid hold of me" (Philippians 3:12). Paul knew his shortcomings, yet he kept moving toward the accomplishment of his mission, for he knew "I can do all things through Christ who strengthens me" (Philippians 4:13).

Peter Daniels of Adelaide, Australia, helps people realize their potential under God. He has demonstrated himself the potential that is in a person. When he became a follower of Jesus Christ at the age of twenty-six, he could neither read nor write. He was profane, broke, and belligerent. He had been tossed from one broken home to another. God saved him, and Peter grasped a vision of his possibilities and keeps growing with unabated consistency.

Today, Peter Daniels is wealthy, literate, influential, and is one of Australia's outstanding speakers. He has committed his wealth to the expansion of God's kingdom. He has invested his influence in service through four international boards. Peter Daniels asks four questions of those who yearn for meaning in their lives:[4]

1. What is the age you have set as your goal for reaching your full potential that God might maximize your life?

2. Tell me in fifty pages or more what your full potential is in every area of your life. (Daniels requires at least fifty pages. Otherwise, a person could put down a few words which, Daniels says, would be "frivolous." Forcing people to write at least fifty pages drives them to assess the sincerity of their concern.)

3. Accepting your potential as 100 percent, what percentage rating do you give yourself right now?

4. Accepting the deficiency between the two scores, what plan have you made to make up the difference and when will you accomplish that plan?

Responding to these four questions could take the better part of a day. But when a person responds fully and honestly, a clear picture of the situation emerges. Peter Daniels' four questions are designed to develop what I call "inspirational dissatisfaction." These questions are designed to point out the difference between where you could be if you were living at your full potential and where you are now—and what you should do to get to your full potential. Without inspirational dissatisfaction, a person would make peace with the status quo, he would not see a need for change, could not grasp a vision of growth, and could not step out in faith. Inspirational dissatisfaction is an essential step to grasping a vision.

Inspirational dissatisfaction is different from a morose, brooding, cynical dissatisfaction that impels one to withdraw into a shell or, on the other hand, aggressively criticize the alleged reasons for his dissatisfaction. Inspirational dissatisfaction inspires a person to high attainment. Despondent dissatisfaction paralyzes the action nerve, corrodes the spirit, and wrecks the life.

Look again at Nehemiah. Inspirational dissatisfaction preceded his vision and leadership. The wall of Jerusalem was broken down. The gates had been burned. Travelers told of the affliction and reproach of God's people. Nehemiah sat down and wept; he fasted and prayed. He confessed his own sin and the sin of his people. He reviewed the promises of God. He requested from the king a leave of absence and letters of reference in preparation for his return to Jerusalem to rebuild the wall.

For three nights Nehemiah circled the ruins of Jerusalem. He observed, but kept his counsel. A study of Nehemiah's work in rebuilding the wall provides an ideal biography of a leader with vision who sees the need, commits to a mission to realize the vision, and moves toward his potential.

The leader must have an understanding of his potential. He must see clearly the vision he has for his group. Then the followers must catch the vision God has given the leader regarding some great project. Nehemiah didn't rebuild the wall of Jerusalem by himself. Others grasped the vision too.

In a vision given by God, the apostle Peter learned that the gospel was for the Gentiles as well as for the Jews. Under the leadership of the Holy Spirit, he then had to "sell" that vision to his colleagues.

Dwight L. Moody had a vision of building a Bible Institute that would train laypeople to become effective in evangelism. It was a new concept. God gave Moody, the businessman turned evangelist, the vision. Then Moody had to light the flame so that others could see the vision and commit to the mission.

God gave Dr. Han Kyung Chik a vision of a church in Seoul, Korea, at the end of World War II. Initially, only twenty-seven people—refugees all—shared his vision. Today, the church stands 60,000 strong, built not by one person, but by many followers who caught the vision of Dr. Han.

A vision generates direction, order, devotion. It overcomes aimlessness, chaos, lawlessness. Leadership grasps God's will, clarifies it to the group, then motivates the group to act on it. The greatest vision a leader can have is one that participates in God's will for world evangelism and explains to the group how it is to be accomplished.

UNDERSTAND WHAT TO DO WITH THE VISION

You now understand what a vision is, where a vision comes from, why a vision is important to a leader, and who it is that must grasp a vision. What do you do with a vision? The obvious answer is, you commit to act on the vision (that commitment is called a mission) and then design a goals program to achieve the mission and thus fulfill the vision. That commitment includes a determination to overcome difficulties and eliminate obstacles.

A leader dishonors God when he professes a vision and then, when difficulties arise and enemies assault, he complains, "God must not want this, or we would not be having so much trouble." Instead, a leader is committed to his vision.

The importance of that commitment can be seen most dramatically when the vision seems least logical. In 1929, Will H. Houghton, pastor of the 4,000-member Baptist Tabernacle in Atlanta, Georgia, was visiting Europe with his wife and her mother. Halfway through the scheduled itinerary, Houghton felt a compulsion to return to America at once. He didn't know why, but he knew God was directing him to return.

He left his wife and mother-in-law to finish the trip, while he took a fast ship to New York. He arrived on a Wednesday in time to attend the midweek prayer service at Calvary Baptist Church across the street from world-famous Carnegie Hall.

The pastor, John Roach Straton, had just become seriously ill, and Houghton was asked if he would fill the pulpit temporarily. He returned to Calvary Baptist Church in January, 1930, preaching in the city often dubbed "the graveyard of preachers." Straton died in October, 1930, and Houghton accepted the invitation to the pastorate. He was one of the few who thrived as a preacher in New York City.

From Calvary's highly visible pulpit, Houghton came to the attention of James M. Gray, the 88-year-old president of Moody Bible Institute. Gray became convinced that Houghton should follow him as president and reported his conviction to the Board of Trustees. Houghton served as president of Moody Bible Institute until 1946. Had Houghton ignored the vision, it is unlikely he would have fulfilled his leadership potential. However, because of his sensitivity, he was put in a position of leadership where he had a world-changing impact on the lives of millions for the glory of God.[5]

Leaders used by God respond to the vision He gives them.

God gave Noah the vision of an ark, and he built it.

God gave Abraham a vision of a city, and he looked for it.

God gave Nehemiah a vision of a wall, and he built it.

God gave Paul the apostle a vision of evangelizing the whole world, and he covered the earth with the message of Christ.

God gave David Livingstone a vision of Africa, and he opened the way for thousands of missionaries to preach the gospel.

God gave John Sung the vision of evangelism in east Asia, and he changed the spiritual complexion of every nation he visited.

If God has put a desire in your heart, accept the presence of the desire as His oath that it can be realized and commit yourself to the fulfillment of the vision. Failure to act on your vision can lead to personal stagnation, a troubled spirit, and a critical attitude. A God-given vision is an awesome responsibility. Fulfillment can lead you to the heights of tremendous service to God and your fellow-man. Failure to follow the vision will deprive others of the leadership they need.

THE IMPORTANCE OF SOLITUDE

You can't see a vision when the artificial lights of the Broadways, the Rialtos, and the commercial offices of the world blind your eyes, any more than you can see the stars at night when you're standing in New York's Times Square, Tokyo's Ginza, or London's Picadilly Circus.

You're more likely to discern a vision in the cloistered halls of solitude than in the screaming jostle of the metropolitan concrete jungle. Perhaps in the cathedral of the trees, under the silence of the stars, or by the moaning sea, you'll be most likely to see the true light and hear "the still, small voice."

In 1964, I made a visit to West Asia. It brought me into contact with Christian leaders who jolted me with the statement that the traditional mission approach was coming to an end in many Third World nations. I thank God for traditional Western-dominated missions because it was through one such missionary that my father came to faith in Christ Jesus. However, just as colonialism brought many blessings but is no longer viable, so, too, the old mission approach is no longer realistic in most Third World nations.

Shortly after that visit, on the island of Bali in Indonesia, a fire began to burn in my soul. I told my three traveling companions that I would be "out of circulation" for a while. They understood and cooperated. I didn't leave my room. In absolute solitude, the vision of Third World Christian leaders, clergy and laity alike, evangelizing their own people came on the screen before my inner eyes like a technicolor movie. I wrote as fast as I could, my thoughts often tumbling ahead of my words. The informal creed I scribbled that day still remains the basic philosophy of world evangelism on which the Haggai Institute functions.

Within the next twelve months, Jerry Beavan and Tom Haggai made incisive, specific suggestions for the best way to implement the vision. Ernest Watson of Australia, Max Atienza of the Philippines, Han Kyung Chik of Korea, Chandu Ray of Pakistan and Singapore, Ah Tua Teo of Singapore, George Samuel of India, and many others all contributed to the fulfillment of the vision.

But it all started in the sanctuary of solitude! Had I spent all my days in crowded socializing, there would be no Haggai Institute. The vision came from God. It was delineated in solitude.

A famous anthropologist said years ago, "The Western mind says, 'Don't just stand there; do something.' So we in the West are action oriented. The Eastern mind says, 'Don't do anything; stand there.' So the Eastern mentality is more attuned to contemplation than action."

These differences between East and West are being modified somewhat as the East becomes more action-oriented and the West sees the value of contemplation. You must prepare for effective action by clear thinking. And the best thinking is done in solitude.

The late Cecil B. Day, Sr., the creator and founder of Day's Inn budget-luxury motels, liked to find his solitude in his "shack" at Tybee Beach in Savannah, Georgia. Sometimes he went there to fast and pray. When the incoming tides at the Day Companies headquarters became crashing breakers, Cecil would go to Tybee. He would walk along the beach to think and pray, the gentle waves cleansing his mind of the tension that clouded clear thinking. He loved the bustle of the headquarters building in Atlanta, but he couldn't do his best creative thinking in the atmosphere of roaring commerce. After walking the deserted beaches, he returned to the city energetic and creative.

Day's vision for his motel chain came in solitude. At two o'clock one morning in 1970, he awakened, grabbed a yellow legal pad, and began writing. For fourteen hours he penned the thoughts brimming over in his mind. When it was done, he had the core idea for the Day's Inn budget-luxury motel. "The ideas were beyond my capacity," reported Cecil later. "It was God's leadership for an idea that has been called the 'Volkswagen of motels.'"

It is possible to create one's own environment of solitude, even in a crowd. But one must not fall into the trap of eliminating occasional solitude in quiet, undisturbed surroundings just because he may have the ability to create his own quiet environment in the midst of noise.

Many times a leader is forced to make an immediate decision without the benefit of prior reflection and deliberation. It is at this point that the power of voluntary solitude enables him to do his thinking, set his course, and determine his plan of action . . . to the benefit of the group.

In Panama, where I was conducting an evangelistic crusade many years ago, a lady called my name as I was crossing a busy thoroughfare. She said, "Suppose at three o'clock this afternoon you were to face an unavoidable decision which would involve thousands of innocent lives and millions of dollars of other people's money, and you had only two minutes to decide, what would you do?"

"I would follow my best judgment."

Aghast, she said, "You mean you wouldn't pray about it?"

"Dear lady, you have given me two minutes. It will consume every second of those two minutes to grasp as much of the relevant data as possible."

"But, I thought you would pray."

"I have. You see, this morning, I had my quiet time with the Lord. I committed the day to Him. And He, who knows the end from the beginning and with whom there is no past, present, or future, has already prepared me. I therefore have full confidence that in this situation, my best judgment would be the expression of His will."

It is in a situation like that, posed by the lady in Panama, that solitude in the midst of the bustling arena is required.

But whether the leader grasps a vision in a beautiful solitary expanse or in a mental seclusion of his own making, he must commit to fulfilling the vision or his influence will go nowhere.

The Christlike leader needs to continually ask himself: (1) Will the vision produce results of beneficial permanence? and (2) Will the vision move the people toward goals that fulfill their real needs?

For the Christlike leader, a vision is a revelation of God's will. A leader grasps the challenge of the vision, commits to the mission, and implements the goals that will accomplish the mission and fulfill the vision.

But it all starts with a vision—the foundation of leadership.

SUMMARY

Leadership begins with a vision. A vision is a clear picture of what the leader sees his group being or doing. A vision could be of health where there is sickness, of knowledge where there is ignorance, of freedom where there is oppression, or of love where there is hatred. The leader is wholeheartedly committed to his vision, which involves beneficial change for his group.

The leader is aware of the importance of his vision and makes it the driving force behind his leadership. The leader's commitment to act on the vision is called a mission. There must also be a set of specific, measurable steps to achieve the mission. Those steps are called goals. A leader will have one vision and one mission but many goals.

Any worthy vision comes from God, whether it deals with so-called "spiritual matters" or not and whether the person with the vision is a Christian and realizes the source of the vision or not. For the Christian, a vision must start with an understanding of God. The leader must then understand himself and also understand the real needs of others.

A vision is important because it is the foundation of all true leadership. A vision must be grasped not only by the leader, but by the followers as well. Therefore, a major responsibility of the leader is to accurately and effectively communicate his vision to the group. Both the leader and the followers then commit to act on the vision, and proceed to design a goals program to achieve the mission and thus fulfill the vision. The commitment includes a determination to overcome difficulties and eliminate obstacles.

Because solitude is necessary to hear the voice of God most clearly and understand the vision He has given, the leader should set aside times when he can be apart by himself. This will prepare him for those times when he must act in a situation when quiet communion with God is not possible.

A vision is the revelation of God's will. A vision is the foundation of leadership.

3

The Principle of

GOALSETTING

You have the vision. Now sharpen the focus of your vision. Are you setting goals to achieve your mission or do you get sidetracked with nonessentials?

The late Cecil B. Day, Sr., had a vision of developing a business to generate funds for God's work worldwide. The most visible part of his business was the motel chain he founded, Day's Inns. In four years he built 40,000 rooms. That achievement has not been even remotely approximated before or since.

In less than five years after Cecil Day founded the motel chain, the oil embargo threatened to bring American traffic to a halt. The scarcity of gasoline lowered highway traffic dramatically. This cut into his revenue dangerously. Furthermore, the hike in oil prices froze liquidity across the country. When the motels under construction at the time of the oil crisis were completed, the lending institutions had no money to fulfill their commitment for conventional loans. As a result, Cecil was saddled with high-interest construction loans.

He never lost his vision. He visited three bankers a day, five days a week for twenty-one months. He not only maintained his vision, but he continually kept refining and executing his well-thought-out action steps for the goals required to make the vision a reality. When he died in 1978, the entire business was intact, and his vision had been carried out.

A leader must have a vision, but that vision must be fulfilled by goals that work toward the achievement of the vision. He cannot waste time with nonessentials. There's no question that Napoleon had a vision. He saw himself as emperor of all Europe. He motivated those who fought for him. But he failed because his egomaniacal plan could never fulfill his vision for European conquest.

A vision is the foundation of all leadership. The leader's vision requires a commitment to act. That commitment is called a mission. But where the rubber meets the road is with a set of specific, measurable steps designed to achieve the mission. Those steps are called goals. A leader without goals is like a ship's captain without reference points or a cross-country motorist without location signs and mileposts.

In the early seventies, sociologist Daniel Yankelovich said that young people were disillusioned. He said that a number of the best-educated and most promising young adults had lost enthusiasm for their business careers. There was a "crisis of purpose."

After having traveled, worked, and fellowshipped on all six continents, I sadly conclude that a high percentage of people in Christian leadership positions also suffer a "crisis of purpose." They are good, sincere, dedicated people for whom the dilemma of finding purpose through the pursuit of traditional Christian activities remains achingly unsolved. With one breath, they say their life's mission is to "serve the Lord." With the next breath, they lament their tragic inability to specify how or in what way.

To be effective, a leader must constantly sharpen the focus of his vision. He does this with effective goalsetting. The clearer the leader's goals, the sharper his focus and vice versa. Effective goalsetting focuses the leader's vision by spelling out what steps he will take to accomplish that vision.

For a leader to lack goals would be as absurd as for a university physics professor to come into class and ask, "What subject shall we consider today?" The students would suffer. In short order, the university would fire the professor. Unfortunately, there are "leaders" in Christian work who, like that professor, lack goals and therefore lack direction. No wonder their influence dwindles, and God's work is slandered.

Henry Kaiser said, "Determine what you want more than anything else in life, write down the means by which you intend to attain it, and permit nothing to deter you from pursuing it."

Setting goals is like programming a computer. Both tasks take skill because nothing can be assumed or left out. For instance, when one of the Haggai Institute graduates sets up a seminar, the objective may sound simple, but to write a program explaining every step could be very complex.

First, he must determine the objective of the seminar in precise detail. Second, he must determine the faculty. Third, he must determine the participants. Fourth, he must determine the facility to be used. Fifth, he must determine the time, both the length of the sessions and the length of the entire seminar. Sixth, he must determine the funding required. Seventh, he must then enlist the faculty. Eighth, he must secure the facilities. Ninth, he must secure the appropriate materials and equipment. Tenth, he must produce the necessary funding. Eleventh, he must recruit the participants. And there are many other steps.

The vision is important, but the vision will never be realized unless a goals program is put in place and followed faithfully. The vision will stay the same over a long period of time and the mission will correspond to the vision. But the goals should be reviewed frequently in order to adjust them to changing situations so that the vision can be realized.

Perhaps your vision is for the development of a secondary school that will be the finest in the city. You realistically expect that it will take eight years to accomplish this mission. You will need to establish a series of goals for the faculty, student body, curriculum, physical facilities, public relations, and other areas each year. The first year, for instance, one of your goals might be to have three teachers with masters degrees, a student-teacher ratio of 30:1 or lower, and 20 percent of the faculty participating in continuing education. The fourth year, however, might include goals of having ten teachers with masters' degrees, a student-teacher ratio of 22:1 or lower, and 35 percent of the faculty participating in continuing education.

Goalsetting is not easy, and it takes constant review and change. The leader who rises above the others, however, will do so not because of his vision, as important as vision is, but because of the successful implementation of an effective goals program. Without a goals program, the vision is merely wishful thinking.

If goalsetting is so important, the leader needs to be able to do it as if it were second nature. Therefore, we need to look at it carefully. First, we will look at the basis of goalsetting—how to do it and the characteristics of good goals. Then we will examine some problem areas in goalsetting that need your careful attention. Finally, we will show the benefits of goalsetting and show how it will help you to be a better, more effective leader. But before ending the chapter, we also need to see why it is that some people object to goalsetting.

S–M–A–R–T GOALS

Setting goals simply involves writing out the steps it will take to accomplish your vision. It may take five years, it may take twenty years, but the vision must be broken down into steps so that you know what you are to accomplish in each area every month.

A good goal-setting program will be S-M-A-R-T: *S*pecific, *M*easurable, *A*ttainable, *R*ealistic, and *T*angible.

Make Your Goals Specific.

It is not a satisfactory goal to say, "I want to honor the Lord." That's a valid desire, but it does not describe a step that will move you toward the accomplishment of your vision. That would be like Noah saying, "I want to survive the flood" or Nehemiah saying, "I want to protect Jerusalem."

Each goal must be a specific step rather than a vague desire.

Make Your Goals Measurable.

"If you can't measure it, you can't monitor it," says Paul J. Meyer of Success Motivation Institute. And since the purpose of goalsetting is to establish a set of steps for the accomplishment of your vision, it is important to know whether each step has been accomplished or not.

A goal of "increasing efficiency in world evangelism" is not measurable. A goal of training 100 credentialed leaders within a year in the "how" of evangelism is measurable. If 98 went through the training, you know you came close to your goal, even though you fell a little short.

Goals should be measurable, not only in terms of *what* is accomplished but *when* it is accomplished. Every goal should specify when the result will be achieved. You shouldn't just have a goal of increasing the average attendance in your church to 300. You should state when it will be accomplished. The reason for this is that each goal is part of an entire goal system designed to fulfill your vision. The accomplishment of one goal is frequently necessary before other goals can be started.

God drove me to set a goal to assist in world evangelism. This was more than half a century ago. One of the action steps arising from this long and continuing overall goal, this mission, is the writing of this book. It has taken four years of my time. It has taken more of my time than the other six books I have written combined. It required me to work with a publisher so that I knew when the manuscript must be completed if the book were to be in the hands of world leaders by early 1986.

I had an intermediary goal of having the manuscript done by May, 1985. I then set goals for myself of when each chapter should be done:

one per month for twelve months, with one month at the end for review and rewrite. Each of these smaller goals was specific, measurable, attainable, realistic, and tangible.

Some of these smaller goals were only for a month. I had broken down my major goal of writing this book into sub-goals. If my goal were just to write this book, I would have faced an overwhelming task. The tendency would have been not to start. But by breaking it down into chapter goals of one month each, I could tell quickly whether I was accomplishing this task.

Make Your Goals Attainable.

A man with a bass voice should not expect to become a soprano soloist. A seventy-year-old woman should not expect to bear a child. An illiterate should not expect to become a famous author within a three-month period. Don't waste your time trying to teach a horse to fly or a snake to sing "The Hallelujah Chorus."

> Although there is much to be said in behalf of courage, enthusiasm, and "the old school try," these attributes may cause more harm than good if they permit emotion to overrule common sense or encourage the commitment of time, effort, and money to objectives that are unattainable.[6]

Set high goals, but not unattainable ones. The Holy Spirit will give you wisdom in setting goals. He will direct you to commit to goals you could never attain in your own strength but which you can attain with His power.

This is an admittedly difficult subject for the Christian. What is attainable? We are to have faith in God. And we are told that with His power all things are possible. However, some Christians are presumptuous, thinking that God should help them do anything. God's help and power come only with those things that are in His will. But He can and does make the impossible possible.

Moses sent twelve spies into Kadesh Barnea to spy out the land. They reported a land flowing with milk and honey and abounding in incomparable fruit. They all agreed it was a desirable land, but ten of the spies soured the report and terrified the Israelites by their description of the "giants" in the land. "We are not able to go up against the people," they said.

However, two of the spies, Caleb and Joshua, brought the minority report. They, too, saw the giants, but they insisted the land was God's provision and He would see them through to victory. The goals of Joshua and Caleb were unattainable in terms of human ability. But they were attainable to those who moved ahead by faith in the wisdom and strength of God. Caleb and Joshua were the only spies permitted to enter the promised land forty years later.

Make your goals attainable, but also remember that as a Christian you have the power of the Holy Spirit inside you, and you do not have to look only to your human strength.

Make Your Goals Realistic.

State what results can be realistically achieved, given your available resources. For a college senior to say, "My goal is to be the president of the university within twelve months" is unrealistic. If he says, "My goal is to be college or university president in twenty years," that will be more realistic, especially if he sets down the intermediate goals: What further training must he get? Where should he take this further training? What steps should he take vocationally in preparation for the presidency? If a man who has barely enough to pay his survival costs today sets his goal to be a millionaire tomorrow, he is unrealistic. To set a goal to be a millionaire in twenty years may be realistic. Here again, concrete and precise measures must be determined and taken.

If a person wants to evangelize an entire nation within a period of five years, he is unrealistic. One reason is that the population keeps exploding. To set a goal to train one evangelist for every 1500 people in the country over the next twenty years may be realistic. This goal is concrete. It is precise. The measures determined and taken must be realistic.

Make Your Goals Tangible.

As you think about your goals, there will be some accomplishments that are intangible. You can achieve these intangible goals by achieving related tangible ones. The goals you set before yourself should always be tangible.

For instance, if you're impatient, you can't achieve the intangible goal of "developing patience" by affirming it or by will power, although both are fine in their place. How will you know when you have enough patience? Set some specific, tangible goals that breed patience. For instance, you could say,

"I won't complain for the next ten days when my wife is late."

"I won't blow my horn for the next ten days when the driver in front of me ignores the traffic light that has changed to green."

"I will smile when my plane is delayed and I may miss an important engagement."

"When an employee repeats a mistake, I will quietly and kindly repeat the correct instructions."

A goal such as "I want to be spiritually minded" doesn't tell you much because it is not tangible, and it is open to a great deal of interpretation. But you can set such tangible goals as:

"I will devote the first thirty minutes of each day to a quiet time of Bible reading and prayer."

"I will not only give the first part of each day to spiritual matters, but I will also devote the first day of each week and the first tenth of every dollar to the Lord and His work."

"I will tell someone what the Lord has done for me at least five days out of every week."

"At least once a week I'll inconvenience myself, if need be, to visit someone in need, for the purpose of encouraging and helping that person in Jesus' name."

Making your goals tangible is the only realistic way of achieving intangible goals.

In addition to making your goals SMART, there are a number of other principles that are useful.

Predicate your goals on your own behavior rather than hoped-for behavior from others. I can list a score of hospitals, churches, Christian organizations and universities that based their goals on hoped-for money from wealthy people, only to be doomed to disappointment at the death of the anticipated philanthropist.

Many leaders have been seriously detained in the pursuit of worthwhile goals because they had a Pollyanna confidence in an employee's performance that did not materialize. In some instances it was the fault of the leader for failing to provide sufficient training, or provide proper supervision, or for not insisting on performance reviews twice a year or quarterly.

Ideally, your goals should be based on things that are under your control—things you and the people who work with you can do. But this is one area that is a unique problem for Christian and nonprofit organizations who depend on volunteer help. You cannot always get the same cooperation from volunteer workers that you can get from those who are employed. This is why in most businesses a manager can direct people's work, but in many Christian organizations, excellence in leadership reveals itself by the motivation of people to serve.

Let your mind soar. Don't limit God or the wonderful things He has in store for you by permitting your own previous experience or the observation of other people's performance to stifle your vision.

Evangelist D. L. Moody asked a pathetically small audience, "How many of you believe God can fill the chairs in this hall with people?" Every hand went up.

"How many of you believe God *will* fill the chairs in this hall with people?" Fewer than thirty hands went up.

"You see," he chided, "it takes no faith to say God *can* do it; it takes great faith to say God *will* do it."

Let your mind soar and have your goals be the expression of your noblest qualities—a desire to be and to do your maximum for God.

Write out your goals in detail. Lord Bacon said, "Writing maketh an exact man." Writing crystallizes your thoughts and makes your ideas specific. Writing also brings the senses into play and sensory-rich images are photographed on the brain.

State your goals positively. The mind cannot picture a vacuum. To say, "My goal is that I'll stop procrastinating" is ineffective. Goals need the motivational force of a positive mental image of yourself doing what you want to do or being what you want to become. How do you visualize "stopping procrastination"?

Make sure your goals include behavioral changes. You must set goals of becoming, of developing whatever characteristics you lack. Working toward internal changes is an essential factor in goalsetting. Your behavior patterns must be compatible with your goals.

You can't expect to lose weight (if that is your goal) when your habit impels you to eat fats and sugars throughout the day. You must change your behavior. You can't launch a new program or enterprise if you permit fear of risk to paralyze you. You must have a behavioral change by developing courage before you can proceed.

Make your goals personal. To set your own personal goals requires a robust character, especially when the goals are different from the norm in your society. It's still impossible for a David to fight in Saul's armor. And it's equally impossible for you to lead with goals handed to you by someone else.

This principle is true throughout an organization. Each person in the organization should set his own goals. The manager may provide guidance for goalsetting, and the goals of each person should certainly contribute to the overall goals and objectives of the organization; but if each person sets his own goals, he will be more likely to achieve his goals and less likely to blame others if his goals are not met.

A young black boy named Carver discerned his vision early in life, and that vision governed his goalsetting, no matter what others thought.

Since he did not know his family, he picked the name George Washington Carver because he liked it. While wandering about the southern part of the United States as a boy, he shuddered to witness a mob beat out the brains of a black man and burn his body in the public square.

Little George had no residence. He slept in barns until one day a laundry lady asked him to help her. He taught himself between school sessions. Finally Highland University, after reviewing his high school grades, accepted him. When the president saw him, he heartlessly barked, "We don't take niggers." George Washington Carver went to Simpson College where he led his class scholastically.

Carver's paintings of flowers won prizes at the World's Fair Colombian Exposition. His musical genius won him a scholarship to the Boston Conservatory of Music. But he chose to specialize in agricultural chemistry in graduate school.

"I can be of more service to my race in agriculture," he said. "I want to help the man furthest down—the Negro—by teaching him how to help himself." That was his lifelong mission. Everything else he achieved was simply the fulfillment of goals toward the accomplishment of this mission.

Declining a prestigious teaching position at Iowa College, he packed his shabby suitcases and proceeded to Tuskegee Institute where he gave his people new goals by showing them the possibility of success. Working incredibly long hours in a shanty-type laboratory, he discovered ways to make plastics from soybeans, rubber from peanuts, flour from sweet potatoes. Thomas Edison offered him a salary in six figures. A rubber company and a chemical firm offered him blank-check retainers to work for them. But he stuck to his mission. He pursued his goals. He stayed at Tuskegee for $1,500 a year.

George Washington Carver could have been a multimillionaire, but he *never* deviated from his goals. He has been called the "Wizard of Farm Chemistry" and is one of the few Americans ever chosen to a fellowship by the London Royal Society for the Encouragement of Arts, Manufactures, and Commerce.

What is your vision? Whatever it is, do you know how you will get there? Write out each goal step by step. Leave no assumptions unstated. This will force you to analyze the resources you need—money, time, personnel—and adjust your plan so that it is a realistic one that reveals potential problem areas.

As you make goalsetting a practice, there are several specific problems you need to watch for.

GOAL CONFLICTS

Writing down your goals forces you to establish priorities, for often two very desirable goals will come into conflict. Buying a new home may conflict with sending your child to university. Prioritize your values to determine which is the most important. Your value system will determine whether to delay the purchase of the new home or postpone the sending of your child to a university.

Sometimes the conflict can be resolved by time. In 1912, my father fled from persecution in the Mideast, arriving in the United States when he was fifteen. Five years later, he wanted to leave for school to prepare for the ministry. His mother said, "You are the only Christian in the family. Your brothers are lost and going to hell. How can you leave to study about how to bring other people to Christ when you neglect your own brothers?"

Because it was an old-world family, the mother had the last word, the father having died previously. There was no recourse but for my father to accede to her suggestion. Furthermore, what she said made sense to him. He delayed his schooling for three more years, during which time his brothers and his brother-in-law came to the Lord.

Conflicts of goals can occur not just between two very desirable goals, but between the goals of different people involved in fulfilling the vision. Your vision may be for a great university that educates many young people in a Christian context. The faculty and staff members may all share the same vision, but their own personal goals of professional advancement or financial security may conflict with the goals that will accomplish the vision for the university. It is the leader who resolves these conflicts.

Harold Geneen, former chief executive officer of ITT, points out that "leadership is the ability to inspire other people to work together as a team under your direction in order to attain a common objective, whether in business, in politics, in war, or on the football field. No one can possibly do it all alone. Others in the organization must want to follow your lead." The leader challenges people to work at those goals that fulfill a vision. Geneen says, "I wanted to get people to reach for goals that they might have thought were beyond them. I wanted them to accomplish more than they thought possible. And I wanted them to do it not only for the company and their careers, but for the *fun* of it."[7]

STATED AND UNSTATED GOALS

In a perfect world, everyone would be candid and straightforward. But we don't live in a perfect world, and sometimes we deceive even ourselves. Thus, as you seek to fulfill your vision, you will write down a series of goals, but you may have other goals toward which you work. You may not express them, even to yourself. In addition to causing confusion, such unstated goals frequently hinder the accomplishment of the stated goals.

Perhaps your stated goals are the steps needed to build an evangelistic church. And yet one of your unstated goals is to provide employment for the members of your family. You wouldn't tell anyone that, but if you're not careful, the unstated goal will cause you to make decisions that are not in the best interest of accomplishing your stated goals. For instance, you may decide to develop an elaborate brochure not because the church really needs it, but because your sister owns a printing company and needs the business.

As more and more people follow your vision, each person with his or her own unstated goals, it becomes increasingly important to keep the stated goals in front of everyone involved and be aware of the possibility of unstated goals conflicting with stated ones.

HOW TO GET STARTED

Here's the way I did it. You might find it helpful. I knew my life mission. Now, what goals were necessary to accomplish that mission?

Every day I would take a yellow, lined pad and write down every conceivable step I felt must be taken to move toward the accomplishment of the mission. There was no particular logic or sequence. I wrote as fast as the ideas came to my head.

Prior to each of these sessions, which lasted anywhere from fifteen minutes to an hour and a half, I had my quiet time and earnestly asked God to guide me. I took great comfort in the words of James: "If any of you lacks wisdom, let him ask of God, who gives to all liberally and without reproach, and it will be given to him" (James 1:5). And I kept reminding the Lord that I qualified for that wisdom because I lacked it.

Every week or so I would review the items I had written down. I would eliminate some, combine some, and alter some. In reviewing, I would come up with other ideas. This continued for the better part of a year.

In addition to the items I had writen down, I made a list of my assets and a list of liabilities. I wrote down every quality or performance I could think of that indicated a personal liability. I also wrote down every criticism I could remember. On the other side of the sheet, I wrote down every asset as I perceived it. In addition, I listed every commendation I had received. This helped me to understand myself as never before, and it helped me to delineate the life mission to which I felt God had called me.

I blush with embarrassment when I confess that it was not until I was in my thirties that I finalized my crystallized expression of my life mission and the goals to attain it. Oh, yes, I had been called to preach when I was six years old. I knew from the time I was ten I wanted to be involved in a worldwide ministry. In that sense, my vision has remained unchanged. But I was nearly thirty-five before I finally worked out my life program under what I believed to be divine direction.

I specified the achievements I felt were necessary—both personal achievements and achievements of others who would be working with me—if the life mission were to be accomplished. This involved every conceivable area of life and activity, including place of residence, personal lifestyle, travel requirements, mental development, social activities, financial goals, family goals, organizational goals, and, of course, spiritual goals. Some items I found to be mutually exclusive. It was then I had to determine my value system and make a decision with regard to priorities.

A leader has one life-dominating vision which he converts to a life-compelling mission. But his goals are many. A vision must be broad enough to be permanent. Goals will change and develop.

Goals change because conditions change. Your life vision and mission remain constant. You alter goals as the changing times require. John Naisbitt gives an illustration in *Megatrends* that Christians should ponder.

In America in the early 1900s, the most successful business was considered to be the Pennsylvania Railroad. When a widow was left with some money, often she was advised to invest it in Pennsylvania Railroad stock, with the encouraging words, "You can always count on the old Pennsy."

In 1905, industrial analysts hailed the Pennsylvania Railroad as the largest and best-managed company in the U.S. Meanwhile, the railroad business moved into almost the same obsolescence as the buggy whip. Why? Naisbitt points out that if the executives of the Pennsylvania Railroad had been asked, "What is your business?" they would have answered, "Railroads." They should have realized they were in the transportation business rather than railroading. They then could have expanded their business to include heavy trucking, highways, jumbo jets, buses, helicopters; but these railroad men remained, as Harvard professor Theodore Levitt has written, "imperturbably self-confident."[8]

The evangelization of the young people of London is an important vision. It is a vision that will be permanent because the need for such a ministry will always be there. But the goals will change. Today, one set of goals might have to do with the development of a drug rehabilitation program—a need that didn't exist as strongly thirty years ago. In the 1960s and 1970s, the development of a coffee house ministry might have been a valid goal, but no longer.

The danger is that instead of making your vision permanent and your goals changing, you will make the vision changing and the goals permanent. This is what happens when an institution—such as a church— outlives its usefulness and yet people want it preserved. Perhaps a neighborhood has changed its character and the church refuses to adapt to the new neighborhood. The institution is preserved because of "the great things God has done here in the past." The vision has changed, but the goals have remained the same. How tragic that is.

I cannot insist too strongly that setting goals is not a one-time exercise. It is an ongoing discipline. Life is not static; it is dynamic. Your goals must be constantly modified. Therefore, you need to stay on top of your goals so that a changing environment will not catch you by surprise. And while you are working on your immediate goals, be sure to keep your eyes on your long-range goals, too.

BENEFITS OF GOALSETTING

I said that it is only through the establishment of a goals program that you can hope to accomplish your mission and thus fulfill your vision. Without a goals program, a vision is merely wishful thinking. The fulfillment of the vision is the primary benefit of goalsetting, but there are many other benefits as well.

Goals simplify the decision-making process. If the decision to be made relates positively to the leader's particular goal, the answer can be "yes." If it does not relate positively to his goal, the answer is "no." If the answer is yes, but he hasn't time for both the new activity and current activities, he must determine which of the two good decisions must be acted on, consistent with his value system and priorities. In this way, the leader conserves energy by concentrating on well-defined goals.

Goals tone up mental and physical health. Most stress comes from confusion and fear. Goals tend to eliminate confusion and override fear. Psychiatrist Dr. Ari Kiev says,

> I have repeatedly found that helping people to develop personal goals has proved to be the most effective way to help them to cope with problems and maximize their satisfaction. . . . With goals, people can overcome confusion and conflict over incompatible values, contradictory desires, and frustrated relationships . . . all of which often result from the absence of rational life strategies.
>
> Without a central goal [a mission], your thoughts may become worrisome; your confidence and morale may be undermined, and you may be led to the feared circumstances. Without a goal, you will focus on your weaknesses, and the possibilities of errors and criticism. This will foster indecision, procrastination, and inadequacy and will impede the development of your potential.[9]

John Wesley was assaulted, beaten, maligned, and yet he remained calm and cheerful. Goals kept him stress-free. He could say, "For I consider that the sufferings of this present time are not worthy to be compared with the glory which shall be revealed in us" (Romans 8:18).

Some of the world's leading medical personalities now emphasize the importance of goals as a deterrent to sickness and as a stabilizer of health. A recent book, *Getting Well Again,* written by Dr. O. Carl Simonton and his wife, Dr. Stephanie Matthews Simonton, and James Creighton, makes a case that goalsetting and striving constitute one of the most important and successful therapies in combating cancer. They say the most effective tool for getting patients well is to ask them to set new life goals. In so doing, they conceptualize and visualize their reasons for living. It is a way by which they reinvest themselves in life.[10]

Goals generate respect. Almost universally, people who know where they're going attract a following. Goals inspire willing followership.

Goals provide a system of measure so one may enjoy the feeling of accomplishment. It is absolutely necessary for the psychological satisfaction of each individual that he or she have a feeling of being worthwhile—usually through accomplishment. The achievement of goals will do this.

Goals produce persistence. The late Bob Pierce, founder of World Vision, told me a story that changed the course of my own life and work. When Pierce was a young man, a respected clergyman told him, "I have studied leaders and organizations. I have devoured biographies and autobiographies. I have immersed myself in history. I have carefully observed the contemporary leadership of my day. I've come to the conclusion that one factor distinguishes the organization that wins. It's staying power.

"In many cases," Pierce said this clergyman told him, "organizations headed by leaders more qualified by virtue of educational achievement, name recognition, natural gifts, and powerful relationships withered and died, while those of seemingly lesser advantages went on to spectacular achievement. The latter simply exercised staying power. When they were hanging on the ledge, ready to crash into the abyss, fingers bleeding as their nails were pulled off from their fingers, the people who won were those who just kept clinging. Somehow, some way, God intervened; He honored their staying power and gave them deliverance." Their goals produced persistence.

Goals, under God, deliver the leader from bondage to the plaudits of people. Conceivably, no greater peril threatens leadership effectiveness than slavery to the plaudits of the crowd. Such slavery borders on idolatry. Shortly before his death, Dr. J. C. Massee, whose Sunday sermons were reported each week in the Boston papers during his seven-year ministry from 1922–1929, said, "The most virulent disease threatening American evangelicalism is the mad passion for applause." He then quoted John 5:44, "How can you believe, who receive honor from one another, and do not seek the honor that comes from the only God?"

Just before his retirement in the early 1960s, the editor of the *Boston Herald* told me, "Massee was the most quotable preacher in Boston during my forty years in the newspaper business, but he seemed impervious to acclaim." Massee preached to 2,600 morning and night throughout his Boston ministry. A higher calling than fame, implemented by clearly defined goals, kept him free from bondage to the fickle response of the crowds.

THE FEAR OF GOALSETTING

If goalsetting is so wonderful, why don't more people do it? I must admit that the primary reason is probably that effective goalsetting is hard work. It takes determination. It takes commitment. But there are at least four reasons why people are afraid of goalsetting.

(1) *The fear of imperfect goals.* Some do not set goals because they are afraid their goals will not be perfect. Actually, a penchant for perfection is perilously close to an irreverent assumption of personal omniscience. Of course your goals will not be perfect. And it's true you may not perfectly reach a given goal. Nevertheless, you have an obligation, under God, to know precisely what you ought to do.

(2) *The fear of defeat.* The fear of defeat is first cousin to the fear your goals may not be perfect. Of course you may suffer defeat. But in the defeat, most probably you will learn some great lessons that will make your ultimate success all the greater. Usually the soundest Christian character is created through temporary defeats.

Defeat is a destructive force only when it is accepted as failure. When you accept it as a needed lesson, it is always a blessing. Defeats are God's great crucible in which He burns the dross from the human heart and purifies the spiritual mettle so that it can withstand the harder tests. In my study of history, I have concluded that the achievements of each man and woman seem to be in ratio to the intensity of the obstructing forces he or she had to surmount.

(3) *The fear of ridicule.* When I was twenty-two years old, I bought a little book, *Thirty Days to a More Powerful Vocabulary,* [11] by William Funk and Norman Lewis, and I started working on my vocabulary. I had realized that the larger a person's vocabulary, the wider the scope and the deeper the penetration of his thinking. Doubtlessly, I was a bit too free in using these new "double-jointed" words. A man whom I considered to be like an older brother quipped, "To understand John Haggai preach today, you must take along a volume of systematic theology and Webster's Unabridged Dictionary." That hurt!

Just as I was about to abandon my vocabulary-building discipline, a country preacher said to me, "John, you are working on vocabulary." I winced. He noticed and said, "Don't be embarrassed. I admire you. At first you will possibly seem a little stilted, but I want to encourage you not only to proceed, but to maintain the discipline as long as you live. It will widen your capacity for knowledge and understanding."

What a blessing that man was to me. I proceeded to enlarge my vocabulary, but my friend's criticism moderated my enthusiasm for displaying the newly acquired words.

Prior to the pastor's encouragement, I had abandoned the idea of pursuing speed-reading and memory courses. But, after overcoming the fear of ridicule, I proceeded with both.

The moment you set a goal, you can anticipate opposition and possibly some ridicule. For one thing, those who know they should be doing the same thing are condemned within their own hearts if they are shirking personal development. They have an alternative: either do what they know they should do or ridicule you. So look on this kind of ridicule as a disguised compliment.

(4) *The fear of considering goalsetting presumptuous.* Some may not set goals because of the verse which says, "Keep back your servant

also from presumptuous sins" (Psalm 19:13). But goalsetting meshes perfectly with the sovereignty of God.

Several years ago, I was lecturing to a group of Brazilian Christian leaders. The editor of a large denominational publishing house queried, "Dr. Haggai, how do you reconcile goalsetting with the sovereignty of God? Is not goalsetting a presumption on God's will?"

We had been discussing goals as they related to the number of people we wanted to see evangelized in the Third World. I asked him, "How many children do you have?"

"Three."

"May I assume your great passion is that they might give their lives to the Lord and live God-honoring, Christ-centered lives?"

"Of course."

"May I also assume that you and your dear wife are praying fervently, instructing the children, and creating the atmosphere in your home most conducive to leading them to such a spiritual commitment, while at the same time maintaining care not to pressure them? In other words, you want the decisions to be their own decisions. Am I correct in this?"

"Yes. Our great desire is that they may know the Lord."

"May it not be said, then, that you and your wife have set a goal, and that this goal relates to the salvation of your children? If that be true, do you think you are profaning the sovereignty of God? Within the parameters of God's sovereignty, He gives freedom for our choice."

We do not profane God's sovereignty by setting goals. Rather, we are to set our goals with reference to His will as we understand it. The goals then are the steps we take in carrying out the will of God!

The Living Bible paraphrases Proverbs 24:3–4, "Any enterprise is built by wise planning, becomes strong through common sense, and profits wonderfully by keeping abreast of the facts."

AN ONGOING DISCIPLINE

Goalsetting is an ongoing discipline of the true leader. Failure at this point destroys the confidence of the followers because it destroys the credibility of the leader.

If you lack a goals program, outside conditions and other people will take over the control of your life, whether you like it or not. If you are not in charge of you, somebody else will be—or some other thing. Specific goals with measurable standards will keep you on target toward the accomplishment of your life mission.

Let me give you an illustration. Hundreds of world leaders participate in the Haggai Institute program each year. Prior to their being accepted, they agree to conduct training sessions for fellow countrymen when they return to their homes. They agree to attempt the training of at least 100 people. Now that can be a goal within the framework of their life mission.

One might state the goal in this way, "My goal is to train twenty credentialed Christian leaders for effective evangelism within the next twelve months." To achieve that goal, one must put down supplementary goals:

1. Determine how to contact and recruit the leaders.

2. Determine who will help do the training.

3. Determine the curriculum (in many cases, he will feel he can adapt much of the material discussed at the Haggai Institute training session).

4. Determine how to schedule the sessions so as not to cripple the regular work.

5. Determine the cost and set a procedure for raising the funds (Haggai Institute does not fund any activity of its graduates).

Each of these steps must be accompanied by time targets.

On occasion, some have had to alter their initial plans because of an unusually destructive monsoon or unexpected interruptions in their civic life or in their church programs. To keep their activities up to date, however, they don't hesitate, in such situations, to change their intermediate goals, but they refuse to change their large goal.

Today's persistent acceleration of change in people, places, and things demands nothing less than a clearly defined goals program. What is brand new today becomes obsolete tomorrow. *And the leader must always know what day it is! His followers are counting on it.*

SUMMARY

A vision is the foundation of all leadership. The leader's vision requires a commitment to act, which is called a mission. But the vision and mission are put into practice with a set of specific, measurable steps designed to achieve the mission. Those steps are called goals. The vision and mission will remain constant, but the goals should be reviewed monthly or more often. At that review you should assess what goals have been accomplished, examine those that are not completed, determine what corrective measures should be taken, and set new goals.

A good goalsetting program is a S-M-A-R-T one. The goals are *S*pecific, *M*easurable, *A*ttainable, *R*ealistic, and *T*angible. Each goal must be a specific step rather than a vague desire. Goals should be measurable not only in terms of *what* is to be accomplished, but *when* it is to be accomplished. Goals should be high ones but attainable, recognizing that the Holy Spirit can help you attain the "impossible." Evaluate your available resources so that the goals are realistic. Achieve intangible goals by stating and achieving related tangible ones.

In addition to making goals SMART, you should predicate your goals on your own behavior rather than hoped-for behavior of others. You should let your mind soar. Don't limit God. Write out your goals in detail. State your goals positively. Make sure your goals include behavioral changes. Make your goals personal.

As you make goalsetting a practice, there are several specific problems you need to watch for. Sometimes two very desirable goals will come into conflict with each other. Prioritize your goals. Be aware of unstated goals and the influence they can have on your own and other's effectiveness at carrying out the stated goals. Be aggressive about modifying your goals to changing situations.

Goalsetting brings many benefits. Goals simplify the decision-making process. Goals tone up mental and physical health. Goals generate respect. Goals provide a system of measure so you may enjoy the feeling of accomplishment. Goals produce persistence. And goals, under God, deliver the leader from bondage to the plaudits of people.

In spite of the many benefits of goalsetting, many people do not do it. Some fail to set goals because it is hard work. Others have a fear of imperfect goals or a fear of defeat or a fear of ridicule—or a fear of goalsetting being considered presumptuous. All of these fears can keep a person from practicing goalsetting.

Goalsetting is an ongoing discipline. You cannot do it once and ignore it. Today's persistent acceleration of change in people, places, and things demands nothing less than a clearly defined goals program.

4

The Principle of

LOVE

J. R. Ewing, the star of "Dallas," the most popular television series in television history, failed at being a leader because he does not move people toward goals of beneficial permanence. He destroys people. He may have vision. He may have a mission. He may even have a goals program, but he lacks a basic ingredient for leadership—love.

Christ makes leaders both fearless and strong as well as loving and self-giving. "For God has not given us a spirit of fear, but of power and of love and of a sound mind" (2 Timothy 1:7). The strongest power in leadership is love.

Napoleon Bonaparte's intellectual greatness and his own intense egotism make his alleged tribute to the supremacy of leadership by love particularly striking. He said, "Alexander, Caesar, Charlemagne, and myself founded great empires; but upon what did the creations of our genius depend? Upon force. Jesus alone founded His empire upon love, and to this very day millions would die for Him."

In his book *Managing,* Harold Geneen makes an important distinction between a leader and a commander. The leader leads his people; the commander tells his people, "I want this done by this date, and if it is not done, then heads will roll!"[12] The commander rules by fear; the leader guides by love.

Vision sets a leader apart from a manager. And love sets a true leader apart from a power-holder. W. C. H. Prentice said that too often we confuse leadership with popularity, power, showmanship, or wisdom in long-range planning. Most so-called leaders today—both within and without the church—are not true leaders but power-holders. And maintaining one's position by popularity or power not only fails to emphasize love, but it sees demonstrating love as a definite weakness because one can't love without making oneself vulnerable. One can't love while keeping one's options open. To truly love—whether it is one's spouse, children, or the people one leads—one must give himself unreservedly in such a way that he can be hurt, that he can be rejected. But the fundamental principle on which a power-holder operates is to protect himself—*not* to be vulnerable.

Love as a characteristic of leadership seems to be out of place. Yet there cannot be true leadership without love. This is a reality in all true leaders, whether Christian or not. But its highest example is found in the person of Jesus Christ. And since Christians are to imitate Christ, they should be in a better position to exhibit love as leaders.

WHAT IS LOVE?

The love of which I speak is not a sentimental emotion. It is the outgoing of the totality of one's being to another in beneficence and help. *Love* as used here refers to a mind-set, an *act of the will.* It is not the exercise of emotions.

A world leader sitting across the table from me in my office said, "You must have great love for the Third World."

I stunned him by saying, "If by that you mean that right now my veins are pulsating with the rich, excitement-charged blood of deep emotion, no. At this very moment, I have no more emotional warmth toward the Third World than I do toward this table. But I have great love for the Third World; you're right.

"I have great love for my son who died in his twenty-fifth year. As I talk with you, I may feel no great emotion about him. However, if I talk about him for a few minutes, reflecting on our experiences together as a family, I shall be nearly overcome emotionally—which, of itself, indicates no greater love. My love doesn't increase with emotion and decrease without it!"

My friend looked at me wide-eyed. He finally grasped what I was saying. Few seem to understand the meaning of true love—the kind of love that is described by the Greek word *agape.*

Agape love is Godlike love. The word *agape* is essentially a Christian word, haloed with a glory given it by God. He used it to express His own attitude toward *all* men and women.

A continuous emotional "high," like that experienced at the birth of a child, the commitment to a marriage relationship, or a victory on the athletic field would destroy us. The psyche, as well as the body, could not handle it. True love, while often including this kind of emotion, far exceeds a temporary ecstasy.

True love involves the totality of one's being. God, and only He, expresses it perfectly. He gave His all. The Man on the middle cross was God. In life, Jesus expressed it when He said, "I am among you as the One who serves." In death, He expressed it when He said, "No one takes [My life] from Me, but I lay it down of Myself."

The love of which I speak includes unconquerable consideration, charitableness, benevolence. It means no matter what anyone does by way of humiliation, abuse, or injury, the Christlike leader works toward that person's highest good. Indeed, without this kind of love, leadership fails the ultimate test—permanence.

Love relates to real needs. Love will not pander to perceived needs that are not real needs. The leader knows what the real needs of the group are because he loves the people in his group. And his love is real, not a self-serving imitation.

When a man who was crippled cried to Peter and John for money, they did not give him money; they healed him. They met his real needs, not his perceived needs.

The child who is never disciplined, whose parents do not love him enough to impose restrictions (to meet his real needs) feels rootless and does outlandish things in order to get attention and appreciation. Even though a child may be angry with the parents for some discipline imposed, studies have proved that the disciplined child feels a sense of belonging. Eventually, he may come to realize that the truly loving parents have the child's highest good at heart.

The same is true with adults. The leader, expressing genuine love, seeks to lead his followers toward those things that meet their real needs, even though the measures taken at the time may not seem palatable.

Love is *active*. It demands expression. It is never passive. Love is *transitive*. It demands an object. Love is *serving*. Love is *sacrificing*.

True love is under the control of one's will rather than a fortuitous flash outside one's control. So there is no excuse for a loveless leadership.

The Christlike leader loves God, himself, and his neighbor. He is emotionally whole because he is spiritually healthy.

The leader sustains a winning attitude by faithfully obeying Christ's two commandments, which mark the starting point for superior leadership. A lawyer cross-examined Jesus: " 'Teacher, which is the great commandment in the law?' Jesus said to him, 'You shall love the Lord your God with all your heart, with all your soul, and with all your mind. This is the first and great commandment. And the second is like it: You shall love your neighbor as yourself' " (Matthew 22:36–39).

In our Lord's two commandments, three areas of love surface: first, love of God; second, love of neighbor; and third, love of self. The love God has demonstrated toward us furnishes us the ultimate illustration of what our love is to be like. His love is the communication of His being to us in beneficence and help. The word *beneficence* means the practice of doing good: active goodness, kindness, or charity—literally, well-doing. Loving God, as commanded here by Christ, means the communication back to God of that which He has given to us. This is demonstrated by our love of our neighbor—which is to be modeled after God's love for us. Jesus talks about it as giving a cup of cold water or visiting someone in jail "in My name." And our love of ourselves arises from the fact that God loves us. It is by understanding and believing that God loves, forgives, and accepts us as we are that we can have a healthy self-esteem.

LOVE GOD

Christ says you must love "your God." You, as a leader, must so live as never to leave a question in anyone's mind as to who your God is. God says, "You shall have no other gods before Me" (Exodus 20:3). Anything or anyone that has a greater formative influence in your life than God is an idol. An idol can be a habit, a person, a thing, just as much as a graven image. Loveless leadership is idolatrous leadership because it replaces God with an idol. The Christlike leader despises idolatry.

Isaiah said, "In the year that King Uzziah died, I saw the Lord sitting on a throne, high and lifted up" (Isaiah 6:1). Uzziah had to die before Isaiah saw the Lord. Uzziah had been an idol to Isaiah. Isaiah had transgressed God's commandment "You shall have no other gods before Me." Uzziah had been a god to him. Other gods are helpless. They only succeed in blurring the leader's necessary focus.

Loveless, self-centered idolatry had stifled Isaiah's leadership. Idolatrous leadership, no matter how brilliant and disciplined, ultimately fails. But poor, egomaniacal man spurns the lessons of history and thinks he will achieve where others failed. Leader after leader has thought that he could make himself like God and has demanded worship and reverence. In fairness, sometimes the idolatry comes from the people with little encouragement on the part of the leader. For instance, Sukarno's fall in Indonesia in the 1960s paralyzed some Indonesian Christians with fear because they had idolized him. Some courageous men lovingly denounced their idolatry. God, who "raises up kings," raised up President Suharto, and the nation entered upon a period of tranquillity and stability.

Love for God must be exclusive, "with all your heart, with all your soul, with all your strength, and with all your mind." Jesus is saying, "Your love for God is to be concentrated and exclusive, surpassing, and all-consuming. You are to love God with your intelligence, your emotions, and your volition—with the totality of your personality."

LOVE YOURSELF

Loving God with the totality of your personality and accepting the love God has for you is the foundation for loving yourself. A proper understanding of self-love is a teaching that has not been emphasized among Christians because of a reaction to a Greek emphasis on "high-mindedness." Aristotle had promoted a concept that fostered pride and regarded those who were humble as contemptible, mean-spirited, and without energy and goals. He exaggerated the importance of an air of loftiness.

In response to this, many Christians taught that we should be humble, but they taught humility in the sense of downgrading ourselves or running ourselves into the ground. We will discuss a correct understanding of humility in the next chapter. Being truly humble, however, is *not* inconsistent with loving yourself. God wants us to have a healthy self-esteem. He wants us to love ourselves. A healthy self-love is essential to good leadership.

In his book *Seeds of Greatness,* Denis Waitley, who served as a consulting psychologist to the American astronauts, says, "The first best-kept secret of total success is that we must feel love inside ourselves before we can give it to others." He then explains, "If there is no deep, internalized feeling of value inside of us, then we have nothing to give or to share with others."[13]

Loving yourself means that you are contributing to your highest needs with beneficence and help. This is not narcissism. It is not putting yourself ahead of everyone else. Rather, it is putting God first. For instance, when you take proper nutrition, sleep, and exercise, you are fortifying your body, which is the temple of God. When you are contributing to your intellectual development with proper knowledge, you are loving yourself. When you exercise your will to avoid engagements that dishonor Christ, you are engaged in the highest form of self-love.

The fad of loving yourself that floods the airwaves and the bookshelves today is too often a preoccupation with self, rather than a preoccupation with God and with your neighbors.

Because the Spirit of God lives in us, He gives confidence and a proper self-esteem. True self-confidence issues from the domination of the Holy Spirit and a subsequent confidence in His leadership.

LOVE YOUR NEIGHBOR

Loving God and accepting God's love for you is the foundation for loving yourself. And loving yourself is the foundation for loving your neighbor, for a healthy self-esteem releases you from spending your energy building up your own self-confidence through power games and putting down others. It lets you give of yourself freely. It lets you experience the outgiving of the totality of your being to another in beneficence and help.

Often we want to love our neighbor, but we don't know how to express it. Ted Engstrom, president of World Vision International, gives ten very practical and powerful principles of expressing love in his book *The Fine Art of Friendship.* [14] These ten principles tell us how to express love to our neighbor.

1. "We must decide to develop friendships in which we demand nothing in return." Love is unconditional. If it's not unconditional, it's not love, but self-serving manipulation. Sadly, manipulation is more common among so-called leaders than is true love.

2. "It takes a conscious effort to nurture an authentic interest in others." Our natural tendency is to be self-centered (which is *not* the same as having a healthy self-esteem). It therefore takes a conscious effort to love.

3. "Each of us is a one-of-a-kind creation. Therefore, it will always take time—often a long time—to understand one another." Leaders are usually busy people, and yet love takes time. There is no substitute.

4. "Commit yourself to learning how to listen." Do you *really* listen to people, trying to understand what they're saying, or do you listen to give an answer—letting another talk while you plan what you will say next? The one who loves listens with understanding.

5. "Simply be there to care, whether you know exactly what to do or not." Loving one's neighbor involves fulfilling, in a visible way, Christ's promise, "I will never leave you nor forsake you." Be available.

6. "Always treat others as equals." Just because God has put you in a position of leadership does not mean He has made you "better"

than others. It is the leader most of all who needs to heed the words of Paul "not to think of himself more highly than he ought to think" (Romans 12:3).

7. "Be generous with legitimate praise and encouragement." Such words build up the self-esteem of others. Words of criticism and discouragement, however, kill enthusiasm and love in others.

8. "Make your friends Number One, preferring them above yourself." This is another point at which we see a clear difference between the leader who loves and the power-holder who manipulates. The leader puts others first. The power-holder "looks out for Number One" (himself!) by "pulling his own strings" and "winning through intimidation."

9. "Learn to love God with all your heart, soul, mind, and strength. Then love your neighbor as yourself."

10. "Emphasize the strengths and virtues of others, not their sins and weaknesses." To illustrate this point, Ted Engstrom tells the following story:

It seemed that Joe had just about had it with his wife of three years. He no longer thought of her as attractive or interesting; he considered her to be a poor housekeeper who was overweight, someone he no longer wanted to live with. Joe was so upset that he finally decided on divorce. But before he served her the papers, he made an appointment with a psychologist with the specific purpose of finding out how to make life as difficult as possible for his wife.

The psychologist listened to Joe's story and then gave this advice, "Well, Joe, I think I've got the perfect solution for you. Starting tonight when you get home, I want you to start treating your wife as if she were a goddess. That's right, a goddess. I want you to change your attitude toward her 180 degrees. Start doing everything in your power to please her. Listen intently to her when she talks about her problems, help around the house, take her out to dinner on weekends. I want you to literally pretend that she's a goddess. Then, after two months of this wonderful behavior, just pack your bags and leave her. That should get to her!"

Joe thought it was a tremendous idea. That night he started treating his wife as if she were a goddess. He couldn't wait to do things for her. He brought her breakfast in bed and had flowers delivered to her for no apparent reason. Within three weeks the two of them had gone on two romantic weekend vacations. They read books to each other at night, and Joe listened to her as never before. It was incredible what Joe was doing for his wife. He kept it up for the full two months. After the allotted time, the psychologist gave Joe a call at work.

"Joe," he asked, "how's it going? Did you file for divorce? Are you a happy bachelor once again?"

"Divorce?" asked Joe in dismay. "Are you kidding? I'm married to a goddess. I've never been happier in my life. I'd never leave my wife in a million years. In fact, I'm discovering new, wonderful things about her every single day. Divorce? Not on your life."[15]

These ten practical and powerful principles will let you not just *feel* love, but *express* it so that others will know that you love them. But, as Erich Fromm says in *The Art of Loving,*[16] the practice of love, which he calls an art, requires discipline, concentration, patience, and it must be of supreme importance to you. Basic to this is the fact that the expression of love requires the indwelling power of the Holy Spirit.

LOVE AND THE LEADER

Love God; love yourself; love your neighbor. Jesus commanded this for all Christians. But it is particularly important for leaders. The leader, expressing genuine love, motivates his followers to move toward that which is beneficially permanent and fulfills their real needs. Only love is permanent. The last part of the greatest words ever written about love says, "And now abide faith, hope, love, these three; but the greatest of these is love" (1 Corinthians 13:13). Love is the greatest because only love is permanent. Faith ultimately will be fulfilled in heaven; hope, too, will ultimately be realized in heaven. However, love will continue throughout all eternity.

Practicing love is particularly important for a leader because leaders deal with people. Unlike the mechanic who deals primarily with things or the mathematician who deals primarily with ideas, the leader deals with people. And people need to be dealt with in love.

Practicing love is particularly important for a leader also because motivation by threat or influence is inconsistent with true leadership. That is the way of the dictator or power-holder. But love is the motivating factor most consistent with true leadership.

For a leader, practicing love is not something that he aspires to for himself only. Rather, he wants to build love into the lives of those who follow him as well. He should be a role model, showing how love works, demonstrating its development, its practice, and its benefits.

The Christlike Leader Eloquently Expresses Love

Just as the majestic tree expresses its life in fruit, the Christlike leader expresses his leadership in love. Paul the Apostle talks of the "fruit of the Spirit" in Galatians 5:22, 23, and he uses the singular. It would seem, therefore, that he is talking about one fruit. Punctuation is not inspired of God and I would therefore like to put Paul's words this way, "But the fruit of the Spirit is love: joy, peace, long-suffering, kindness, goodness, faithfulness, gentleness [humility], self-control. Against such there is no law."

The eight qualities mentioned are all expressions of love. Leadership imbued with these qualities moves those that are led toward the fulfillment of their *real* needs. And it moves them with grace.

In the rest of this chapter, we will look at the first six expressions of love. The last two—humility and self-control—will be considered in the next two chapters since they are two important principles of leadership themselves. These eight qualities will shine through the leader who is practicing love. Here is what his followers will see.

Joy

Joy is love's music. Only love can keep one cheerful in all circumstances. Jesus told His disciples, "These things I have spoken to you, that My joy may remain in you, and that your joy may be full" (John 15:11). But it is not a superficial giddiness that is meant here.

Our self-centered nature and society have led us to believe that happiness and joy come when we get what we want and our "needs" and "wants" are filled. We are told that joy is a new car, a bigger house, healthy children, and a bit of fame. But these things will never bring joy because we will always want more. Joy comes not from getting, but from giving. My friend Peter Gillquist expressed it this way, "Every time we have the chance in *any* way to flesh out the love of God to others, our joy cycle gets fulfilled all over again."[17]

St. Francis of Assisi expressed the Christian's way to joy through love in his famous prayer:

"Lord, make me an instrument of Thy peace.
Where there is hatred let me sow love;
Where there is injury, pardon;
Where there is doubt, faith;
Where there is despair, hope;
Where there is darkness, light;
Where there is sadness, joy.
Oh Divine Master, grant that I may not so much seek
To be consoled as to console;
To be understood as to understand;
To be loved as to love;

For it is in giving that we receive;
It is in pardoning that we are pardoned;
It is in dying that we are born to eternal life."

PEACE

Peace is love's agreement. The Bible speaks of two kinds of peace that come to a person as the result of a loving relationship with God. There is "peace *with* God" and the "peace *of* God." The first refers to the making of a peace treaty after a war is over. "Friendship with the world is enmity with God. Whoever therefore wants to be a friend of the world makes himself an enemy of God" (James 4:4). But when you become a child of God through Jesus Christ, no longer are you at war with God—no longer are you His enemy—but you are at peace with Him.

The second phrase—the "peace of God"—refers to the inner tranquillity you can have in the midst of a confusing and falling-apart world because you know that God is in charge. The fruit of the Spirit, which is love, produces peace.

There is a third aspect of peace in the life of the leader. He is to bring peace to others in this world of turmoil, for he has been given a "ministry of reconciliation."

It is often the ploy of the loveless, self-centered power-holder to create factions, skillfully foment ceaseless conflict, unrelentingly keep the parties off balance so he can control the group. This callous *modus operandi* fails in the end. The loving leader, the one who works for harmony, may lose some votes, but ultimately win the decision—for everybody's benefit. He's willing to be vulnerable. He knows that unless he's vulnerable, his leadership will never be viable. He doesn't waste adrenaline on paranoid efforts to exterminate criticism.

In 1970, I spent three weeks with one of the influential leaders of the world's largest Presbyterian church, the Young Nak Church in Seoul, Korea. I asked many questions about its celebrated senior minister, Dr. Han Kyung Chik.

"Does he ever encounter opposition in session meetings?" I asked.

"Many times."

"How does he respond?"

"Usually he'll say, 'You are good and godly men. I know you desire the will of God. Perhaps I was premature in bringing this matter up. Or, maybe it's an error to consider it. Let's pray some more about it."

"And how does Dr. Han respond to unjust criticism?"

"I remember one time when a session member made what to me was a savage attack on Dr. Han's judgment. Dr. Han wept. He said, 'Apparently I did not pray sufficiently before taking this course of action. Forgive me. I shall pray more earnestly about this.' Within a year, the entire session saw the wisdom of Dr. Han's proposal and adopted it, although he never again brought it up."

What makes this so powerful a lesson to me is that Dr. Han spends hours every day in prayer. For more than half a century he's been at prayer no later than 5 o'clock every morning. Neither I nor any of the critics are worthy to tie his shoes! His great and surpassing and sustained leadership finds its roots in love—and peace, love's agreement.

LONG-SUFFERING

Long-suffering is love's endurance. The meaning of the New Testament word for long-suffering is "to endure with unruffled temper." The long-suffering person is long-tempered. This person incarnates the words of the apostle Paul in 1 Corinthians 13, "love suffers *long* and is kind."

Dr. Han says, "When you lose your temper, you lose everything." How true that is. I recommend that every leader read, reread, and memorize Rudyard Kipling's poem "If." It begins, "If you can keep your head when all around you are losing theirs and blaming it on you. . . ."

Any leader worth "his salt" possesses a temper. The effective leader, in reliance upon God, controls his temper. The effective leader will not stoop to respond, no matter what the provocation, with smug complaisance, worldly courtesy, patronizing contempt, or a brutal vindictiveness. Rather, he responds with love's endurance—long-temperedness.

KINDNESS

Kindness is love's service. The original word for kindness in the New Testament does not refer to sentiment but to service, to helpfulness in small things—doing the little things that help, reinforce, and support. Kindness is love's service.

When I was a teenager, I listened to the spellbinding Dr. Walter A. Maier on the Lutheran Hour's "Bringing Christ to the Nations" broadcast. Sunday after Sunday I sat before the radio transfixed by the greatest radio preacher on earth. I scraped up two dollars and mailed it to him with a letter. I apologized for such a small offering but told him it was all I had. I assured him of my faithful "attendance" to his broadcast and of my fervent prayers for him and his ministry.

I was astonished a few days later when I received from him a two-page typewritten letter. It was no "canned" letter. He had typed it himself. No secretary could have been that bad! He answered my letter in detail. He told me how important my gift was. He encouraged me with the fact that "every dollar reaches 1,500 people with the gospel through our program, so your gift will reach 3,000 people!" He shared some personal insights and anecdotes. In my ecstasy, I said to myself, "When I get older, if anyone writes me, I shall be as kind to them as Dr. Maier has been to me."

Maier's response demonstrated kindness, love's service. No wonder his leadership influenced millions with dimensions of beneficial permanence.

GOODNESS

Goodness is love's deportment. Goodness is the manifestation of Godlike virtues in a person. Goodness is Joseph's fleeing from Potiphar's wife when she tried to seduce him. Goodness is Jesus' showing compassion to the woman caught in adultery without condoning her sin. Goodness is George Washington praying on his knees in the snow at Valley Forge and Abraham Lincoln on his knees in the White House—each asking God for guidance and strength to do the right. Goodness is one of Egypt's great Christian leaders living modestly on an income that does not even make provision for a car, giving himself totally because he loves the Egyptian people, even though he could enjoy a prestigious position with a good income and impressive perks.

God Himself is referred to as abounding in goodness. And goodness marks the strong leader. It reveals the strength which opposes everything evil and immoral. It drives the Christlike leader to dependence on God. This leader asks God for:

- a disposition to hate what is evil,
- a compulsion to follow after that which is good,
- wisdom to judge rightly in all things,
- increased thoughtfulness and sensitivity in dealing with all people.

The Greek word that is translated *goodness* in the New Testament never appears in secular Greek writings. Neither the Greeks nor the Romans grasped the meaning of *agape* love, nor of its offspring, goodness. They saw love and goodness as qualities to be avoided. Instead, the Greeks worshiped the intellect and the Romans worshiped power.

Love is the father of goodness. Therefore, it functions only in the area of beneficence and help. Goodness finds its anchor in love, not in legalism, nor in lackeyism. Neither the legalist nor the lackey provide beneficence or help.

The legalist forces his so-called "goodness" on others. The martinet, always poised to jump with criticism on every person who deviates from his chart of "proper" behavior, preempts leadership.

The lackey forfeits leadership not only by obsequiously agreeing with those he perceives to hold power and favor, but by shamelessly adopting their "goodness" code in an attempt to acquire their power and curry their favor. Both the legalist and the lackey violate love and, therefore, leadership.

Goodness in leadership produces a deportment that is kind but just, tender but tough, fair but firm.

FAITHFULNESS

Faithfulness is love's measure. Faithfulness has to do with a leader's staying true to his trust, to his commitment to others, to himself, and, above all, to God. It's a characteristic of the reliable leader. Faithfulness is Noah's building an ark in spite of the jeers and criticisms of others. He and his family were saved in the flood because of that ark. Faithfulness is Abraham's willingness to sacrifice his only son Isaac because he believed God would deliver him. And He did—by providing the substitute of a ram.

Faithfulness is Savonarola's defiance of the vested interests of Florence, Italy, in his proclamation of the Truth. He was hanged and his body burned, but his leadership continued hundreds of years after his death. That's the power of faithfulness in life and leadership.

Do you keep your promises? Do you pay your bills? Do you honor your appointments? Do you stay on course with your commitments? Is your word your bond? Do you go the second mile?

Motel magnate Cecil B. Day opposed everything false. He refused to alter verbal agreements at the closing of real estate transactions, even when the alterations were legally permissible and when they would profit him.

Faithfulness is love's measure. People will not willingly follow an unreliable leader. They want one who is trustworthy.

The attitude of *agape* love gives vitality and credibility to the leader's influence. Love in the leader produces in the group a desire to follow him. Love accomplishes what neither fame nor force, muscle nor manipulation can attain.

When the late Dr. E. Stanley Jones preached on love in India, a church leader complained that though he had saturated his leadership with love, one of the laymen was making a lot of trouble and threatening to split the church. The frustrated clergyman asked Dr. Jones what to do since love hadn't worked. "Increase the dosage," retorted Jones.

Leadership by love works! In business and politics, in the professions and education, the church, and the home—in every area of life, the leadership of love is the outgoing of the leader to others in beneficence and help. Leadership based upon this foundation cannot fail.

Jesus, the only *perfect* leader, set the example and promises the strength to follow it.

And that's the leadership our changing world cries for. It's the *only* leadership that holds out any hope. There is no limit on the number of such leaders needed. You have a wide open opportunity to help set the course of this changing world in the right direction. And your resource is the ultimate Super Power—LOVE!

SUMMARY

Just as vision sets a leader apart from a manager, love sets a true leader apart from a power-holder. There cannot be true leadership without love. True love is not merely a sentimental emotion, but it is an act of the will in which the Christlike leader works toward the highest good of others.

Scripture says that you are to love God exclusively "with all your heart, with all your soul, with all your strength, and with all your mind." You are to love yourself with a self-confidence that issues from the domination of the Holy Spirit in your life. And you are to love your neighbor, giving yourself freely to others in beneficence and help.

The Christlike leader expresses love because love infuses his leadership with a beneficial permanence that draws others to him. The expression of love is found in Galatians 5:22–23. The qualities listed there will be present in the life of the Christlike leader who shows love.

* *Joy* is love's music.
* *Peace* is love's agreement.
* *Long-suffering* is love's endurance.
* *Kindness* is love's service.
* *Goodness* is love's deportment.
* *Faithfulness* is love's measure.

Leadership by love works! It is the outgoing of the leader to others in beneficence and help. Leadership based upon this foundation cannot fail.

5

The Principle of

HUMILITY

Contrary to what many think, humility gives tensile strength to leadership.

To please a certain official, Abraham Lincoln once signed an order transferring certain regiments. Secretary of War Stanton, convinced that the President had made a serious blunder, refused to execute the order. "Lincoln's a fool!" he roared.

When Lincoln heard what Stanton had said, he replied, "If Stanton said I am a fool, then I must be, for he is nearly always right. I'll step over and see for myself."

Lincoln did just that. When Stanton convinced him the order was in error, Lincoln quietly withdrew it.

Part of Lincoln's greatness lay in his rising above sensitivity to the opinions of others concerning himself. One could not offend him easily. In his humility, he welcomed criticism. And he demonstrated a strength that few leaders ever match.

If you hope to rise to your potential as a leader, you'll do well to learn to meet criticism with tranquillity and pleasantness. This approach strengthens your spirit, gives added thrust to your work, and, above all, honors God.

To paraphrase the words of the late A. W. Tozer in his book *The Pursuit of God,* [18] the humble man is not a human mouse, suffering a sense of his own inferiority. In his moral life, he may be as bold as a lion and as strong as Samson, but he doesn't fool himself about himself. He has accepted God's estimate with regard to his own life. He knows he is as weak and as helpless as God has declared him to be. Paradoxically, he relies on the confidence that in the sight of God, he is more important than the angels. In himself, he is nothing; in God, he is everything. That's his motivating motto. He is not overly concerned that the world will never see him as God sees him. He is perfectly content to allow God to determine His own values. The humble man patiently waits for the day when everything will get its own price tag, and real worth will come into its own. In the meantime, he will lead for the benefit of mankind and for the glory of God, happily willing to wait for the day of final evaluation.

Humility—or meekness—is love's mood. It is love's prevailing attitude, spirit, and disposition. The humble person is free from pride or arrogance. He submits himself to others and is helpful and courteous. The humble person does not consider himself to be self-sufficient. And yet he recognizes his own gifts, resources, and achievement. He knows that he has been the object of undeserved, redeeming love. Therefore he cannot build up himself for he knows it is "all of grace." But being humble does not exclude confidence, for we are told in Scripture to "cast not away your confidence" (Hebrews 10:35).

The humble person does not take offense or fight back. He turns the other cheek to the one who hits him. And yet humility is not cowardice, for humility requires high courage. Humility makes you willing to take a lower place than you deserve, to keep quiet about your merits, to bear slights, insults, and false accusations for the sake of a higher purpose. Jesus displayed humility for "when he was reviled, [He] did not revile in return; when He suffered, He did not threaten."

Christ gave life, vitality, and glory to the word *humility*. We learn of humility through His teaching, His example, His character. He did not come in the pomp of arrogance or of pride, although He could have done so. He did not ask Herod for the key to the city. Nor did He have His associates engineer a testimonial dinner in His honor. He came in lowliness of mind, according to the prophecy in Psalm 22 and Isaiah 53.

Humility is the lowliness that pervades the leader's consciousness when he contemplates God's holy majesty and superabundant love in contrast to his own unworthiness, guilt, and total helplessness apart from divine grace. This is the kind of humility Christ welcomes. This humility makes religion neither stiff nor heavy nor pompous, but simple, relaxed, joyful, honoring to God, and helpful to people.

While it is difficult for most people to display humility, it is particularly difficult for a leader because his experiences discourage humility.

Most leaders have a ceremonial role to fill. It is the leader who must meet and entertain visiting dignitaries. It is the leader who represents his followers at official events. It is through honor given to a leader that the group also receives honor. When Prime Minister Rajiv Gandhi is treated elegantly, with honor and respect, at an official state visit in another country, all of India is being treated elegantly with honor and respect. Because of this, it is not easy for a leader to demonstrate humility. And yet humility is an extremely important principle of leadership.

One recoils at the task of writing on humility when he recognizes that even the discussion of humility can induce pride. It can be said that just as the honest person does not discuss honesty nor the pure person discuss purity, so the humble person does not discuss humility for the simple reason that humility possesses no self-consciousness. Humility is the "eye which sees everything except itself," according to Ritschl.

Someone asked Dwight L. Moody, "Are you saying that the humble person doesn't think much of himself?" Moody retorted, "No. He doesn't think of himself at all." Humility is unconscious of itself. The man who is humble doesn't know he is humble.

False Humility

Even worse than a lack of humility in a person's life is a false humility in which a person is very proud about acting in a humble way. The English author and poet Samuel Taylor Coleridge correctly said that the devil's "favorite sin is pride that apes humility."

And yet the person with false humility is fooling only himself, for people see through the pompous, self-adulatory, and arrogant person who feigns humility. The truly humble person will avoid contrived posturing. He will not play games like those who are always willing to sit at the foot of the banquet table, provided they come late enough for everyone to see them do it.

After a soloist has thrilled an audience with a glorious rendition marked by beauty, skill, and impact, it would be false humility to deny such surpassing ability in response to the comment, "That was a beautiful solo." It would be hypocrisy. The musician, recognizing that the voice, the health required to practice long hours, and the tutelage all were gifts from God, accepts the comment with grace and gratitude.

In the first century, there were some teachers at Colossae called Gnostics. They said one could obtain perfection beyond the capabilities of ordinary Christians through special knowledge ("gnosis") and through observing Jewish circumcision, feast days, new moons, and sabbaths. To these Jewish observations, the Gnostics added their own precepts and rituals. They taught that the observance of these rituals led to a special communion with angels. The rationale was that since angels are above this world, the ascetic, by divorcing himself from the things of this world, draws near to the angels and is therefore qualified to associate with them. The apostle Paul branded this as a false humility that detracts from the true worship that is due to Christ alone: "Let no one defraud you of your reward, taking delight in false humility and worship of angels, intruding into those things which he has not seen, vainly puffed up by his fleshly mind. . . . These things indeed have an appearance of wisdom in self-imposed religion, false humility, and neglect of the body, but are of no value against the indulgence of the flesh" (Colossians 2:18, 23).

Paul accused these Gnostic teachers of wanting to appear humble while they were actually laying claim to superior insights into divine truth and superior piety in their own lives. They claimed they were doing more than God required.

Unfortunately a similar false humility is all too common today. Some people imply they have a direct line to God, a line not available to other Christians. Four such people in a church business meeting, all having opposing views, create chaos. They each insist, "God told me we should follow my suggestions." Each claims to have the mind of Christ. Obviously, it takes God-honoring humility to come to a position of agreement.

The man or woman of true humility *never* criticizes an alleged lack of humility in another. Judgmentalism is foreign to true humility. But it is extremely difficult for the leader to see judgmentalism in himself. Sometimes it surfaces in the advice he gives. The leader is not omniscient, and humility will protect him from indiscriminate counsel.

Whether it be dress or speech or behavior, anything that draws attention to itself and away from Christ is displeasing to God and violates humility. It promotes pretentiousness and projects vanity.

In every age, true humility has been a rare quality. Even Christ's disciples in the first century did not always exhibit humility. Listen to them when they were interrupted by the woman of Canaan seeking healing for her daughter: "Send her away, for she cries out after us" (Matthew 15:23). Or listen again as they argue about who would be greatest in the kingdom of heaven. They did not exhibit any outgoing of beneficence and help to others.

WHY IS HUMILITY IMPORTANT?

The psalmist ascribes humility to God Himself:

> Who is like the Lord our God,
> Who dwells on high,
> Who humbles Himself to behold
> The things that are in the heavens
> and in the earth?
> —Psalm 113:5–6

God, "the High and Lofty One . . . whose name is Holy" (Isaiah 57:15) dwells in the humble heart.

There can be no real love without humility. Paul told the Corinthians that love does not parade itself and is not puffed up. Augustine said that in importance, humility is first, second, and third.

The spirit of humility frees the leader to concentrate on the real needs of others. He doesn't dissipate his energies wondering what kind of impression he is making. Refusing to "think of himself more highly than he ought to think," he does not feel insulted no matter what is said. Nor does he languish under the fear of being treated in a disrespectful manner.

> "Great peace have those who love Your law,
> And nothing causes them to stumble" (Psalm 119:165).

Humility is important for a leader because people follow more enthusiastically the leader whose motives they consider to be non-self-serving. All other things being equal, the humble leader comes closer to achieving his objectives. Why? Because his objective is the highest good of the group, not his own self-aggrandizement. The humble leader's joy comes from seeing the group move toward the fulfillment of its real needs. Leadership lacking this quality, this expression of love, inevitably loses credibility.

THE RESULTS OF HUMILITY

The Christlike leader will pray for and strive after humility because he knows it is a characteristic Christ Himself demonstrated and one He expects of His followers. But there are also a number of results that come to the one who demonstrates humility that should make it a characteristic that anyone would seek after.

Serenity

Humility fosters serenity. Activity to the point of frantic confusion, uncertainty, worry, and fear are all too common today. People feel as if they need to depend on themselves, but self-sufficiency does not give them calmness and strength. What a contrast is the leader who exhibits serenity, tranquillity, and poise because of his humility. He is not self-conscious, and he is not offended by what people may say that is not complimentary. He is too busy serving with all humility to give thought to offenses real or imagined.

The late Corrie ten Boom dubbed herself "Tramp for the Lord." Unlike the tramp who does nobody any good, Corrie moved across the world serving others with gladness of heart and with deep serenity in the midst of threatening problems.

I know two ladies who demonstrate this contrast. One is a medical doctor who, although she comes from great wealth and could live a life of ease and affluence, has chosen to bury herself in service to thousands who are hurting and diseased half a world away from her home. She lives amidst constant danger. But the serenity in her heart reveals itself in her face and deportment. She endures slights and savagery, derogation, and danger. But she continues without self-pity. She actually revels in her opportunities to serve. Five minutes in her presence reveals to the most casual observer both her humility and the resulting quiet serenity.

In contrast to this young doctor is another woman I know who focuses all attention on herself and her family. She serves nobody. Though she is a highly trained academic, her energies and training are dissipated in a passion for self-protection. Her face is a maze of misery and a mask of distress. She has retreated into a bottle of alcohol. She forms a striking contrast to the serenity the doctor exhibits because of her humility.

Enlargement of Life

Too often humility is associated with lethargy, apathy, indecision, and inactivity. Nothing could be farther from the truth. Instead of limiting the leader, humility will enlarge his life. It will lead to learning, faith, and service.

Because the humble leader will not act as if he is self-sufficient and will not have to pretend he knows all the answers, humility puts the leader in a position to draw insights from others. The person who lacks humility and pretends to be self-sufficient, however, won't accept any ideas; he restricts himself to his own little world. Instead of leading to the shriveling neglect of personhood, humility opens the door to the expansion of personality and individuality.

Humility results in an enlargement of life because the humble person is faithful and content where he is and so God can give him more.

Banishment of Fear

Humility tends to banish fear because humility is love's mood, and "perfect love casts out fear" (1 John 4:18). The humble leader knows that God is in control of the world and all that is in it. His confidence is not in himself but in God, and if God is in charge, he has nothing to fear.

Humility calls the leader to courage in adhering to truth and righteousness, no matter how pervasive the evil or how unrelenting the resistance to the truth. Because God is in charge, the leader can stand up without fear. Christ's unflinching exposure of the Scribes and Pharisees in Matthew 23 is a challenge to the humble leader, for he recognizes that assertion has a legitimate place when it comes to the defense of truth and righteousness. Humility that arises from a dependence on God and a confidence in the faithfulness of God banishes fear.

Success

Humility leads to success. Sometimes we may shy away from success (perhaps in false humility!), but it is a legitimate goal. God told Joshua to meditate on the Word of God "day and night, that you may observe to do according to all that is written in it. For then you will make your way prosperous, and then you will have good success" (Joshua 1:8).

Assuming that you know about something when, in fact, you know nothing is a dangerous cover for ignorance and confusion. Those who think themselves to be "wise and prudent" (see Matthew 11:25) are impervious to new light. Pride and prejudice prohibit spiritual enlightenment and intellectual advance. The true scholar and the legitimate leader react like Newton, the man who discovered gravity, who said, "The great ocean of truth lay all undiscovered before me." Like scholarship, leadership requires docility, not dogmatism. The man who knows everything, learns nothing, and so it is a humble attitude that sets the stage for the knowledge and know-how that lead to success.

Availability of Unlimited Resources

It is a divine principle that strength is made perfect in weakness. God's resources are available to the humble leader who is willing to recognize his weakness. The person who fails to understand this principle weakens himself and dishonors the Lord.

The apostle Paul said, "I can do all things through Christ who strengthens me" (Philippians 4:13). Another translation, which I find exciting, is "I am almighty in the One who continually keeps pouring His power in me." When Paul says, "I can do all things" or "I am almighty," it would be the raving of an egomaniac were it not moderated by what comes after: "in the One who continually keeps pouring His power in me."

The one who comes humbly to God—who comes as a little child—finds God's strength, wisdom, resources, and discernment available to him without limit.

Serenity, enlargement of life, banishment of fear, success, and availability of unlimited resources all come about through humility. There are also many other results of humility. The point is, however, that humility does not lead to a suppression of your personality and an abandonment of achievement goals. Nor does it stifle leadership. Rather, humility is the way to enlarge your personality, to achieve, in His strength, the goals God has given you, and to enhance your leadership.

HOW IS HUMILITY NURTURED?

If you wanted to lose five kilograms, you would go on a diet. If you wanted to be closer to the Lord, you would spend more time in prayer and study of His Word. If you wanted to become more knowledgeable about the history of Egypt, you would study books and listen to lectures. But how do you become more humble? Talking about humility seems to make us less humble—not more humble—because humility possesses no self-consciousness.

It is possible to develop humility, but you must do it indirectly. You must recognize those paths that lead to humility and then concentrate on those paths, not on humility itself. Humility will come. But to concentrate on humility will make achieving it impossible.

How is humility nurtured? Here are five paths to humility:

By Enthroning Christ in Your Heart

If Christ lives in your heart, humility will shine through to the degree that you yield yourself to Christ. You will want to glorify Christ, not yourself. Humility is the expression of love, which is the fruit of the Holy Spirit. Love germinates and develops as a result of the Spirit's life-giving power.

The first path to humility, therefore, is making Christ the Lord of your life. Although you are born again only once, you must constantly renew your commitment to yield yourself to the lordship of Christ because self-will is constantly trying to dethrone Christ and rule your life.

By Obeying Christ

The person who enthrones Christ in his heart will want to obey Him, for Christ said, "If you love Me, keep My commandments" (John 14:15). In obedience to Christ some very practical steps are taken toward humility.

For instance, in 2 Timothy 2:24–25, Paul says, "And a servant of the Lord must not quarrel but be gentle to all, able to teach, patient, in humility correcting those who are in opposition. . . ."

The true leader must not quarrel. He must be gentle to all, not just to those who are polite to him. He must be patient. He must lovingly share the truth. The Holy Spirit produces humility through such a commitment to obedience. There is no place for a pompous, self-promoting arrogance in the Christlike leader. At one time Paul was proud, but having been brought low at the feet of his Lord and Master, he was able to exhort others. "If it is possible, as much as depends on you, live peaceably with all men" (Romans 12:18).

Christ said many things for our instruction and guidance; we cannot review them all. But they are summed up in His words to His disciples: "If you keep My commandments, you will abide in My love, just as I have kept My Father's commandments and abide in His love. These things I have spoken to you, that My joy may remain in you, and that your joy may be full. This is My commandment, that you love one another as I have loved you" (John 15:10–12).

By Assuming the Attitude and Behavior of a Little Child

To the Greek philosophers, the ideal man was a magnificent physical figure. He was one who excelled in both sports and the intellect. Christ, however, said that the ideal disciple was as a little child. A child is trusting and innocent, not arrogant. A child knows others are more important than he is, but he also has an unshattered belief in his own ability to do things. A child is obedient.

The Christian who wants to become more humble must assume the attitude and behavior of a little child.

By Following Christ's Example in Prayer

Christ taught His disciples the simplicity and humility of prayer. And what He taught them, He also practiced. He frequently retired into remote privacy to pray, submitting Himself, the Son, to God the Father. Over and over again the Gospels tell us of Christ's prayer life.

One evening at sundown, people brought the diseased to Jesus to be healed. All the town was there, and they must have stayed a great while. And yet "in the morning, having risen a long while before daylight, He went out and departed to a solitary place; and there He prayed" (Mark 1:35).

At another time, having fed 5,000, Jesus told His disciples to get into a boat and go to the other side of the Sea of Galilee while He sent the people away. "And when He had sent them away, He departed to the mountain to pray" (Mark 6:46).

Before choosing the twelve apostles, Jesus "went out to the mountain to pray, and continued all night in prayer to God" (Luke 6:12).

Christ bathed His ministry in prayer. He prayed to God because He needed fellowship with God. He included praise and adoration of the Father in His prayers. He prayed for the needs of Himself and others. In the prayer He taught His disciples, He also showed us that we should ask for forgiveness and confess our sins in prayer. Humility comes by following Christ's prayer example.

By Following Christ's Example in Personal Relationships

Consciously, in the strength of Christ, avoid elitism, intolerance, class distinction, and self-promotion. Here again, we profit from observing the little child who is not impressed with a person's bank balance, social position, or educational attainments.

A friend of mine, an outstanding Christian leader, exploded with rage because his office had sent only a junior staff member to meet him at the airport. Later he reflected and repented. I applaud the humility his contrition showed. He's a leader!

Christ demonstrated His humility in the choice of His followers and friends. He didn't go to the "Who's Who" of Palestine to select the people whom He would choose as disciples. In fact, in 2 Corinthians 1:26 and 27, Paul says, "Not many wise according to the flesh, not many mighty, not many noble, are called. But God has chosen the foolish things of the world to put to shame the wise, and God has chosen the weak things of the world to put to shame the things which are mighty."

Christ showed His humility by His sympathy with little children and those of modest circumstances who begged Him for help. He demonstrated appreciation for the smallest offering and the simplest service (see Matthew 10:42).

In 1969, a businessman who had climbed to a top executive position with an international oil company came to the first Haggai Institute session. When he arrived at the airport, the late Dr. Ernest Watson, then dean of the Haggai Institute, met him and went with him to the baggage claim area. The oil company executive turned to Dr. Watson and said, "Where is the servant to carry my bag?" Without any reply, Dr. Watson, a man then 66 years old and a recognized world leader, smiled and picked up the bag, carrying it to the car.

On arrival at the room, the gentleman complained, "There is only one glass in my room, and I need two." Patiently and without any rebuttal, Dr. Watson secured a second glass for him. During the sessions, God did a work of grace in that executive's heart, and his spirit seemed significantly tempered by the work of the Holy Spirit who used Dr. Watson as an example.

By Serving Others

The twelve apostles came together at the Last Supper. Ordinarily a servant or a slave would have been present to wash the feet of the guests, but apparently there was not one on this occasion. Peter did not offer to do it, nor did John, nor Thomas—nobody offered to wash the other's feet. Everybody's business was nobody's business, and so nobody offered to wash anybody's feet. They had taken their positions, reclining around the table. Our Lord then rose; laid aside His outer garments, took a towel, and girded Himself with it. He then poured water into a basin and went from one disciple to another washing their feet. After He had done that and was again reclining with them, He told them He was among them as a slave, a domestic who does the most menial work. They had seen this demonstrated for themselves (see Luke 22:27).

Jesus Christ, the ultimate example of leadership, lived a life of humility. The Lord of earth and heaven dressed in the garb of a rustic! He who poured out all the waters of the earth—the Amazon, the Euphrates, the Nile, the Mississippi—bent over a well to ask a Samaritan woman for a drink. He who spread the canopy of the heavens and set the earth for a footstool, spent the night with Simon a tanner. He whose chariots are the clouds, walked with sore feet. Look at Him hushing the tempest on Galilee and wiping off the spray of the storm, sitting down beside His disciples as though He had done no more than wipe the sweat from His brow in His father's carpenter shop.

He took the foot of death off the heart of Lazarus and broke the chain of the grave against the marble of the tomb, after which He walked out with Mary and Martha without any more pretension than a plain citizen going into the suburbs to spend the evening. Look at Him jostled as though He were a nobody, pursued as though He were an outlaw, nicknamed—sitting with crooks and sinners. He was the King of heaven and earth, with His robes trailing in the dust!

The leader will always endeavor to do good to others. The leader need not go to the ends of the earth to start serving—he can start in his own house. The leader, from morning to night, should be moving people toward goals that fulfill their real needs. It should be his constant ambition to imitate our Lord Jesus Christ by being willing to bear other's burdens. Is this difficult? Absolutely. But serving others is an essential path to follow on the road to humility.

The Christlike leader will follow these five paths to nurture humility in himself in all areas of his life:

In the social area of life, he will "in honor give preference to one another" (Romans 12:10).

In the intellectual area of life, he will subordinate his intellect to the mind of Christ that it might be maximized in serving others.

In the financial area of life, he will understand the true meaning of Wesley's heart when he said, "Earn all you can and save all you can to give all you can for as long as you can." The effective leader will invest his money, counting on God to multiply it, even as the Lord multiplied the fishes and loaves so that He could feed the multitude.

In the physical area of life, he will, in humility, observe the laws of health in order that he may more effectively serve those for whom God has made him responsible. He will recognize the importance of consistent exercise that strengthens the heart and lungs and maintains the best possible circulation. He knows the body is the temple of the Holy Spirit.

In the area of family life, he will demonstrate humility in his relationship with his spouse and conduct himself so as not to provoke his "children to wrath" (Ephesians 6:4).

Love and its mood—humility—are essential principles of Christlike leadership. They are not often found among so-called leaders who are not Christlike. That is why their cultivation is so essential. These principles set the Christlike leader apart from other leaders. Only that person who subjugates himself to the place of a servant and lets Christ continually pour His power into him is equipped to deliberately exert that special influence within a group to move it toward goals of beneficial permanence that fulfill the group's real needs.

Professor Dr. Eliseo Pajaro of Manila, Philippines, who died 6 October 1984, was one such person. From boyhood, Pajaro shone as a musical talent of exceptional promise. He developed into a man of charm, achievement, and spiritual depth. He earned his Ph.D. at the Eastman School of Music in Rochester, N.Y., and not long afterward attained full professorship at the University of the Philippines.

In 1959, Pajaro became the first Filipino to receive a grant from the Guggenheim Foundation for a year's study in the United States. During that time, he composed an opera which won the Filipino Presidential Medal of Merit. Twice he received the Republic Cultural Heritage Award. His entire adult life was punctuated with honors.

Dr. Pajaro was a professor, a composer, a conductor, a performer, but above all, a leader whose thumbprint shall remain indelible and intelligible on the pages of Filipino history, culture, music, and spirituality.

When Pajaro retired in 1980, he gave his energies to composing Christian cantatas. He completed four. Just prior to his death, he told me he planned next to write a cantata for Haggai Institute.

A year before his death, I attended a Haggai Institute (Philippines) dinner meeting which included some of the elite of the Philippines: representatives of government, academia, the judiciary, the church, medicine, the media, and multinational businesspeople. I was struck by the unobtrusive way Dr. Pajaro took a chair in the back row. People rushed to sit by him. His face, a marvelously open countenance, revealed his wholehearted response to every speaker. His wife, also a retired professor, and an H.I. alumna, had a major part on the program. He beamed. Afterward, he was crowded by many of these celebrated leaders. They all wanted a word with him.

It would never have crossed Dr. Pajaro's mind to tell people he was humble. A humble man does not concentrate on his humility. When I congratulated him on his achievements, he thanked me; he didn't deny them, but he made it clear that God had so blessed him he must honor God with his talent. To use his gift for the glory of God was his quiet passion.

Eliseo Pajaro embodied the principle of humility. His influence continues after his death, independent of any public relations program or publicity scheme. He demonstrated a humility that gave his leadership a continuing beneficial influence so that "he being dead, yet speaks."

SUMMARY

Humility is love's mood. It is the lowliness that pervades the leader's consciousness when he contemplates God's holy majesty and superabundant love in contrast to his own unworthiness, guilt, and total helplessness apart from divine grace. The humble person is free from pride or arrogance. He puts himself in submission to others and is helpful and courteous. The humble person does not consider himself to be self-sufficient and yet he recognizes his own gifts, resources, and achievements. Both love and humility are characteristic of true leaders.

Even worse than a lack of humility in a person's life is a false humility in which a person is proud about acting in a humble way. The person with false humility is fooling only himself, for people see through the pompous, self-adulatory, and arrogant person who feigns humility. In every age, true humility has been rare. Even Christ's disciples did not always exhibit humility.

Serenity, enlargement of life, banishment of fear, success, and availability of unlimited resources all come about through humility. Contrary to what is usually thought, humility does not suppress one's personality nor stifle leadership. Rather, it is the way to enlarge one's personality and to achieve—in God's strength—the goals He has given.

Talking about humility seems to make us less humble—not more—because humility possesses no self-consciousness. Therefore, to develop humility, you must concentrate on other paths that lead to humility. Enthrone Christ in your heart. Live in obedience to God and His Word. Assume the attitude and behavior of a little child. Follow Christ's example in prayer. Follow Christ's example in personal relationships by avoiding elitism, intolerance, class distinction, and self-promotion. Serve others.

The cultivation of love and its mood—humility—is essential for the Christlike leader because they are characteristics not often found among so-called leaders who are not Christlike. Only that person who subjugates himself to the place of a servant and lets Christ continually pour His power into him is equipped to deliberately exert that special influence within a group to move it toward goals of beneficial permanence that fulfill the group's real needs.

6

The Principle of

SELF-CONTROL

Religious leaders, some of the world's leading intellectuals, and hundreds of others stood ten and twelve deep trying to get into a packed Miami, Florida, auditorium in 1945 to hear a young evangelist, Bron Clifford. Dr. M. E. Dodd, minister of the prestigious First Baptist Church of Shreveport, Louisiana, introduced Clifford as "the greatest preacher since the apostle Paul." Clifford held the audience spellbound. That was normal. That same year he kept Baylor University students on the edge of their seats for two hours and fifteen minutes with his address, "Christ and the Philosopher's Stone." President Pat Neff, himself an outstanding orator, had ordered the bells switched off so the evangelist would not feel time-bound.

At the age of twenty-five young Clifford touched more lives, influenced more leaders, and set more attendance records than any clergyman his age in American history. National leaders vied for his attention. He was tall, handsome, intelligent, and eloquent. Hollywood invited him to audition for the part of Marcellus in *The Robe*. It seemed as if he had everything.

Less than ten years after the Miami meeting, Clifford had lost his leadership—and his life. Drinking and fiscal shabbiness did him in. His story is one of the saddest I know.

Before Clifford died, Dr. Carl E. Bates, a Christian leader, visited him and tried to help him. Dr. Ernestine Smith, a surgeon in Bates' church, had done exploratory surgery on Clifford and knew he was near death. She had asked her pastor to visit him.

72

Clifford was alone, with nobody to look after him. He had left his wife with their two Down's syndrome children. Bates was appalled to find Clifford occupying a grubby room in a third-rate motel on the western edge of Amarillo, Texas. Dying of cirrhosis of the liver, he was too sick to continue his last job, selling trucks for Plains Chevrolet in Amarillo.

Bron Clifford died unwept, unhonored, and unsung. The ministers of Amarillo took up an offering among themselves to buy an inexpensive casket and ship his body back east where it was buried in a potter's field.

Clifford lacked one essential quality necessary for sustained leadership: self-control. And it is lack of self-control that brings most of the griefs in other leaders' lives, too.

WHAT IS SELF-CONTROL?

Self-control is love's mastery. It is a way of life in which, by the power of the Holy Spirit, the Christian is able to be temperate in all things because he does not let his desires master his life. The concept of self-control does not just mean that the Christian abstains from certain habits such as contentiousness, quarreling, or drunkenness. It means that all aspects of his life are brought under the mastery of the Holy Spirit. It means his life is characterized by discipline.

The Greek word for self-control comes from a root word meaning "to grip," or "to take hold of." It describes the strength of the person who takes hold of himself, who stays in full control of himself. Paul talks about athletes being "temperate in all things" when they are in training. Eating, sleeping, and exercise are all carefully regulated when one is preparing for a race or a game.

Aristotle used this same word to describe the "ability to restrain desire by reason . . . to be resolute and ever in readiness to endure natural want and pain." He further explained that the man who is self-controlled has strong desires which try to seduce him from the way of reason, but he keeps them under control.

When I was a boy, my father told me the story of Esther in the Old Testament. I never tired of it. In that story, Haman, who was made head officer of the Persian empire under Xerxes, expected everyone to bow before him and pay homage to him. When Mordecai, Esther's uncle, did not bow or pay homage, Haman "was filled with indignation." He was furious. He could have arrested Mordecai on the spot. "Nevertheless Haman restrained himself"—he exerted self-control—so that he could plan an elaborate plot to have Mordecai hanged. Haman's plot backfired, but I have always been fascinated by the way in which Haman restrained his natural desire for the moment. That was self-control.

SELF-CONTROL AND THE LEADER

Self-control is an essential attitude and characteristic for a leader. Without it, the leader diminishes his effectiveness, and he will lose the respect of his followers. With it, people view him as one who has the determination and strength to be in charge.

In spite of its importance, self-control is an attitude that is difficult for a leader to develop, as it is for those who are not leaders. For instance, the effective leader has a vivid and clear vision of what his group will be like in three or five years. The leader lives in the future. With his top assistants, he actively plans goal programs that will accomplish his vision. But self-control requires that expenditures and attitudes be geared to today's reality so that he doesn't get into trouble by spending money before he has it. The effective leader will have many people looking to him for wisdom and insight, but self-control insists that he not think more highly of himself than he ought to think. The successful leader always runs the risk of believing his own press releases—of thinking he can do no wrong. But self-control should result in an attitude of humility and caution. Successful leadership requires self-control, and yet successful leadership makes it difficult to practice self-control.

It is this tension that makes understanding self-control so important for the Christlike leader. No leader can influence others if he doesn't control himself. When Paul listed the qualifications of bishops in Timothy 3, most of them related to the bishop's control of himself or of his family:

A bishop then must be blameless, the husband of one wife, temperate, sober-minded, of good behavior, hospitable, able to teach; not given to wine, not violent, not greedy for money, but gentle, not quarrelsome, not covetous; one who rules his own house well, having his children in submission with all reverence (for if a man does not know how to rule his own house, how will he take care of the church of God?); not a novice, lest being puffed up with pride he fall into the same condemnation as the devil. Moreover he must have a good testimony among those who are outside, lest he fall into reproach and the snare of the devil (1 Timothy 3:2–7).

Lack of Self-Control Destroys Leadership

Time and time again otherwise competent leaders have been destroyed because of a lack of self-control. Bron Clifford was one such tragic example. For some, their greed and extravagance have caused them to embezzle money or cheat their organization. Others have been lured by sexual temptations that have destroyed the leader himself, his family, and his leadership ability. Talking too much and too indiscreetly has cost other leaders the respect of their followers and the loss of confidential information. Gluttony or alcohol abuse has cost others their leadership positions because of the destruction of their physical bodies. Pride and self-indulgence have cost many their leadership position because their judgment became corrupted.

No one is immune to temptations caused by lack of self-control. But leaders are particularly susceptible. What one needs to be aware of is that such loss of self-control is most likely to happen in those areas where one is the strongest, has the most confidence, feels most secure. That's exactly where trouble strikes. The apostle Peter was known for his boldness and self-confidence. He vehemently proclaimed that he would defend Jesus Christ against all opposition. It was Peter who took a sword and cut off the high priest's servant's ear when the soldiers came to arrest Christ. And yet it was Peter who denied Christ three times that same night. Too much confidence in your strong points can sabotage your self-control in the very areas of your strength.

When the leader has no control over his own spirit, the smallest consequences annoy him. The shabbiest allurements draw him into the side alleys of leadership-destroying trivia. The smallest provocation angers him. Victimized by his own undisciplined passions and losing self-control habitually, the leader loses the confidence of the group. He sinks into complete uselessness. The self-indulgent person makes himself the slave to the self-controlled person.

Self-Control Gives Courage to Stand Alone

The first step toward effective leadership is a vision—a clear picture of what the leader sees the group being or doing. The leader may listen to others, but God gives the vision to him alone. He must not be diverted from his vision by the opinion and subtle pressures of the crowd. Self-control gives the leader the courage to stand alone.

John Templeton, Wall Street's most successful financier in the field of mutual funds, spends comparatively little time in New York City. He lives on the Bahama Islands. One of the reasons he gives for distancing himself is so that he might do his own thinking without being swayed, however imperceptibly, by prevailing Wall Street wisdom. I believe that this consistent self-control is one reason Templeton has created so many ideas that have brought immeasurable help to people around the world.

Self-control gives the leader courage to stand alone when others are questioning his vision. The habit of self-control will teach a leader the importance of relying on his own evaluation and understanding of situations rather than relying on popular opinion. Most shiver at the thought of individual responsibility or liability. They don't determine their stand until they first test the direction of the wind, consult a popular poll, or detect a consensus.

Strong character is an individual thing, requiring individual nurture. An attitude of self-control develops strong character and strong character can be defined as the power to stand alone. Holiness never counts its companions; it never intimates that its validity is in proportion to the number of its admirers.

The leader realizes the importance of standing alone because continual contact with his followers weakens him. He will sink to their level. He will accommodate to their habits and fancies. Instead, he should limit the spiritual development of his character to being on God's plane. Being part of the group is far easier and more comfortable than rising above the group, but that would fail to meet the group's highest needs by giving it a vision that will result in change of beneficial permanence.

In solitude, where you recognize your need of God, you become strong. But solitude demands self-control. Alone in a desert with God, John the Baptist viewed things that matter most—and viewed them in true perspective. He never became drugged on his own fame. He knew his mission. He knew his relationship with the coming Messiah: "He must increase, but I must decrease." He paid the price in love's mastery, self-control, to exert the special influence that motivated great crowds to fulfill their real needs.

The real test of a leader's courage and ability to stand alone comes in times of crisis. Crises remove all subterfuge, double-talk, and posturing. It is in times of crisis that the leader's self-control is so important because lack of control will only aggravate most such situations.

Self-Control Draws Followers to the Leader

People want a leader whom they can trust. The effective implementation of any of the principles of leadership—vision, goalsetting, love, humility, self-control, communication, investment, opportunity, energy, staying power, authority, and awareness—will draw people to the leader. They want a worthy example to follow and these principles accomplish that. They want to have confidence in the strength of their leader, and the attitude of self-control especially will convey the leader's strength. They want to believe that the change the leader will bring about really will be ones of beneficial permanence. Living these principles communicates that.

Probably no foreigner exerted greater leadership over the people of Shaohsing, China, in the early twentieth century than Dr. Claude H. Barlow. This self-effacing medical missionary was the personification of self-control.

A strange disease for which he knew no remedy was killing the people. There was no laboratory available for research. Dr. Barlow filled his notebook with observations of the peculiarities of the disease in hundreds of cases. Then, armed with a small vial of the disease germs, he sailed for the United States. Just before he arrived, he took the germs into his own body and then hurried to the Johns Hopkins University Hospital, where he had studied.

Claude Barlow was now a very sick man. He turned himself over to his former professors as a human guinea pig for their study and experimentation. A cure was found, and the young doctor recovered. He sailed back to China with scientific treatment for the scourge and saved a multitude of lives.

When he was asked about his experience, Dr. Barlow simply replied, "Anyone would have done the same thing. I happened to be in the position of vantage and had the chance to offer my body." What humility! What self-control! What love!

No wonder multitudes followed Claude Barlow's leadership when he returned. He demonstrated love's mastery. He risked his life, to say nothing of his reputation and future ministry, by attempting the impossible. He motivated the people by his own love, the outgoing of his total being to them in beneficence and help. And the capstone quality of this love was its mastery, self-control.

It is this kind of leadership that will draw the followers to the leader.

HOW TO DEVELOP AND EXERCISE SELF-CONTROL

Like all of the principles of leadership, self-control must be carefully developed and nurtured. It doesn't just happen. And there will never be a time in this life when the leader can say he has arrived and does not need to continue nurturing his love, his ability to communicate, or his self-control.

Through Dependence on God

The exercise of self-control must be done in dependence upon God. "Will-power has no defense against the careless word, the unguarded moment. The will has the same deficiency as the law—it can deal only with externals. It is not sufficient to bring about the necessary transformation of the inner spirit."[19]

The ultimate resource derives from the transformation of the inner spirit. I'm referring to the resource available to the Christlike leader who has been changed into a new creation by Jesus Christ. Belonging to Him, you can look to Him for guidance and depend on Him for help. You can develop and exercise self-control through dependence on God.

Through a Life of Discipline

A life characterized by self-control begins with an attitude of discipline. This discipline is not just in one or two areas of life, but all areas. Those who are disciplined in small things tend to be disciplined in large things as well, whereas those who are undisciplined will be that way in many areas of their lives. Regular exercise takes discipline. Maintaining an organized study takes discipline. Getting out of bed on time takes discipline. Discipline is necessary to have a daily devotional time. You may think the small areas are unimportant, but a lack of discipline in little things will affect your ability to maintain discipline in large things.

The word *discipline* for the Christian also has a specialized meaning in the sense of the classical disciplines of the spiritual life. In our age of self-gratification, these disciplines have for the most part been abandoned. They are viewed as too rigorous, too other-worldly, too time-consuming. These disciplines include meditation, prayer, study, solitude, service, confession, and worship.

What better way for a Christian leader to begin a life of self-control than with the cultivation of these disciplines of the spiritual life!

Through Making Decisions Ahead of Time

When Daniel, Shadrach, Meshach, and Abed-Nego were chosen for special training in Babylon, they purposed in their hearts that they would not defile themselves "with the portion of the king's delicacies, nor with the wine which he drank." Thus when they were actually faced with the opportunity to eat the king's food and drink the king's drink, they didn't have to make a decision under pressure. They had already made up their minds. They knew they wouldn't do it.

Self-control is made easier when you purpose in your heart how you will act in certain situations. For instance, I have decided that I will be honest if a clerk gives me too much change for a purchase. If I buy something for $3.00 and give the clerk a $5 bill, I don't have to think twice about returning the extra money if I receive $7.00 in change. It's automatic. I don't give myself the opportunity to rationalize that the store charges too much for its goods and so the error simply evens things out. Too often, if we are faced with a decision under pressure, it gives us a chance to question whether we should do what we know is right or not and we will find an excuse to do what we know to be wrong.

Self-control works best when you make your decisions ahead of time and live according to those decisions.

Through Gratitude for Adversity

It fascinates me that of all the New Testament writers, only Paul used the word *adversity*. Adversity was his constant Spirit-administered discipline. He could have become bitter about his adversities, but he rejoiced in them because he knew they were given for his benefit. He could finally say, "I take pleasure in infirmities, in reproaches, in needs, in persecutions, in distresses" (2 Corinthians 12:10).

At the peak of his career, God sent Paul a "thorn in the flesh" to buffet him lest he be "exalted above measure." What a blessing! God had equipped Paul with gifts of character, energy, and power. He possessed the capacity to command, to lead, to organize. His was a great mind which could articulate the truths of God so as to be understood by both the literati and the illiterate. However, had it not been for the presence of his infirmity, he may never have achieved for God such splendid work. He may have surrendered to self-centered confidence rather than developing self-control. He may have relied upon his extraordinary endowments instead of casting himself completely on the power of God.

Scripture assures us that suffering produces joy and "the testing of your faith produces patience." Adversity is God's refining fire. In the crucible of suffering you have the greatest opportunity to develop and exercise self-control. During Job's suffering, his wife urged him to "curse God and die." Job responded, "Though He slay me, yet will I trust Him." That kind of self-control comes as the result of adversity. You should show gratitude for those experiences God gives you that will build self-control. He gives you those experiences because He loves you and wants to see you develop love so demonstrated through self-control.

Through Ruling Your Spirit

A friend told me that he could not possibly control his temper. He attributed his ungovernable explosions of anger to his parents and grandparents. He said there were some people, like himself, who could not be expected to rule their own spirits. I asked him if he were in a heated argument with his wife and the doorbell rang, would he continue shouting. He saw my point that he really could control his temper when he wanted to. You can rule your spirit, and ruling your spirit is essential to developing self-control.

In exercising self-control, you must learn to take all sorts of punishment and abuse without retaliating in kind. This is the price you pay for leadership. When an angry person starts to vilify and abuse you—justly or unjustly—just remember that if you retaliate in a like manner, you are being drawn down to that person's level; you are allowing that person to dominate you! And in so doing, you are forfeiting your leadership, for you have allowed that person to control your emotions rather than controlling them yourself.

The Christlike leader rules his spirit. "He who is slow to anger is better than the mighty, and he who rules his spirit than he who takes a city" (Proverbs 16:32).

You will find support in developing and exercising self-control by reflecting on God's work in your own life. The mercy Paul received from God, for instance, motivated him to exercise self-control. How could Paul ever despair of others when he himself had found such mercy? How could he abandon his course when the same grace by which he was saved was given to him so abundantly to guide him and sustain him? How could he become impatient with others when he reflected upon God's long-suffering which had hovered over him and had overcome his rebellion? God's goodness provides a powerful incentive to self-control.

From the beginning to the end of his career, Paul was constrained by the one overriding thought that he had been redeemed to serve—to help meet the *real* needs of others.

Through Controlling Your Thoughts

The effective leader realizes that self-control is really a matter of thought-control, and he insists on doing his own thinking. Thinking about your vision, your mission, your goals, and the needs of your group several times daily—especially upon awaking and before retiring—will go a long way toward guaranteeing your exercise of self-control.

Picture the way you will act as a leader characterized by self-control. How will you react to people in various situations? How will self-control contribute to your goals and mission? Picture your group as you see it one year and three years from now. Putting these images clearly in your thoughts will help you act them out in reality. In addition to picturing yourself in situations as you would like them to be, replay in detail situations where you have already demonstrated self-control.

Athletes are trained in this way. They are told to relax and visualize their best performance—how they felt, what they heard, odors they noticed, the taste of the water or dirt or air, what they saw. They are told to input all of these sensory-rich impressions into their brain so that in their next contest they can reproduce and even improve their performance. Big league salesmen and notable orators have been doing this for years.

Develop your self-control by taking time each day, preferably just after your prayers and before retiring at night, to replay victories of self-control when the normal response would have been anger, fear, or intimidation.

You have the potential ability to make your thoughts do your bidding. Two impulses set your brain in motion: self-suggestion and outside suggestion. It is humiliating to realize that you are influenced by the outside suggestions of others whom you permit to place thoughts, without your examination or question, in your consciousness. You have it in your power to determine the material you will think about. Act on this ability. It will develop your self-control.

Deliberately choose the thoughts which you want to dominate your mind. Decisively deny admittance to all outside suggestions that don't square with your values and commitments. Paul commanded us to do this when he said to think on "whatever things are true, whatever things are noble, whatever things are just, whatever things are pure, whatever things are lovely, whatever things are of good report" (Philippians 4:8).

You are the product of your thoughts. You must exercise self-control if you are to influence others with your suggestions instead of yourself being influenced by random suggestions from outside. You learn to swim by swimming. You learn to exercise self-control by exercising self-control. And the key is through controlling your thoughts.

Optimum Self-Control Is Spirit-Control

Domination by the Holy Spirit makes possible the self-control that God and good leadership require. Spirit domination and lack of self-control are mutually exclusive. One cannot exist with the other. The

Holy Spirit produces in the submissive heart a disposition, a strength, a mind-set that makes an otherwise unreachable self-control possible.

WHAT SELF-CONTROL ACCOMPLISHES

You can't permanently defeat the leader who exercises self-control. Obstacles ultimately seem to melt away in the presence of such a leader. In short, love conquers, and self-control is love's mastery.

Self-control is usually seen as a restriction, a discipline that produces a harsh, joyless existence. In reality, however, just the opposite is true. Self-control produces in any person results that will make him a candidate for leadership.

Freedom

Self-control produces a wonderful freedom that comes from bringing self-centeredness and fear into subjection. Self-control cuts down on nagging decisions about whether you should do the things you know you should avoid and whether you would skip the things you know you should do. You have already made up your mind. You don't have to decide. Self-control is God's practical way of giving us freedom from the domination of sin and sinful thoughts. The freedom produced by self-control comes from knowing you have mastered your habits instead of letting them master you.

You need to experience this freedom to appreciate it because you are told every day by the world that freedom comes not from self-control but from self-indulgence. In reality, self-indulgence leads to slavery, whereas self-control leads to freedom.

Confidence

Self-control produces a confidence and assurance that you are capable of leadership.

When I met His Excellency Rajiv Gandhi a year before he became India's prime minister, I was impressed. When I returned home, I was asked if I thought he would succeed his mother, Madam Indira Gandhi.

"I think so."

"Can he fill the role?"

"I'm convinced he has the intelligence, the savvy, the charm, but I'm not sure he has enough 'fire in his belly.' He's a brilliant and gentle man, the kind you'd like as a friend, but I'm not sure he has the stomach for the rough and tumble of politics."

How wrong I was! Through the exercise of self-control, Rajiv

Gandhi has consolidated power and achieved a support base unequaled by any Indian prime minister before him, including his illustrious mother and scholarly grandfather. Self-control created in him the confidence to lead.

Joy

Joy comes from knowing you are being obedient to the will of God. Consistent, constant obedience takes self-control. That is why self-control can produce a deep, lasting joy. Richard Foster says, "Joy is the keynote of all the disciplines. . . . When one's inner spirit is set free from all that holds it down, that can hardly be described as dull drudgery. Singing, dancing, even shouting characterize the disciplines of the spiritual life."

Stability

Few people like change. We want things to stay the way they are. People look to leaders who will provide them with stability. A disciplined life does not mean there will be no change for you and your followers, but it does mean that the change will be purposeful and controlled. It does mean that there will be stability.

Leadership

Self-control produces freedom, confidence, joy, and stability. Those qualities will catapult a person to a place of leadership. Self-control also insures the flowering of every other quality of love: joy, peace, longsuffering, gentleness, goodness, faithfulness, and meekness. Through self-control, all aspects of the Christlike leader's life are brought under the mastery of the Holy Spirit.

One of the most important principles of effective leadership is certainly that of self-control. Begin today to develop it in your life.

A twenty-seven-year-old man, Dawson Trotman, with only one year of Bible school and one year of seminary, organized the Navigators, an evangelistic organization that majored on conversion and spiritual growth through complete commitment to Christ, the Bible, and others.

Daws Trotman embodied self-control in his prayer life, in his Bible study, and in putting others first to a degree I have rarely witnessed. After extended time with God, he was driven to take the promises of God seriously and to act on them. He was a constant challenge to me, and he was a leader whose leadership still exerts special influence around the world.

Trotman was bright, artistic, and highly articulate, but he emphasized the importance of complete commitment to the Lord Jesus Christ and to the Bible. He was an exhorter. No exhorter of significance is ever responded to with neutrality. People either love him or hate him. Trotman suffered some vicious attacks over the course of his life and ministry. But he continued on, fully believing the promise, "Great peace have those who love Your law, And nothing causes them to stumble."

In 1956, Daws was at Schroon Lake, New York. A girl was drowning. He dived into the water, saved the girl, but it cost him his life. He drowned as a young man. He left an organization that now ministers powerfully in more than 50 countries with a staff numbering more than 2,500.

Bron Clifford is a vapor long since dissipated. Dawson Trotman is a power continuing to influence the world. The difference in the two men is one of self-control.

SUMMARY

Self-control is a way of life in which, by the power of the Holy Spirit, the Christian is able to be temperate in all things because he does not let his desires master his life. Self-control is usually seen as a restriction. And yet it is impossible to permanently defeat the leader who exercises self-control. Self-control is love's mastery.

The Christlike leader knows that self-control is important because lack of self-control destroys leadership. The leader needs to be particularly careful that loss of self-control does not come in those areas where he is the strongest, has the most confidence, feels the most secure. That is exactly where trouble strikes. Self-control gives courage to stand alone. It allows the leader to be not diverted from his vision by the opinion and subtle pressures of the crowd. Self-control draws followers to the leader. People want to follow those who demonstrate self-control.

Like all the principles of leadership, self-control must be carefully developed and nurtured. This is done through dependence on God, a life of discipline, making decisions ahead of time, gratitude for adversity, ruling one's spirit, controlling one's thoughts, and by letting the Holy Spirit live in the leader.

Self-control is usually seen as a restriction, a discipline that produces a harsh, joyless existence. In reality, however, just the opposite is true. Self-control produces in any person results that will make him a candidate for leadership. Self-control produces freedom, confidence, joy, and stability. Those qualities will catapult a person to a place of leadership.

7

The Principle of

COMMUNICATION

Leadership begins with a vision. The commitment to that vision is a mission, which is then fulfilled by setting and accomplishing certain goals. But the leader does not do this in isolation. The leader's task is to communicate the vision, the mission, and the goals to his followers in love and humility.

The leader must be a communicator. He may have other skills because of the field in which he works, but he is to be first and foremost a communicator. Good musicianship, for instance, is a requisite for a good choir director, but many great musicians have failed as choir directors because they could not communicate effectively to the members of the choir.

The ability to effectively communicate, through speech and writing, is possibly the leader's most valuable asset. There are seven rules of effective communication which, if mastered, will help leaders maximize their effectiveness.

RULE ONE: RECOGNIZE THE IMPORTANCE OF EFFECTIVE COMMUNICATION

"What could be easier than communicating?" you might ask. "I do it every day." But communication is not as simple as it appears, and you may be only repeating words when you think you are communicating. And yet communication is the way the leader unifies and directs the group.

In simplest terms, communication takes place when a message has been transmitted from one person to another with both people understanding the message in approximately the same way. But there are an incredible number of barriers to effective communication. Suppose Mr. X wants to tell Mr. Y something. The figure[20] below represents Mr. X's communication to Mr. Y.

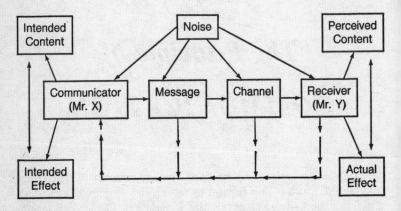

Mr. X wants his message to have a certain effect on Mr. Y. Perhaps he is compiling a mailing list and mixes up some of the addresses. Mr. X wants Mr. Y to correct the mistake. He chooses certain words to tell Mr. Y that the list is incorrect and what he should do to make it right. The technical word for this is "encoding." The encoded message has both an intended content (the list is wrong) and an intended effect (Mr. Y fixes it). Next, Mr. X transmits the message to Mr. Y through a channel. Perhaps he speaks to Mr. Y or perhaps he writes him a memo. Mr. Y then decodes the message so that he will perceive the content Mr. X is trying to communicate. The effectiveness of the communication depends on how similar the perceived content is to the intended content and the actual effect is to the intended effect.

It is important for the leader to recognize that the effectiveness of the communication depends on the *perceived* content and *actual* effect— not on his intended content, no matter how eloquently given, nor on the intended effect, no matter how pure and noble his intentions. It is the communicator's task to *make sure* the perceived content and actual effect are right, not just assume the content is understood and the effect is carried out.

Mr. Y's perception of the content and the actual effect of the message depends on many things other than the words. If Mr. X speaks Swahili and Mr. Y understands only Japanese, obviously the message will not be communicated. If the room is so noisy that he can't understand what Mr. X says, Mr. Y may smile politely and do nothing. The intended effect is not achieved. If Mr. Y has just heard that his father died and has had several other things go wrong that day, he may get angry with Mr. X. Again, the intended effect is not achieved. In addition to his words, Mr. X can communicate a great deal by his nonverbal behavior—how he stands, his facial expression, where he places his hands.

Effective communication is both an art and a science. It's an art that requires the same earnest attention, persistent practice, and careful technique as the mastery of painting, sculpture, or music. It's a science based on the tenets of psychology.

Learning to communicate effectively is important to you as a leader because you will never reach your leadership potential without it. I am convinced that only bad attitudes account for more failures of leadership than faulty communication.

Effective Communication Overcomes Isolation

Members of a group can be isolated from each other by geography, language differences, or attitudes such as class distinction, religious sectarianism, racial segregation, nationalism, or political partisanship. Isolation destroys the group and group achievement, and so the leader is compelled to overcome the isolation of members of the group. Through effective communication, the leader must encourage the kind of understanding, tolerance, and sympathy that will bring those in isolation into unity with the rest of the group.

Effective Communication Is a Factor in Reproduction

Communication is the means by which the leader reproduces leadership principles in others. He wants others in the group to catch the vision and work toward the goals that will fulfill the mission. "He who does the work is not so profitably employed as he who multiplies the doers," a man named Morley said in the early part of the last century.

"No man ever began a movement which was destined to stand the test of time but that he placed great stress on the task of teaching those who followed after him," said Dr. Herschel H. Hobbs. "Thoughts are things, beliefs are biotic, and ideas are imperishable. Leaders may come and go, personalities may live and die, but mental and spiritual concepts are immortal. These are the dynamics for changing the course of history and the lives of men and women."[21]

It is the reproduction of great thoughts, beliefs, and ideas in others through effective communication that sets a leader apart.

Effective Communication Tends to Safeguard Freedom of Speech

Those of us who live where there is freedom of speech may not fully appreciate it, but such freedom is a treasure to be guarded and defended. And yet when speech becomes insipid and banal, all the legislative enactments in the capitals of the world will not make it effective. A person in a leadership position who violates the rules of effective communication tragically imposes a greater limitation on freedom of speech than any external restriction that tyrants can impose. Free speech cannot long endure without effective speech. The leader should therefore make the development of communication effectiveness his lifelong passion and discipline.

Effective Communication Presents Worthy Thoughts Worthily

A popular assumption is that you need only "to have something to say" in order to communicate. What a dreadful fallacy! Unless that "something to say" is communicated effectively, it might as well be scattered to the wind. Having a concern only with what is being said is focusing attention on the *intended* content and *intended* effect of the communication. They are important, but the effective communicator focuses instead on the *perceived* content and *actual* effect.

How often speech fails to attain its purpose! The professor seeks to impart his important knowledge, and he finds the students confused. The lawyer pleads earnestly before the jury to accept his valid facts, but he loses the case. The salesman extols his superb products, but he makes no sales. The father wisely counsels his son, but the son shows no change in attitude or action. The political leader presents his just policies to the crowds, but he loses the election. And the preacher declares the eternal truth of the Word of the Lord, and the congregation falls asleep! In each instance, potential leadership was desecrated because effective communication was violated. Worthy thoughts were not given a chance because they were not presented worthily. The perceived content did not match the intended content, and the actual effect was not the same as the intended effect.

The effective leader leaves nothing to chance. Although he will certainly be open to the enlightenment and leading of the Holy Spirit, he prepares his verbal communication as thoroughly as the concert master prepares his musical communication. It is not enough to have worthy thoughts. Those thoughts must be communicated worthily.

Progress would be tragically stopped if all communication were prohibited. The wheels of industry would screech to a halt. Schools would shut down. Governments would collapse. Families would disintegrate. Alliances would crumble. Famine would decimate humankind across the globe. How sorely would evangelization of the world suffer if all communication were prohibited!

Communication is the means by which we transfer truth. Communication can move and mold men, individually and collectively. Communication lays the very foundation for spiritual decisions. It relates intimately to a person's relationship with God. If effective communication is so important, does it not follow that leaders, redeemed and called of God, ought to give sober attention to the most effective way of utilizing this powerful tool? The leader cannot ignore the rules of effective communication.

RULE TWO: ASSESS YOUR AUDIENCE

The leader's task as an effective communicator is (1) to make the perceived content of the message in the mind of the receiver as similar as possible to the intended content of the message that is in his own mind and (2) to make the actual effect of the message on the receiver be as close as possible to the intended effect. To do this, the leader must know the receiver—his audience.

Several years ago, I received a phone call from a young man named Jackson. He asked me for some counsel. I identified him as a young man in his mid-thirties, living in Texas, the son of a close friend whom I had known for twenty years. We set the date to meet. To my astonishment, it was someone other than the person I expected. The man who met me was also in his thirties. He also lived in Texas. His father had also been a close friend of mine for more than twenty years. However, because I had misassessed my audience, my preparation was substantially different for the young man I thought was coming than it would have been for the young man who actually came. I had failed to assess my audience.

You must know your audience thoroughly if you are going to communicate effectively and lead the people in it.

First and most basic, you must identify the audience makeup. Learn such demographic facts as gender, age, ethnic background, education, vocation, lifestyle, religious affiliation and degree of commitment to it, hobbies, and anything else that would be particularly relevant to what you want to communicate.

Second, assess your audience's attitude toward its environment and important issues. Are they happy with the social, political, cultural, and educational conditions where they live? Do the working conditions and family conditions of the area meet with their approval?

I painfully recall a dinner I had with several business leaders in a Third World nation. Their head of state had just delivered a major address. Although I disagreed with some of what he said, I told the businessmen that I was enthralled by his oratorical style. They looked at me in stony silence with eyes that seemed to say, "We didn't know you were so stupid!" They felt so strong an antipathy for the man that nothing I could say would have been construed as positive.

Third, assess your audience's attitude toward each other. Are they comfortable with each other, jealous of each other, suspicious of each other, supportive of each other? Are they homogeneous or heterogeneous?

Fourth, assess their attitude toward the subject you are dealing with. Are they familiar with your subject? Are they agreeable to what you will say? A subject such as "How to Kill Rats" might rivet the attention of farmers, but bore college students to death.

If your audience is totally unversed in your subject, you'll probably begin with the known and progress to the unknown. If your audience is not interested in the subject, you will have to show how the discussion is going to affect them and fulfill their real needs.

Finally, assess your audience's attitude toward you, the leader. Communication is a two-way street. You should tailor your communication by the feedback you get to what you say.

When I was conducting large crusades, it was standard operating procedure to send my associates ahead to learn as much as possible about the audience. Even then, on occasions we slipped up. In 1974, I made an impassioned plea in Australia for each person to vote during an upcoming election. In America, people are not compelled to vote. It is strictly voluntary. I was trying to impress my audience with the importance of every citizen taking advantage of this precious privilege of a free society. After the meeting I was told that voting was compulsory in Australia! In fact, people are fined if they do not vote. I had wasted twelve minutes of each person's time simply because I had not properly assessed the audience. Multiply twelve minutes by 2,000 people, and the 400 hours wasted still embarrasses me.

My definition of leadership presupposes a thorough assessment of the audience. How can a leader move the group toward goals of beneficial permanence that meet its real needs if he does not know who the group really is, where the members of the group really are in terms of self-image and living philosophy, and what they really want to accomplish?

RULE THREE: SELECT THE RIGHT COMMUNICATION GOAL

The first requisite to effective communication is a clear understanding of the goal of the communication. No one builds a building without asking what the function will be, and no one takes a journey without knowing where he is going. If the leader fails to target a precise goal when he communicates, the followers will respond with indifference.

Once a stranger in America stopped a man on the road and asked him, "Where does this road lead to?" The man answered, "Where do you want to go?"

Again the stranger persisted, "Where does this road lead to?"

"My friend," replied the other, "this road leads to any place in the United States."

It is the same with communication. The leader must know his destination if he wishes to arrive there. He must have a goal when he starts out. His goal may be to inform, to impress, to convince, to entertain, or to actuate. The leader usually will have the goal of actuating, but he will try to actuate the group by informing, impressing, convincing, or entertaining.

When the leader is explaining the impact of a newly enacted law on the group's activities, his goal is to inform. When he is handing out awards to the high achievers and reciting some of the historic "highs" of their achievements, his goal is to impress. When he lectures on the superiority of computerization, his goal is to convince. When he makes an after-dinner speech, his goal may be to entertain. And when he is speaking to the members of the board about the importance of spending $100,000 to purchase computers and another $100,000 a year to recruit computer technocrats, his communication goal is to actuate.

Whether you're writing a memo, composing a magazine article, preparing a sermon, presenting a radio talk, or motivating students or employees, knowing the proper communication goal will conserve time, accomplish the task more effectively and thus strengthen your leadership.

To Inform

If your goal is to inform, it means you will create understanding. This is the goal of all who seek to convey information purely as information. In this instance, the duty of the communicator is discharged when he presents the ideas so that the audience can understand them clearly. This is the goal of the witness in court. This is the great function of a dictionary. When "to inform" is your goal, you state the ideas and stop there. You state no bias, no slant.

To Impress

Impressiveness connotes vividness. The message to be conveyed is not simply to be understood, but to be *felt*. The lecturer on literature desires that in the presentation, the genius of Kahlil Gibran will not only be understood, but that it shall arouse pleasurable emotion. The evangelist, in preaching on the love of God, is concerned not only that it be comprehended, but that it will stir the soul. This is the goal of speakers at school graduations, funerals, festivals, anniversaries.

When the specific purpose is to arouse in the listener emotional association, the goal is to impress.

To Convince

When the leader has the goal of convincing, it means that he is not content for his group only to understand or feel, but he wants each person to accept the subject matter as truth. Each one must say, in effect, "That is so"; "You are right"; "I believe." This goal, however, doesn't require action. It simply relates to matters of opinion, such as which of two political philosophies exercises the greater influence or which is the better policy for world evangelization.

In every case where the dominant motive of the communicator is to secure acceptance of his idea, the goal is to convince.

To Entertain

Entertainment as a goal is concerned with amusement. This is the leader's goal when he wants to arouse pleasant feelings, interest, mild delights, or even hearty laughter.

In 1971, Hockaday, an elite girl's school in Dallas, Texas, asked me to speak. The officials warned me that the last several speakers were interrupted by the girls; they would hum on one note, causing a distraction that made the public address impossible. I told them I thought we would get along just fine.

Within fifteen seconds, through the use of humor, I had captured their attention. Twenty-seven minutes later, they gave me a standing ovation. I was actually able to say everything that was on my heart. It was the entertainment factor that neutralized the girls' antagonism. To this day, some, now mothers and career women, write to tell me what a turning point that session was to their lives.

To Actuate

When the leader has a goal of actuating the group, it means that he wants his hearers to *do* something. He wants them to take action. His dominant purpose is to move the group to act: to be, to go, to give, to bring, to join, to do.

To actuate is surely the main concern of the evangelist, the trial lawyer, the political speaker, the merchant, and the salesman—and the leader. To actuate may demand, as preliminary steps, the goals of informing, impressing, convincing, or even entertaining. But it is more than all of these. The goal of actuating seeks to make the hearer not only see, feel, and believe, but to make him validate his understanding, his feeling, his belief by his works.

The Epistle of James underlines this communication goal: "But be doers of the Word, and not hearers only, deceiving yourselves" (James 1:22).

Differences in Goals

The distinction between the various goals becomes unmistakable when we consider them in relation to a particular topic.

If my subject is Samson and I explain his conquests and his final defeat but ultimate victory without any effort to secure approval or disapproval, then the goal is *to inform.*

If I wish to arouse the emotions by showing how Samson backslid, how he was double-crossed by those whom he trusted, and how in his closing hours he honored God, then my goal is *to impress.*

If my purpose is to make the listener or reader believe that victories are possible in the strength of God and use Samson as an illustration, then my goal is *to convince.*

If I am using some of Samson's exploits such as sending the foxes through the Philistines' corn as an illustration of humor in the Bible and my dominant motive is to create pleasure, then my goal is *to entertain.*

If I am addressing a group of young people urging them to make a complete surrender of their lives to God, and use Samson as an illustration of the importance of putting God first, then my goal is *to actuate.*

Be clear, precise, and focused if you want people to follow you. This will come by having a clear communication goal. Selecting the right communication goal liberates the leader from the awful pit of indefiniteness.

Rule Four: Break the Preoccupation Barrier

Before you can communicate effectively, you must capture your audience's attention. But everyone is preoccupied. You will rarely find anyone who wants to know what you think. Moreover, everyone is bombarded with thousands of messages a day, each clamoring for their attention: "Buy Shell gasoline"; "Here's the latest in the Mideast crisis"; "You need to take a vacation in Australia"; "The price of gold went up today." Your first move, then, if you want to communicate, is to master the skill of breaking the preoccupation barrier. The key is in assessing your audience.

In 1975, I had a special speech to give. For days I thought and prayed for a way to break the preoccupation barrier. The major perceived problem troubling the largest number of people at that time was the financial crisis caused by the skyrocketing oil prices.

I began the address with these words: "I'm going to give you ten commandments for surviving the financial crisis." In seconds, you could hear an onionskin drop on the carpet, so quiet was the audience of 2,500 persons. When it was announced that the message would be available on cassette or in printed form, the telephone operators were kept busy for the next twelve hours trying to handle all the requests.

The title and cover of a book are given the task of capturing attention. Of all the books I've written, one has outsold all others combined. It has been in print for more than twenty-five years and has been translated into eighteen languages. The title is *How to Win Over Worry.* Apparently the title breaks the preoccupation barrier.

It is possible to get people's attention by forcing them to listen, but that insures neither a faithful following nor an effort on the part of the listener to decode the message. Forced attention violates the very foundation of leadership. But attention captured by self-interest lasts. This is a principle ineffective leaders ignore and good leaders grasp. A leader can force some followers to listen, but effective leadership occurs only when the leader breaks the preoccupation barrier and earns the right to be heard.

To break the preoccupation barrier, the leader must ask himself, "What are the disturbing problems the people are facing?" He then identifies the problem in a way that the listeners or readers will recognize. Next he promises a solution and fulfills the promise.

Writers of magazine articles need to quickly break the preoccupation barrier. One writer who did this effectively had the following first sentence: "You who are reading this article may die before you finish it."

It was an article on heart disease, and the writer knew what would get people's attention. The sentence is personal. It sets up a potential problem that the reader will want to know about. It is universal. If the first sentence had been, "Heart disease strikes most often at men and women around forty," the writer would have lost a large audience. Only people around forty would be tempted to read it. Or if the first sentence had been "Heart disease causes more deaths than any other ailment," the writer would have captured very few people because the sentence would be too general. Instead, the writer's sentence was striking and it was personal.

Russell Conwell built one of America's largest churches, established one of the world's leading universities, and founded Temple University Hospital. How did he raise the funds? He delivered his classic address, "Acres of Diamonds," more than 6,000 times. What made him so powerful a communicator? For one thing, he knew how to break the preoccupation barrier of his hearers.

> Friends, this lecture ("Acres of Diamonds") has been delivered under these circumstances: I visit a town or city, and try to arrive there early enough to see the postmaster, the barber, the keeper of the hotel, the principal of the schools, and the ministers of some of the churches, and then go into some of the factories and stores and talk with the people, and get in sympathy with the local conditions of that town or city and see what has been their history, what opportunities they had and what they failed to do—and every town fails to do something—and then go to the lecture and talk to those people about the subjects which applied to their locality.[22]

Conwell broke their preoccupation barrier in the first seconds of his lecture because he knew their problems and he had the solution. He could do this because he took the right steps to assess his audience.

RULE FIVE: REFER TO THE KNOWN, THE AUDIENCE'S EXPERIENCE

Jesus had many important teachings, some of which were abstract and a bit difficult to understand. Therefore, Jesus told parables, stories that referred to situations that were in His audience's experience. For instance, to those who were familiar with farming, He told the parable of the sower and the parable of the wheat and the tares.

Communication is not "unloading" on your audience. Communication carries with it the idea of involvement with others, and the leader is involved with people. The word *communication* has its root in the Latin word *communis,* which means "common." To be an effective communicator, you must impose on yourself the discipline of seeing things from the viewpoint of your people. This may be the most important lesson in communication.

The leader refers to what his listener knows—that which the listener has seen, heard, read, felt, believed, or done and which still exists in his consciousness, his inventory of knowledge. The known includes all those thoughts, feelings, and events which to him are real. It includes direct experiences—those he has experienced with his own senses—as well as indirect experiences which, while not felt and seen directly, are nonetheless accepted as second-hand knowledge. We have never seen Julius Caesar, but we accept as reality the statement that he lived and did certain things.

Only by referring to the experience of your audience will you develop credibility. You judge the truth or error of a statement by the criterion of your own experience, and what's true of you is true of others. Reference to experience is the way you make the unknown known.

You must habitually ask yourself, "How would I feel about this if I were in the audience? Would I understand this point with the background they have? Would this sound reasonable if I had been through their experiences? Would it be interesting to me if I were they?"

There are several factors to consider about people's experiences. First, we tend to remember those impressions that were initially intense. In 1975, in Tehran, I was doubled over by the pain of a kidney stone. Using that experience won't relate to most people since most have never had a kidney stone attack. But most people have had a toothache. I can use the experience of a toothache to communicate the idea of pain much more powerfully than that of a finger scratch because a toothache is far more intense.

Second, an experience will be vivid in proportion to the number of times it's repeated. Those coming from the northern hemisphere have a deep conviction that mid-year is warmer than winter. It is vivid not so much because of the original experience but because of the frequency of the experience. They have experienced summer every year of their lives. Those living south of the equator have the opposite experience; mid-year is the colder season.

Third, an experience will be vivid in proportion to the number of times it's recalled. A war veteran may have served in only one campaign, but the battles and the sieges all have their original intensity if he has frequently recollected them and retold them, keeping the mental pictures fresh. One of the great justifications for giving Christian people an opportunity to testify frequently is that it focuses their attention on the great things God has done for them. Recalling God's blessings strengthens their commitment by making those blessings more vivid.

Fourth, other things being equal, an experience is vivid according to its nearness in time. Do you remember what you had for breakfast this morning? Of course. Do you remember what you had for breakfast ten years ago? Probably not. You can remember the raging headache you had yesterday with much deeper feeling than you can the pain you had four months ago.

Just as a singer has a repertoire of songs, you must acquire a repertoire of vivid general experiences common to the average person you lead if you are to communicate with influence. These experiences must have the characteristics of intensity, recency, and frequency in recurrence and recall. Impress on your own mind those experiences. Develop the habit of seeing with the eyes of those with whom you communicate and hearing with their ears.

People today refuse to be commanded, threatened, or maneuvered into an opinion. They say, "Only through my knowledge, only through my life, shall you secure my approval. I am a person. Bring your thought in line with my mind frame, and I may join with you."

You must always ask yourself, "What references to the listeners' experience will bring my idea, with the necessary vividness, most quickly in line with the listeners' knowledge? What will cause them to say, 'I see,' 'I feel,' 'You are right,' 'I will do it,' 'I am pleased'?" Then you will know what arguments come closest to the lives of your listeners, what appeals come nearest to their hearts. Knowing this, you are able to distinguish that which appeals to all from that which appeals to a few, and in great moments you can touch the universal chord.

RULE SIX: SUPPORT YOUR ASSERTIONS

Abstract ideas tend to chloroform people's attention. Or worse, people frequently resist abstract ideas altogether. Usually people don't believe a statement unless there is proof. And they don't act on a suggestion unless it's given logical and emotional support.

A salesman may tell me I need a computer/word processor in my study at home. I disagree. "The cost is prohibitive. I don't have the space. And I have not been trained in how to use one," I say.

He doesn't let the matter drop. He explains that his company will give me full instructions. He shows me how little space the equipment requires. He convinces me that I'm losing money by my archaic method of dictating, reviewing, and editing. He leads me to persuade myself that failure to secure the equipment is throwing money in the trash. Today, I'm writing this book on a computer/word processor because a salesman supported his assertion, "You need a personal computer/word processor."

Most of a leader's communication centers on assertions. Without supporting them, he appears to be didactic, pontifical, even dictatorial. "Support" refers to any and all material used to clarify, amplify, verify, or in any way make the assertion illuminating and valid. The assertion is the skeleton; the support gives flesh and blood—life.

You may use several forms of support. Sometimes you'll use one form; other times you'll use two or more in combination:

1. Cumulation
2. Restatement
3. Exposition
4. Comparison
5. General illustration
6. Specific instance
7. Testimony

Cumulation

You will not likely change a person's mind, inspire his devotion toward a new concept, or make him contribute to a worthy cause with an isolated statement. You need to employ a succession of statements bearing on the same point. Cumulation means "a heaping up." It's a progression of thought. It adds to the information given, offering additional proof.

If I say, "Many over sixty have done great accomplishments," my audience may question the assertion. But I may win their agreement if I use cumulation by telling of Benjamin Franklin, who was ambassador to France when more than eighty; Gladstone, who was prime minister of England at eighty-three; Chiang Kai-shek, who governed the Republic of China when he was more than eighty; and Verdi, who wrote operas when he was eighty.

Cumulation uses a succession of details, instances, and illustrations to direct the followers' attention repeatedly to the original statement until the required goal has been attained.

Normally you cannot accomplish your purpose with a single statement. You cannot make the doctrine of the Trinity clear with one sentence. You cannot stir deep feeling by simply saying, "Milton was great." If you insist that apartheid in South Africa is wrong and say nothing more, you'll not convince anyone of the validity of your opinion. An isolated declaration will not usually affect your followers.

Using cumulation, however, gives your followers the necessary time and logical and emotional support to convince them of what you are saying. Each detail, each fact, each illustration "heaps up" support to accomplish your purpose.

Restatement

Restatement offers no additional proof, puts forth no reasons, and gives no details. Restatement tends to force the listener or the reader to concentrate on the original assertion as an entity. It subtly says, "Focus your attention on this; grasp it fully." You should use restatement when you believe greater concentration on the assertion itself is required.

When the leader's goal is to inform, restatement may be necessary to break through this obscurity that results from unfamiliarity with the meaning of the words or the complexity of structure.

The statement "He (Voltaire) had exercised a function and fulfilled a mission" is obscure; it does not communicate the precise meaning of "fulfilled a mission." Therefore Victor Hugo restated it: "He had evidently been chosen for the work which he had done by the Supreme Will which manifests itself in the laws of destiny as in the laws of nature." [23]

Often restatement can be valuable as a conclusion. If the argument has been lengthy, the leader can rapidly review his several ideas and drive them home as a whole.

However, let me warn you not to use restatement indiscriminately. Nothing annoys a person more than a writer or speaker who restates an idea that is already clear and vivid.

Exposition

Exposition sets forth in simple and concise terms the meaning of an assertion.

The late Justice Louis D. Brandeis, for instance, explained the meaning of the word *profession:* "The peculiar character of a profession as distinguished from other occupations, I take to be these: First, a profession is an occupation for which the necessary preliminary training is intellectual in character, involving knowledge and, to some extent, learning, as distinguished from merely skill. Second, it is an occupation in which the amount of financial return is not the accepted measure of success." This is exposition.

Comparison

You may support your assertion by pointing out similarities between that which your audience already knows and that which it does not know. You connect the known with the unknown.

Here's how Thomas Edison explained electricity and the long-distance telephone: "It's like a dachshund (this is a dog with short legs but a disproportionately long body) long enough to reach from Edinburg to London; when you pull his tail in Edinburg, he barks in London."

You greatly increase your credibility and authority when you use comparison that refers to the experience of your audience.

General Illustration

General illustration gives details about the idea expressed in the original assertion. It amplifies, although it does not individualize.

You might say, "My alma mater is a good school. Today it's turning out some of the nation's best leaders in the fields of robotics, genetic engineering, aerospace, and computer science." The assertion about the quality of the school is clarified by the general illustration that follows. You mention robotics, for instance, but you do not name any particular leader in that field.

Specific Instance

Specific instance concerns itself with specifics—dates, times, places, names, incidents. It differs from general illustration in that it is individual, absolute, and precise.

You might make the assertion, "Greece had great men." You could clarify and support the assertion with the general illustration, "It had authors, philosophers, poets, experts in medicine." Specific instance supports the same assertion by saying, "It had Demosthenes, Aeschylus, Plato, Aristotle, Sophocles, Homer, and Hippocrates."

Testimony

Testimony is the form of support in which an authority figure verifies what you are saying. It gives you the added credibility of the person whom your audience accepts as an authority. Testimony is used widely in advertising as, for instance, when an athlete says he eats a particular brand of breakfast cereal.

Testimony corroborates the leader's assertion in the mind of the follower. Testimony will be stronger than your own assertion when your audience looks on the person or work quoted as more authoritative than you. Interestingly enough, it is not necessary for the person to be authoritative on the matter at hand—although he should be. The athlete, for instance, may not know anything about breakfast cereal but still be able to sell it effectively.

If you want to use testimony effectively, you should know your audience, have a familiar knowledge of recognized authorities and authoritative works, and constantly be alert to and gather testimony that can be used.

Let me give one caution: it is possible to use quotations and testimonies so frequently you destroy your audience's confidence in your own credibility and authority. My former professor, Dr. P. B. Fitzwater, said, "People don't come to hear through your lips what somebody else said. They come to hear what you say!"

Yet there are the occasions when testimony is essential and powerful. Added to the other forms of support, testimony can be clear and compelling.

RULE SEVEN: MOTIVATE ACTION BY THE APPEAL TO DESIRE

Most of the time the leader's communication goal will be to actuate, even though he may use one of the other goals to achieve that end. The leader should stimulate action by appealing to desire, by understanding and using the motivation that people already have.

People don't want facts for facts' sake. You can give your son a pile of facts about health, and he will be indifferent. Then one day he comes home from school all fired up to compete in a 1500-kilometer race. He goes into training and avidly studies all the facts about health he can get. What made the difference? Desire. Perhaps his coach said he had to do it or he would fail. Perhaps he wants to impress a certain young lady. But there is in him a desire to compete.

To most effectively motivate people to action—to move them toward goals of beneficial permanence that meet their real needs—you need to understand people's desires and how to fulfill them.

You do not buy a life insurance policy because the Department of Vital Statistics predicts that one out of every four people now alive will be dead in ten years. Rather, you buy the insurance because you don't want your wife to be destitute, your children deprived of an education, the estate you have built up decimated, and your reputation (after death) to be one of irresponsibility. Life insurance salesmen know that and have learned the most effective ways to appeal to these desires.

Many thinkers have tried to analyze our desires. Fifty years ago, Professor A. E. Phillips classified all desires under seven headings: self-preservation, property, power, reputation, affection, sentiment, and taste.[24] In his book *The Magic Power of Emotional Appeal,* Roy Garn refers to four basic desires: self-preservation, money, romance, and recognition.[25] The late Alan H. Monroe of Purdue University listed eighteen major desires.[26]

In one of the most significant studies of desires, Abraham Maslow suggested that there is a hierarchy of needs. The basic needs, he said, are physiological and security needs—food, clothing, shelter, security. Next, says Maslow, are social needs—needs to belong. The highest level of needs are self-actualization needs. These include the need for ego fulfillment. Maslow suggested that once a lower-level need is satisfied, a person can attend to the next higher level of need but that you can't preach an ideology to a person with an empty stomach.[27]

In this book, I will look at needs from the standpoint of self-preservation, property, power, reputation, and affection.

Self-preservation

Self-preservation is the desire for long life and health and all that makes living more pleasant and fulfilling. It includes the desire for freedom from sorrow, pain, and death. It includes the desire for heaven as opposed to hell.

Self-preservation is the primary desire that induces the majority of actions. It determines that we eat and drink. It recruits armies and organizes police forces. It demands emission controls on automobiles and environmental protection concerns on the part of industry.

Property

Property refers to the desire for wealth, goods, lands, and money. It is not just the desire for survival, but the desire to have things—whether we "need" them or not.

This desire is prevalent from the cradle to the grave. The baby cries for the toy. The worker wants an increase in salary. The capitalist wants a greater return on his investment. The child wants a bicycle.

Power

Power refers to the desire to possess skill, force, and energy. It refers to the desire for ability to be and to do. It includes the desire for strength (moral and physical), authority, and influence. Under this category come nearly all ambitions.

Reputation

Reputation refers to the desire for the good opinion of others. It is rooted in self-respect and pride. All normal people seek the favor of others. They find pleasure in being known as upright, honest, kind, generous, and scholarly.

This is a powerful desire. Some men would rather risk their life than lose a good reputation. It is this desire that makes the lazy industrious, the stingy generous, and the deceptive honest.

Affection

Affection refers to the desire for the welfare of others—a loving concern for the needs of loved ones, a town, or a nation.

No one is a leader who cannot induce others to act, and no one can induce others to act if he ignores the employment of appeal to basic desires. When Jesus said, "Give and it shall be given unto you," He appealed to the desire of property. When the apostle Paul said, "Knowing, therefore, the terror of the Lord, we persuade men," he appealed to the desire of self-preservation. When Solomon said, "Train up a child in the way he should go, And when he is old he will not depart from it," he appealed to the desire for affection.

This appeal to desire can be manipulative. However, in moving your group toward goals of beneficial permanence to meet their real needs, you must make clear that the action you're suggesting will, in fact, contribute to fulfilling their *real* needs.

Since the leader transfers his thoughts to his group through communication, it follows that only effective communication can make clear to the group their real needs and move them toward the appropriate goals to fulfill those needs. Effective communication, through speech and writing, is possibly the leader's most valuable asset. You can and must acquire it.

Make communication an ongoing study, your life-long passion and discipline. Practice, practice, practice! Study human reactions. Know what your followers are thinking. Think of ways to refer to their experience in the achievement of your objectives. Through effective communication, you will out-achieve others who may be more intelligent or more personable, but who have not developed their communication abilities.

SUMMARY

The leader must be a communicator. The ability to communicate effectively through speech and writing is possibly the leader's most valuable asset. Seven rules of effective communication will help the leader develop that asset.

1. *Recognize the importance of effective communication.* The leader is not just concerned with the words he says, but with the content his listeners perceive and the effect the content actually has as a result of his communication. The leader's task is to create understanding. Effective

communication overcomes isolation, is a factor in reproduction, tends to safeguard freedom of speech, and presents worthy thoughts worthily.

2. *Assess your audience.* The foundation for carrying out all the other rules of effective communication is to assess your audience. Learn its demographic characteristics. Assess its attitude toward its environment and important issues, assess the audience's attitude toward each other. Assess its attitude toward your subject. Assess your audience's attitude toward you.

3. *Select the right communication goal.* Having a goal clearly in mind will conserve time, accomplish the task more effectively, and thus strengthen your leadership. The leader will almost always have the goal of actuating—motivating the group to take action. But he will try to actuate the group by one of the other goals: informing, impressing, convincing, or entertaining.

4. *Break the preoccupation barrier.* Capture the audience's attention. Earn the right to be heard. To break the preoccupation barrier, identify the leading problems the people in the audience are facing, promise a solution to those problems, and then fulfill that promise.

5. *Refer to the known, the audience's experience.* Only by referring to the experiences of your audience will you develop credibility. To do this, you must acquire a repertoire of vivid general experiences common to the average person you lead. A number of factors make these experiences more memorable: intensity, how often the experiences are repeated, how often they are recalled, and recency.

6. *Support your assertions.* Abstract ideas in themselves do not capture people's attention. Abstract assertions should therefore be supported and brought to life through cumulation, restatement, exposition, comparison, general illustration, specific instance, and testimony.

7. *Motivate action by the appeal to desire.* The leader wants action. He wants to effect change. The most effective way to do that is by an appeal to the dominant desire of the particular audience. The leader should appeal to his audience's healthy self-interest, which can be expressed in needs of self-preservation, property, power, reputation, and affection. No one is a leader who cannot induce others to act, and no one can induce others to act if he does not employ an appeal to basic desires.

Make communication an ongoing study, your life-long passion and discipline. Through effective communication, you will out-achieve others who may be more intelligent or more personable, but who have not developed their communication abilities.

8

The Principle of

INVESTMENT

The small Zambian Baptist Church was poor. The members loved their pastor, Rev. Godfrey Mulando, but they were unable to pay his salary. This love was mutual, and the pastor had dedicated himself to lead his people into a close daily walk with God. However, he had been warned not to preach about money or he would frighten the people away.

When Mulando went to Singapore for leadership training in the "how" of evangelism, he was so struck by what he heard of God's commands and promises on the subject of money and possessions, he was convicted that his people should also know this truth.

When he returned to Zambia, he began to teach his people: "Stewardship is part of the gospel. A person cannot fully know God unless he knows the concept of stewardship and practices it. Worship is not complete unless you give something. When the wise men came to worship the baby Jesus, for example, they brought precious gifts."

The members of the congregation were dedicated people and they were not frightened away by God's commands to give. Rather, they were thrilled at what they heard and also ashamed of their own disobedience. They asked their pastor why he had not taught these things before. He was forced to admit that he himself had not known them.

For the first time, the people of Masala Baptist Church in Ndola, Zambia, began to tithe and give joyously of themselves and their money. In addition to meeting church expenses, they accepted responsibility for their pastor's salary and house rent. They bought the pastor a motorcycle to facilitate his visitation and evangelistic work. They also wrote to the missionary society and said, "No more money, just send your prayers and your love."

They discovered they could not outgive God, and not only were their personal lives blessed, but God also blessed the church. It grew. As the members saw God honoring His promises, they began to share their joy, themselves, and Christ with friends, neighbors, and relatives. They began bringing people to the church. It grew to such an extent the walls had to be knocked down and the building extended. A daughter church was founded in an area lacking in gospel witness. Then another, and another—until there were five churches where there had been only one struggling church.

"When my people started giving, they saw that they had a big role to play in the whole realm of evangelism. Prior to that they were just spectators in the church. When they began to tithe and give to God's work, they began to see their responsibility to witness, to bring in the people, to teach and help them, and they were so excited," said Pastor Mulando.

"Before I went to Singapore in 1974, we were 134 members; and [within only five years] I saw the church grow to 300 members (not counting the daughter congregations and 200 adherents not yet members)."

Pastor Godfrey Mulando and his people had experienced the truth of an important principle of leadership: "Give, and it will be given to you: good measure, pressed down, shaken together, and running over will be put into your bosom. For with the same measure that you use, it will be measured back to you" (Luke 6:38). This is the principle of investment.

MASTER THE MEANING OF INVESTMENT

The principle of investment says that if you invest or give something, you will receive it back many times over. The Scriptures express this principle again and again.

"Whatever a man sows, that he will also reap" (Galatians 6:7). What do you want? Sow it. Invest it. Do you want friends? Invest friendship. Do you want love? Invest love. Do you want respect? Invest by respecting others. The political dictator and corporate autocrat stumble because they invest fear and, therefore, reap fear. Their followers may fawn, but at the opportune time, they will revolt.

"Just as you want men to do to you, you do to them likewise" (Luke 6:31). This is what some have called "The Golden Rule." But as much as people give lip service to it, few seem to try to live by it.

"But this I say: He who sows sparingly will also reap sparingly, and he who sows bountifully will also reap bountifully" (2 Corinthians 9:6). It's not just a matter of receiving back *what* you invest, but also a matter of receiving it back according to *how much* you invest. If you invest little, you will receive a little in return, but if you invest a lot, you will "reap bountifully."

I use the terms *investment* and *giving* interchangeably. To many people, *giving* means a reduction in the giver's net worth. Such people have a scarcity mentality. That is not a proper understanding of giving because giving is an investment. The term *investment* carries the idea of increasing the investor's net worth. Those who understand this have an abundance mentality. They realize that the more they give away in time, money, or encouragement, the more they will receive back of time, money, or encouragement.

The motivation for giving (or investing), therefore, is self-interest, a motive not only commended by Jesus, but the only motive He ever used in the Scriptures.

Too often giving which is seen as reducing the giver's net worth is motivated by charity, sentiment, peer pressure, recognition, and even guilt. Such motivation *never* sustains meaningful philanthropy.

Robert W. Woodruff died at the age of 95 while I was writing this book. He not only built Coca-Cola® into an international giant, but he also influenced education, the arts, politics, social service, and Christian outreach. Among other gifts, he gave the largest single gift ever made to a university: $105 million to Emory University in Atlanta, Georgia.

Atlanta is the only American city with a population of more than one million that racially integrated its schools with no incidents whatever. A lot of credit goes to William B. Hartsfield, who was mayor at the time. However, he was able to put teeth in his program because of the moral and financial backing of Woodruff. Woodruff was self-giving.

As a leader, you are to understand and practice the principle of investment. If your leadership is motivated by love, humility, and self-discipline, you will reap love, loyalty, and devotion from the people you lead. If they recognize that you're investing your very life for their good, they'll be more inclined to follow your leadership. But if the group perceives you to be self-aggrandizing, you'll lose the influence you now have to move those in the group toward goals of beneficial permanence that meet their real needs. They will question the validity of the goals you state because they will question your motives.

The elders of Dr. Han's church in Korea told me that he received his pay on Fridays and often, before he had arrived home, he had given it all away. Finally, they started giving the money to Mrs. Han so she could pay the bills and buy the groceries! Dr. Han's practice of giving accords his leadership the credibility and permanence that leaders who are self-aggrandizing never attain.

But more than understanding investment and practicing it yourself, you are to instill it in the people in your group. As the result of example, of teaching, and of the vicarious experience of seeing reaping according to what you have sown, the people in your group should come to the point where they are living by the principle of investment too.

In their tremendously popular book, *In Search of Excellence,* Thomas J. Peters and Robert H. Waterman, Jr., study what it is that makes an excellent company. Among the eight factors is one that illustrates the principle of investment: "Excellent companies are close to the customer." Such companies have an obsession with quality, reliability, or service. They are committed to making the customer important, giving him the best value for his money, and being ready to serve him in any way he needs. And these excellent companies reap what they sow by gaining customer loyalty and long-term sales and profit growth. Peters and Waterman tell the story of Frito-Lay, a potato chip and pretzel company, to illustrate the point:

> What is striking about Frito is not its brand-management system, which is solid, nor its advertising program, which is well done. What is striking is Frito's nearly 10,000-person sales force and its "99.5 percent service level." In practical terms, what does this mean? It means that Frito will do some things that in the short run clearly are uneconomic. It will spend several hundred dollars sending a truck to restock a store with a couple of $30 cartons of potato chips. You don't make money that way, it would seem. But the institution is filled with tales of salesmen braving extraordinary weather to deliver a box of potato chips or to help a store clean up after a hurricane or an accident. Letters about such acts pour into the Dallas headquarters. There are magic and symbolism about the service call that cannot be quantified. As we said earlier, it is a cost analyst's dream target. You can always make a case for saving money by cutting back a percentage point or two. But Frito management, looking at market shares and margins, won't tamper with the zeal of the sales force.[28]

The result of this sowing of service is that Frito-Lay reaps more than $2 billion of potato chip and pretzel sales per year, it owns market shares of 60 percent and 70 percent in most of America (which is astoundingly high for such an undifferentiated product), and it has profit margins that are the envy of the food industry.

In mastering the meaning of investment, realize that it is important to have a spirit of giving—of wanting to help others. This makes practicing the principle of investment a natural habit. But there are two kinds of people who make up the world: the investors and the takers. By their nature the investors practice the principle of investment; the takers are the ones who do not see giving as an investment and so try to hoard whatever they have. Ultimately, the investors win and the takers lose.

Jesus was the perfect man, the only perfect man who ever lived. Unqualified and generous giving marked every moment of His life here on earth. And those who are effective leaders reflect this passion to give rather than to take.

One of my heroes is John R. Mott, who was born in 1865 and died in 1955 at the age of 90. Mott made the YMCA a significant worldwide organization. He founded the International Missionary Council. He headed up a fund-raising drive for the United War Work Council that raised more than $188 million in less than a year. He recruited more than 240,000 men and women for leadership positions on all six continents during the course of his unequaled career. He was decorated by eighteen nations. He won the Nobel Peace Prize in 1946. You cannot worship at any church of any denomination on any continent that he did not influence.

The key to John Mott's leadership was that he was an investor. He had a commitment to the principle of investment. John Mott represents the highest type of leadership. No personality cult arose around his name. Mott was generous with his concepts, his time, his energy, and his money.

I believe the secret to Mott's self-giving spirit can be found in the intimate relationship he sustained with the Lord. He began each day with an unhurried quiet time of Bible study, prayer, and meditation.

Years ago, I heard the pastor of one of America's largest churches say, "After a long study of history and a lifetime of observation, I have concluded that without exception the men whom God has used most remarkably over the years are those who are generous."

At the risk of being misunderstood, let me say that I believe the reason America is in a position of world leadership is because of its generosity. America has given more money, goods, and services to other nations than all the nations of the world in all the history of the world combined. I believe America's leadership in the world has occurred largely as a result of its investment of concern and resources in the nations of the world.

While investors win, takers lose. In the 1970s, an Indian pastor was invited to attend a meeting in Europe. He said he couldn't afford it. The people holding the meeting offered to underwrite 75 percent of his expenses. He still refused to attend. When the Indian pastor was killed a few weeks later in an automobile accident, it was discovered he had hoarded $160,000. During the course of his ministry he had complained about poverty and had taken advantage of his poor parishioners who, out of love, had sacrificially given extra money to him. He had sown deceit and distrust. And the legacy of his life is one of dishonesty and greed. He did more to harm the Christian witness in his town than all the atheists in India combined.

For nearly forty years, I have watched men and women in leadership slots. The takers ultimately lose. They lose disposition, friends, health, and respect. The investors win. As a leader you need to master the meaning of investment and study how to make giving a habit for both you and those whom you lead.

PERCEIVE THE RIGHT MOTIVE FOR INVESTMENT

If the leader wants to create joy for people in his group, he can accomplish this by motivating them to make the principle of investment the law of their life. But to do this, he has to understand the right motive for investment. The leader knows that his group will act when they have a reason. To motivate people to enjoy the enlargement of life that comes from investment, he must put forth a powerful motive.

Charity, sentiment, peer pressure, recognition, and guilt are not adequate motives for giving. They will work at times, but they are not self-motivating. Duty is a legitimate motive, but it usually fails because most people lack the character to respond. No greater motive can be put forth than the motive of love. Nevertheless, the wise leader knows that while he himself must lead from the motive of love, for many in the group, love is fluctuating and tends to rise and fall with spasms of altruism. Were we already in heaven, doubtlessly love would be the best motive to put forth. But we are still sinful.

The one and only motive that Jesus ever used is the motive of self-interest. Investment is the ultimate path to permanent gain. Every command and promise that Jesus made was based on the assumption of self-interest—that obeying the command would benefit the individual. For example, Jesus said, "Judge not, that you be not judged." He also said, "Do not lay up for yourselves treasures on earth, where moth and rust destroy and where thieves break in and steal; but lay up for yourselves treasures in heaven. . . ."

The principle of investment is so powerful because it has built into it the motivation of legitimate self-interest of the individual. "Give and it will be given to you." Everyone wins.

The farmer gains by giving. He invests his labor and seed and irrigation into the soil. He normally gets back in proportion to what he puts in. The businessman gains by widening the market. He invests money for advertising and entertainment and public relations and necessary travel and labor. He gets his money back multiplied. The athlete invests effort and gains strength and achievement in proportion to the effort invested. The effective leader will appeal to the powerful desire of self-interest to actuate his people to invest.

Some may protest that it's not right to give in order to get. I usually tell such people to argue with Jesus, not with me, for it was Jesus who said, "Give and it will be given to you." If you are a believer, why did you give your life to Christ? Most people will answer that they wanted forgiveness, salvation, and peace. Self-interest is a legitimate motive, one to which Jesus Himself appealed.

You may say you cannot please God with the wrong spirit. That is true, but the effectiveness of the principle of investment does not depend on one's spirit in the matter. If an atheist plants a thousand acres of corn, and a Christian plants one acre of corn, who is going to get the most corn? The "right spirit" has nothing to do with the harvest. The principle of investment is as inexorable a law as the law of gravitation. If I jump off the top of the Empire State Building and an agnostic jumps at the same time, I'm not going to be in any better shape than he is when we hit the ground!

You can identify a person's IQ—investment quotient—by noticing if he continues to invest under all circumstances. For instance, does the board member give as generously when he has been rotated off the board as when he was on the board? Does the church officer maintain the same level of giving when out of office as in office?

The effective leader devotes his life to bringing his group into the joy of giving. He leads by his own example. His life demonstrates to his group the validity of self-interest as the motive to which Christ appealed. The leader will bring honor to God, benefit to the world, blessing to his people, and enrichment to his own life to the degree that he is successful in moving his people to the habit of perennial investment through the motive of self-interest.

Warnings about Care and Covetousness

The principle of investment is like all of God's gifts. The gift is good. But if the principle of investment is used to get more of something that has become a god or something that is evil, we are misusing the benefits of the principle. We are to use the principle of investment to acquire money, but it is necessary to mention Jesus' warnings here against care and covetousness.

Most people hold one of two erroneous ideas concerning money. Some feel that money is inherently evil and only things of the spirit are good. This is the position that was held by many Greek philosophers and Christian monastics. However, money and matter are neither good nor evil. It is how we use material things that determines the goodness or the evilness involved. Those who believe money is inherently evil tend to be overcome with cares and concerns about material things.

The other erroneous idea is the attitude of materialism which makes matter the very center of life. Unhappily, this view has even infiltrated areas of church life. This position leads to idolatry of things, and it is against this attitude that the Bible sounds some of its sharpest warnings: "You shall not steal. . . . You shall not covet your neighbor's house; you shall not covet your neighbor's wife, nor his manservant, nor his maidservant, nor his ox, nor his donkey, nor anything that is your neighbor's" (Exodus 20:15, 17). "For the love of money is the root of all kinds of evil" (1 Timothy 6:10). "Do not lay up for yourselves treasures on earth" (Matthew 6:19). "Man shall not live by bread alone" (Matthew 4:4). Those who have made matter the very center of their lives tend to be ruled by covetousness.

Jesus warned against the perils that arise from these two ideas of material things, money, and the principle of investment. He warned against care and covetousness—the worry that one might not possess enough to meet the bare necessities of life and the desire to possess more and more. These two perils will undermine the discipline needed to employ the principle of investment.

Jesus said, "You cannot serve God and mammon" (Matthew 6:24). The word *mammon* represents wealth and material possessions, not necessarily in particular quantity, but the fact of their existence. According to Jesus, mammon is something about which people should never be anxious, over which they should never worry, something with which they should not be obsessed. Instead, the Christian is to "seek first the kingdom of God and His righteousness, and all these things shall be added unto you" (Matthew 6:33). The covetous leader and the worrying leader ultimately self-destruct.

When Jesus says we cannot serve both God and mammon, He is not saying that mammon is inherently evil. Mammon—material things—can be the vehicle to achieve the highest ends and the most God-honoring objectives. Or you can put mammon to such base uses that it will bring mischief and hurt.

E. Stanley Jones correctly said, "You can serve God with mammon, but you cannot serve God and mammon." [29] When you serve God, you are the bondslave of God, yielding to His absolute supremacy so that everything is regulated according to the divine will. Material things are not abandoned, but are brought into His service. But to serve mammon, to be the bondslave of material possessions (and poor people can be a bondslave of material possessions as well as rich people), is to bring about spiritual impoverishment and, in many cases, even financial disadvantage. When you live to serve mammon, either through worrying about what you shall eat and drink and how you shall be clothed or through covetousness, you dethrone God. And your leadership loses credibility.

Religious leaders often emphasize the need for more prayer if God is to send worldwide revival. But until these same leaders get honest with God on the money question, prayer will continue to be an exercise in hypocrisy and futility. A spirit of care or covetousness mocks prayer. Living according to the principle of investment is the attitude God wants us to have toward material goods. So, too, those who profess a concern for the salvation of the world's needy millions and pray for their salvation while withholding from God the money to give people the Good News are uttering hollow words.

Jesus warns against care, against worry. It is very easy to become concerned because in ourselves we do not know the future. Living by the principle of investment demands vulnerability. When the farmer puts the seed into the ground, he becomes a bit vulnerable. He will not see the seed again for a period of time, during which he will cultivate, water, and employ all of the agricultural techniques he knows to insure an abundant harvest. When one invests his love in another, he becomes vulnerable. When a businessman invests in a piece of property, he becomes vulnerable. Without vulnerability, there is no viability. Without risk, there is no forward movement.

But this is no excuse for care and worry. When one invests in God's work, he is given promises by God that protect the investor. Why it is that otherwise competent leaders fail to see and act upon the investment principle mystifies me. Their failure here robs them personally and their people of advantages otherwise unattainable.

Jesus also warns against covetousness, the desire to possess. The covetous sometimes camouflage their stinginess with such expressions as "prudence," or "good business," or "sound planning." God calls it covetousness—an insatiable desire for worldly gain, an obsession to get more, a preoccupation with having what is not yours.

Covetousness is David, with all his wives and concubines, wanting Bathsheba, the only wife of Uriah. That jeopardized David's leadership.

Covetousness is Saul keeping for himself, in defiance of God's ban, the finest cattle and the blue-ribbon sheep of the Amalekites. Covetousness ultimately destroyed Saul's leadership.

Covetousness is Judas, selling Jesus for thirty pieces of silver. Covetousness destroyed Judas' leadership for he had been the treasurer, a respected position.

Each suffered severe punishment. God has not moderated His view of covetousness. It is still sin. And those trapped by this sin still suffer.

Covetousness can cost you ulcers, friendships, inordinate pressure, family relationships. The costs in litigations, medical care, and forced vacations can offset the short-term gain of covetous maneuvers.

One of the major reasons for covetousness is insecurity. The insecure person, the person who is afraid, is doing his best to protect himself from feared calamity. No matter how much bravado is projected, basically the stingy person, the one who lives only for himself, is terribly frightened. And, of course, a temperament of insecurity and fear does not make for great leadership.

Since God has promised a special blessing to those who honor Him with their material possessions, then the leader sins against his followers by withholding this good news of the joy and enrichment of giving. You can't expect blessings from God if, through greed and covetousness, you block the pathway down which God sends the blessings. In short, covetousness not only betrays love, but it also blasts self-interest. It destroys leadership.

THE TEN COMMANDMENTS OF INVESTMENT

One out of every six verses in the Gospels has to do with the right and wrong use of material possessions. Sixteen of Jesus' thirty-eight parables have to do with the right and wrong use of material possessions.

Money is the most powerful tangible expression of our life. One of the great things about the famed evangelist Dwight L. Moody was his understanding of the place of money in the kingdom of God. He wasn't timid about expressing it. Time after time, he had solicited money from James Farwell. On one occasion, after Moody had asked Farwell for $10,000, Farwell complained, "Mr. Moody, must you always be coming to me for money? You have so many other wealthy friends. I've already given you $85,000 for your work."

Moody replied, "Mr. Farwell, you grew up on a farm just as I did. Did you ever take a pail to a dry cow?"

Moody's leadership developed Farwell, but Moody's influence with Farwell would have died had Farwell not known that Moody was a self-giving person who practiced what he preached. Largely through Moody's influence, Farwell became an outstanding nineteenth-century philanthropist.

The principle of investment deals with one of the most sensitive but important issues in the Christian church. The leader's attitude toward money and material possessions will affect in part the effectiveness of his leadership. Therefore, let me list ten commandments for investment. They will help you understand and master this important principle.

COMMANDMENT ONE: *Recognize That God Is the Provider*

In Genesis 22, Abraham speaks of God as *Jehovah-jireh,* which means "the Lord will provide." God had told Abraham to offer his only son Isaac as a burnt offering on a mountain in the land of Moriah. Evidently Abraham did not tell Isaac what God had said to him, for when they arrived at the mountain, Isaac said, "Look, the fire and the wood, but where is the lamb for a burnt offering?"

You can imagine the emotional turmoil Abraham was going through. He was determined to obey God no matter what the cost. He even went so far as to tie Isaac on the altar and "took the knife to slay his son." But at the same time, Abraham had tremendous faith in God, for when he and Isaac left the servant at the foot of the mountain, Abraham had told the servant they would both "come back to you." It was in the middle of this experience and in answer to Isaac's question that Abraham said, "My son, God will provide for Himself the lamb for a burnt offering." *Jehovah-jireh.*

God provides all the resources necessary to accomplish His will. We can be confident of that. For those who have the gift of generosity, those resources can be an abundance of this world's goods.

It is tragic that over the years we have equated sanctification and poverty. It is true that we are supposed to be willing to be abased. And it is very possible that God may have purposes for us that do not include driving luxury cars or living in elegant homes. But whether we are poor or rich, whatever we have comes from our Provider, God. And, we have the joyful obligation to honor Him and enrich ourselves by acting on the principle of investment.

COMMANDMENT TWO: *Keep Your Mind on the Things You Want and Off the Things You Don't Want As Long As These Are Compatible with the Will of God.*

After telling of his misery and misfortune, Job said,

> For the thing I greatly feared
> has come upon me,
> And what I dreaded
> has happened to me (Job 3:25).

Job feared the worst and he got it.

Our negative thoughts and fears become self-fulfilling prophecies. If you don't believe you will make your sales goal, you probably won't. If you are a pastor and you are afraid your new congregation won't accept you, they probably won't. If you tell a child that he will fail and never amount to any good, you'll probably be right. So many dear people see the glass half empty instead of half full. They don't comprehend that "God has not given us a spirit of fear, but of power and of love and of a sound mind" (2 Timothy 1:7).

You'll ruin your leadership potential by concentrating on the things you don't want. And, such negative attention violates the principle of investment.

But if you keep your mind on the things you want, you'll probably succeed. Keeping your mind on winning the race is the first step to making it a reality. Believing a friend can accomplish a difficult task and telling him he can do it can help to make it possible.

The leader who acts on the principle of investment tends to be positive and optimistic. This gives him personal power and influence.

COMMANDMENT THREE: *Invest What You Want*

This seems like an obvious statement. If you plant cotton, what do you get? Cotton. If you plant wheat, what do you get? Wheat. If you plant corn, what do you get? Corn. If you plant love, what do you get? Love, of course. If you plant friendship, what do you get? Friends.

Most people will agree that the statements in the previous paragraph are true. The awkward part comes when it is asked, "If you invest money, what do you get?" People usually freeze up on this point. Some say, "When Jesus says, 'Give and it shall be given unto you,' it means you give money to God, and He'll give you back peace and joy . . . spiritual blessings. He doesn't mean He'll give you monetary returns." That interpretation is fatuous spiritualizing. Why is money different from cotton or friendship?

Jesus promises that when you give money, you'll get back more money than you gave. When the leader communicates by precept and practice the principle of investment in all areas of life, he strengthens the motivation for the followers to move toward goals of beneficial permanence that meet their real needs.

COMMANDMENT FOUR: *Invest on the Front End*

Suppose a farmer were to say, "If I have a good harvest, I'll then plant the seed." Or suppose a businessman were to say, "When I receive 100 percent of the lease payments for a ten-year period, I'll build the apartment building." You would agree that that is ridiculous!

No, you invest first—on the front end.

Remember the story of the widow of Zarephath? She said that she had just enough oil and meal to make some food for her son and herself. They were going to eat and then die. Elijah said, "Do not fear; go and do as you have said, but make me a small cake from it first" (1 Kings 17:13). Be it said to her eternal credit, she violated worldly wisdom and what would seem to be sound thinking, and she made God's prophet the cake first. "And she and he and her household ate for many days. The bin of flour was not used up, nor did the jar of oil run dry, according to the word of the Lord which He spoke by Elijah" (1 Kings 17:15–16). The widow invested on the front end.

Don't delude yourself by saying, "When my ship comes in I shall give a lot of money to the work of God to help people in need." Start where you are with what you have.

COMMANDMENT FIVE: *Be Patient*

When the farmer plants, he doesn't expect a crop the next day. It takes months. You should be patient. It may be a while. You may have lots of problems before the harvest.

Can you imagine a farmer planting one day and digging down into the ground the next day to see how the seed is germinating? Relax. Keep cool. Exercise faith. Believe God. It's an attitude of patience that oftentimes distinguishes the leader.

COMMANDMENT SIX: *Do Not Be Deterred by an Occasional Crop Failure*

Just because a frost wrecks the peach crop in Georgia, does the peach farmer quit growing peaches? No, he knows that he will prosper as he obeys the laws of peach growing.

Just because a friend betrays you, does that mean you'll never trust anyone else? I hope not. You may say, "I invested love, and I was betrayed. I invested friendship, and I was insulted. I invested money, and I suffered financial disaster." Yes, you may get an occasional crop failure. But the law of planting and harvesting is as unchangeable as the truth of God. If you observe this over the long term, inevitably you will be the one who prospers.

COMMANDMENT SEVEN: *Put Your Money Where You Want Your Heart to Be*

I hear people say, "If people just get right with God, they'll give. So therefore, just build them up in the faith." But the best way to begin to build someone up in the faith is through the motivation of self-interest. And if a person invests money in a particular work, he will become involved in it through self-interest.

Charles W. Shepard, a cotton broker from Gadsden, Alabama, became interested in the work of the Haggai Institute. He gave to it and inspired others to do the same. In one year, he raised more than $30,000. He said to his friends, "Let's help John Haggai. He's strengthening the moral base of America."

In 1968 he and his beautiful wife, Kathleen, accompanied me on a major evangelistic mission in Indonesia. He enthusiastically passed out tracts and was instrumental in winning people of all ages to faith in Christ.

Two years later he was dying of cancer. My father and I visited him in the hospital and I asked Mr. Shepard when it was that he received Christ as his Savior. He said, "I don't know exactly when I became a Christian. But do you remember the first big money I put into the Haggai Institute? Well, I followed that money to see where it was going, and I ran right into Jesus Christ. I don't know exactly the day, but I know He is my Savior, and I'm trusting Him."

Put your money where you want your heart to be.

COMMANDMENT EIGHT: *Rejoice*

Even when things are not going right, rejoice. You can't think clearly when you're frowning and fretting. Don't fret because of evildoers or because of evil conditions.

You may not feel like rejoicing if you have just lost some money in a sour investment or the stock market has just gone from 1,300 to 900. While you can't control your feelings directly, you can control them indirectly by controlling your actions and sometimes by controlling your thoughts. If you don't feel the way you ought to feel, think and act the way you ought to feel, and soon you'll feel the way you are thinking and acting.

Nobody follows a griper. A griper, a complainer, is never dynamic. There are two types of people: thermometers and thermostats. The thermometer person, who registers the temperature of his environment, is up and down like a yo-yo. He reacts according to whatever happens to him. On the other hand, the thermostat person regulates the temperature of his environment. When this radiant personality, manifesting the strength of God, comes in the room, it's like turning on hundreds of lights. Yes, rejoice. Rejoice in your face. Let others, by looking at your face, know of the joy you say is in your heart.

COMMANDMENT NINE: *Expect Results*

The farmer expects results. He may not see any evidence of it for several weeks, but he expects results. The Christlike leader, living by the principle of investment, should expect results too. He should expect that when he invests encouragement in a person, he will see better performance. He should expect that when he goes out of his way to be friendly to people, he will acquire many friends. And he should expect that when he invests money in God's work, God will repay him.

The Bible says, "Abraham believed God." Every Christian believes *in God,* but it seems very few *believe God.* I am calling upon you to believe God in the financial area of your life. Believe God and expect results.

This habit will add an impressive dimension to your leadership. You'll always seem in command—focused, energized, in control of yourself. That inspires confidence and loyalty.

COMMANDMENT TEN: *Give God the Glory*

It is so easy when your investment pays off to think that you were special. You may have worked hard; you may have planned well; you may have sacrificed. But it is God who provided your reward. When discussing divisions in the church, Paul gave the credit for the successes the church had experienced, not to one faction or the other, but to God: "So then neither he who plants is anything nor he who waters, but God gave the increase" (1 Corinthians 3:7). Paul also said, "He who glories, let him glory in the Lord" (2 Corinthians 10:17).

Rejoice in God's provision and cash in on His promises. Take advantage of the principle of investment, but make sure God gets the glory since He is the Provider.

Millions upon millions of dollars haven't been tapped. Tapping them for the glory of God and the benefit of mankind would enrich not only those who would receive the money, but also the people who now have that money in their custody. As a leader, you are to teach the principle of investment by precept and example. To be an effective leader, you must be a person of faith.

When you live to impress people with your importance, to use leadership as a means primarily to gain wealth, honor, power, or pleasure, you'll wind up as did Caesar, Charlemagne, and Napoleon. But when your life and leadership incarnate the principle of investment, you'll leave a mark of beneficial permanence. "But seek first the kingdom of God and His righteousness, and all these things shall be added to you."

In 1978, I had the honor of meeting Archbishop Perreria of Bombay, India. This great Roman Catholic leader impressed me with his humanity and his spirituality. After he heard my lecture on investment, he said, "Dr. Haggai, what you say is splendid, but I cannot preach this to my people. They are so poor they cannot possibly tithe."

"Your grace," I said, "you say they have nothing. Is not the tithe of nothing also nothing? The point is, if they have a desire to honor God with their financial substance, if they have a tithing heart, I am convinced it will not be long until they will have money with which to tithe."

Two years later, the archbishop told me, "I started emphasizing what the Bible says about tithing. The people of my parish responded with gladness and today they are prospering as never in their lives or in the history of this diocese. And the church income is greatly enlarged."

I challenge you, if you have not acted on the law of investment previously, to begin today. Add a new and an exciting dimension to your life—and to your leadership.

SUMMARY

The principle of investment says that if you invest or give something, you will receive it back many times again. You will receive it back based on *what* you invested (e.g., if you invest friendship, you will have many friends) as well as on *how much* you invest ("He who sows sparingly will also reap sparingly").

The motivation for investment—or giving—is self-interest. The investor invests because it will benefit him. This is the only motive Jesus ever used in Scripture.

As a leader, you are to understand and practice the principle of investment. In addition, you are to instill the habit of giving into the people in your group.

There are two kinds of people in the world: investors and takers. The investors (or givers) by their nature practice the principle of investment; the takers are the ones who do not see giving as an investment and so they try to hoard whatever they have. Ultimately, the investors win because they receive back many times what they invested. The takers ultimately lose because they lose disposition, friends, health, and respect.

Like all of God's gifts, the principle of investment is good, but it can be used for good or evil ends. Jesus, therefore, warned against two extremes in our attitudes toward money. He warned against feeling that money is inherently evil and therefore being overly concerned about material things and worrying about them. He also warned against the extreme of making material things the center of one's life and being covetous or having the desire to possess for the sake of possessing. The Christian cannot serve both God and Mammon, but he is to learn how to serve God with Mammon.

Since God has promised a special blessing to those who honor Him with their material possessions, then the leader sins against his followers if he withholds this good news of the joy and enrichment of giving. The leader therefore will master the meaning of investment, perceive the right motive of investment, grasp the importance of investment, and follow the ten commandments for investment:

(1) Recognize that God is the provider.

(2) Keep your mind on the things you want and off the things you don't want as long as these are compatible with the will of God.

(3) Invest what you want.

(4) Invest on the front end.

(5) Be patient.

(6) Do not be deterred by an occasional crop failure.

(7) Put your money where you want your heart to be.

(8) Rejoice.

(9) Expect results.

(10) Give God the glory.

The principle of investment is summarized in the words of Christ: "Give, and it will be given to you: good measure, pressed down, shaken together, and running over will be put into your bosom. For with the same measure that you use, it will be measured back to you" (Luke 6:38).

9

The Principle of

OPPORTUNITY

Your greatest opportunities are cleverly disguised as insurmountable problems.

In the 1970s, Lee Iaccocca was the aggressive, successful president of the Ford Motor Company. He had created the Mustang, a car that sold more units its first year than any other automobile in history. He had led Ford to a $1.8 billion profit for two years in a row. He received an income of $970,000 a year and was treated royally. But he lived in the shadow of Henry Ford II, a man Iaccocca describes as capricious and spiteful. On 13 July 1978 Henry Ford fired Lee Iaccocca.

Less than four months later Iaccocca became president of Chrysler, an automobile company that had just announced a third-quarter loss of $160 million, the worst deficit it had ever had. Iaccocca found that Chrysler was not managed well—each of the thirty-one vice presidents was working by himself rather than working with each other. The oil shortage of 1979 compounded Chrysler's problems as the price of gasoline almost doubled and sales of large cars plummeted. In 1980, Chrysler lost $1.7 billion, the largest operating loss in United States corporate history.

But Iaccocca was turning his obstacles into opportunities. He had been fired. He had become president of a company most people felt would go bankrupt. But without these obstacles, Lee Iaccocca would never have had a chance to prove himself. He was determined not to quit. Union concessions, streamlining Chrysler's operations, development of new products all contributed to Chrysler's recovery.

In 1982, Chrysler made a modest profit. In 1983, it made the best profit in its history. And in July of that year, Chrysler paid off its controversial government-guaranteed loan—seven years before it was due. Chrysler introduced new cars that excited the American public: the economical K-car, convertibles, and the mini-van. Chrysler stock soared from two dollars to thirty-six dollars a share. Its investors made money and gained renewed confidence in the company. Its challenging slogan became known nationwide: "If you can find a better built car, buy it!" Lee Iaccocca became one of the most respected corporate leaders in America, and when his autobiography was published in 1984, it broke publishing sales records.

These opportunities would not have come to Lee Iaccocca if he had not had the obstacles of being fired from Ford and a near-bankruptcy situation at Chrysler. He found in these obstacles his greatest opportunities.

Every setback has within it the seed of an equivalent advance. You only have to look for it.

Joseph was the favorite son of his father Jacob. Joseph was a dreamer, but his dreams angered his eleven brothers who envied, criticized, and mistreated him. They captured him and sold him to some Midianite traders. The Midianites took him to Egypt where he became a slave of Potiphar, a court officer. The brothers, meanwhile, dipped Joseph's tunic in blood and led Jacob to believe Joseph had been killed by wild animals.

In Egypt, Joseph was thrown into jail. He had fled from Potiphar's wife when she made sexual advances toward him. Angered at his refusal to sin with her, she accused him of mocking and attacking her. Joseph was in prison as a slave in a foreign country. The obstacles he faced seemed insurmountable. But God turned them into his greatest opportunity.

Joseph was brought before Pharaoh and he interpreted Pharaoh's dreams. As a result of Joseph's faithfulness and discernment, Pharaoh made him his second in command in Egypt. Joseph was an influential leader with great power.

The significance of Joseph's opportunity was shown when his brothers came to him years later to buy grain because there was a famine in their land. They did not know who he was, and he tested them for awhile before revealing his identity to them. With love and forgiveness he said, "Do not therefore be grieved nor angry with yourselves because you sold me here; for God sent me before you to preserve . . . a posterity for you in the earth and to save your lives by a great deliverance" (Genesis 45:5, 7).

The principle of opportunity says that life is a series of obstacles, and these obstacles hold the key to your greatest opportunities if you only discipline yourself to see opportunities everywhere.

You are not perfect! Nor am I. Nor is anyone. Since you are bound to make blunders—a mistake made through stupidity, ignorance, or carelessness—you must know how to turn blunders into benefits. Anyone can make a mistake. That takes no genius. But it does take outstanding character to refrain from throwing up your hands in despondency. Learn from your blunders. Convert them to unexpected benefits!

Dealing with blunders productively contributes to outstanding leadership because it removes the paralyzing fear of making mistakes. The leader knows he will make mistakes, but he knows he can turn those mistakes to his benefit—and the benefit of the group. The more you succeed in turning blunders into benefits, the greater will become your self-confidence. When that takes place, you will lose the timidity that paralyzes the decision-making process. You will be willing to make decisions and act on the decisions even when risk is involved.

To put the principle of opportunity into practice, you need to learn how to handle mistakes, how to cope with errors, and how to profit from blunders.

First, admit the blunder the moment you know about it. You can never correct a situation if you don't admit that it exists. Moreover, mistakes multiply and get worse if they are uncorrected. Several years ago, a newscast reported that should NASA's Venus probe veer one degree off course, it would miss its target by approximately two hundred thousand miles. The NASA scientists had to carefully and constantly monitor the Venus probe so they could identify any deviation the moment it occurred.

Late in 1969, I learned that our accountant had forgotten my instructions to pay an airline bill of nearly $50,000 for bringing the participants and faculty to the first session of the Haggai Institute. While there were other bills due, they were not so pressing, and so I had made arrangements for them to be handled later. But the accountant had paid the other bills, leaving no money available for the airline.

Like the proverbial ostrich, I stuck my head in the sand, hoping the problem would go away. I didn't want to admit the blunder had been made. As a result, we lost our international airline credit cards. Repeatedly, the airline threatened us with lawsuits. It wasn't until I admitted the blunder, talked to the creditors, and transparently told them what we could do and what we could not do that the fears began to subside, the doubt melted, and the limitations seemed to disappear.

Second, assume accountability for the blunder. I am appalled at how few people want to assume accountability for anything that is not a success. Over the next two weeks, watch for it. You will find that when a stupid mistake or an honest error is mentioned—even if there is no implication that the person responsible needs to be determined—most people's initial reaction is to say in some way, "I didn't do it."

This reaction started in the Garden of Eden. When God caught up with Adam and Eve after they had eaten the fruit of the tree of the knowledge of good and evil, He asked Adam if he had eaten it. Adam's response was exactly like that people give today. He said that it was not his fault: "The woman whom You gave to be with me, she gave me of the tree, and I ate." Eve also responded that it was not her fault: "The serpent deceived me, and I ate."

Blunders are not the end of the world. No one escapes them. In fact, the people with the greatest number of achievements have frequently also scored the largest number of blunders. For years, Babe Ruth held the record for the most home runs hit in a single season of baseball. But he also held the record for the greatest number of failures through strikeouts.

To correct and profit from your blunders, you must assume accountability for them. As a leader, you must also assume accountability for the blunders of the people in your group just as you receive the credit and respect for the group's successes. A good leader does not say, "Sam did that and so it's not my problem" if Sam is a member of his group.

When I was a student pastor, my father visited my church one Sunday morning. I was ready to resign the pastorate and quit the ministry. Dad saw how disconsolate I was. He told me to assume accountability for my blunders. He said, "If you have done poorly in presenting your message, analyze why it was. If the reason lies in your failure to give sufficient preparation or to undergird it with sufficient prayer, or through any other personal faults, confess it, claim God's forgiveness, and go forward ready to honor the Lord on your next opportunity.

"If, on the other hand, the problem is outside yourself, commit that also to the Lord. If anything can be done about it, do it. If it cannot, relax and rejoice that He is more interested in His work than you are."

The world's great and not-so-great all make blunders. A blunder is not the end, but the beginning, if you assume accountability for it. So, what do you do next?

Third, evaluate the damage. Will the damage resulting from this blunder be minimal or major? Think it through carefully. Care must be taken neither to underestimate nor overestimate it. Sometimes we can get upset about a blunder that will make us embarrassed but cause little actual damage. On the other hand, when we cannot escape accountability for a blunder, our second line of defense is sometimes to minimize its importance, whereas we ought to be taking quick and drastic measures to eliminate further damage.

When God directed us to launch the Haggai Institute for Advanced Leadership Training, we took great care to determine the most propitious place to conduct the training. It should be in a neutral nation. If the training were done in the United States, the leaders, on return to some of the countries, would be eyed as Uncle Toms or as mouthpieces for America's CIA. A host of leaders from Asia, Africa, South America, and Australia affirmed Switzerland as the ideal nation.

The offer of some property in Switzerland, at an extraordinarily low price, fell through; but it helped direct our thinking to that country. Finally we found a property on a lake in the German-speaking section.

Conducting the initial seminars of the Haggai Institute in Switzerland turned out to be one of the biggest blunders we have ever made. Switzerland was not the right place. I had no choice but to admit the blunder. I then had to assume accountability for it. I called a major donor who had borrowed $100,000 to get the program started to make an appointment to see him. I would rather have taken a flogging, but I knew I had to do it.

"Why can't you tell me by phone what's on your mind?" he asked. I said, "Regarding this matter I must sit in front of you and look into your eyes." When I arrived at his home and told him the story, this dear man who could have made life miserable for me, broke out in a big grin and said, "John, you learned a great lesson by a much cheaper blunder than I did. We have just lost two million dollars on a bad overseas venture in our business!" What grace!

Our evaluation of the damage of this blunder included a loss of $55,000 in cash because the owner of the original property went back on his word. There had been signed agreements and we were advised to take him to court, but the board decided not to pursue that course of action.

It became clear that I had been influenced to move to Switzerland by superficial observations and the offer of property in a beautiful area at a low price. In other words, I had fallen prey to the trap of taking what is handy rather than securing what is really needed.

Often a church will hire an unemployed woman in the congregation because she's handy and because it can get her at half the price it would normally pay for a secretary. In many cases, the reason she's unemployed is because of her mediocre ability. To my thinking, this is a wicked mishandling of the Lord's money. However, I had fallen into the same trap of taking what is handy rather than securing what is really needed.

In addition to the cash loss, our damage included a loss of some of the momentum of the Institute and the expensive costs involved in finding a new location in another part of the world.

When evaluating the damage done by a blunder, ask yourself such questions as: What effects will it have by upsetting deadlines? How will this blunder interfere with the work of others? Will it adversely affect the "big picture"? How will it affect the testimony I have?

Fourth, do an in-depth study of the possible causes of the blunder. Blunders are the result of (1) an error in judgment, (2) poor planning, (3) insufficient information, or (4) defective follow-up. Examine all these areas in depth. To fail to study the causes of your blunder will only guarantee a repetition of the mistake.

Cross-examine yourself. To put the blame on others is leadership suicide. Identify the problem and isolate it.

Ask if the planning was defective. You may have planned most of the project, but if you overlooked any component, it can set back the entire project.

Ask yourself if you allowed enough time. Or did you select the best time to do it? I once met a godly American who had taken thirty people to an Asian country for an evangelistic thrust. He had not taken into account that it was during the monsoon season and so hundreds of thousands of dollars were wasted simply because of poor timing.

Ask yourself if the project was sufficiently funded. Did you allow for inflation? Did you identify the sources of the funds? A warning that needs to be given here is that if people of the so-called poorer areas of the world are to develop the kind of self-respect that honors God, they must stop wasting their energies writing people in other parts of the world for financial handouts. I have never seen a strong church maintained by foreign monies. Some of the largest church memberships in the world are situated in Korea. Most came out of dreadful poverty. Their strength today can be explained, in part, by their emphasis on the importance of self-support.

Ask yourself if you had adequate personnel. Did you have the various jobs slotted, and did you know exactly the person or persons required to fill each slot? Did you have a sufficient number of people both in the skilled and the nonskilled areas?

Ask yourself if you had the right kind of equipment. For example, if large mailings had to be sent out, did you have the means by which to process them? Or did the lack of equipment or persons mean that the mailing was stretched over such a long period of time as to neutralize the impact?

Ask yourself if you anticipated and made contingency plans for possible obstructions. For instance, in certain countries one must make provision for strikes. Did you allow for sickness or legitimate absenteeism? Did you make plans for securing any necessary government clearances or permissions?

Ask yourself if your information was accurate. Veteran missionary Roy Robertson made a statement to a group of leaders in Indonesia in 1968 that has stuck in my mind: "A genius with inadequate information is at a great disadvantage to a man of mediocre mentality but with superior information." He was so right!

Ask yourself if the blunder was due to a lazy worker who failed to carry out directions on time or whose violent temper caused discord among those who work with you or who did not thoroughly understand what he was supposed to do. In asking this question, however, be careful not to look for scapegoats. That is both unproductive and un-Christian. And it will demoralize an entire staff.

Do an in-depth study of the possible causes of the blunder. If the mistake was important to you and your group, you may have others help you find the answers, but ask the questions and make the evaluation yourself.

Fifth, immediately eliminate the causes for the blunder. Your evaluation in step four revealed the causes of the blunder. Now take action. Write down your plan. Work this into your goals program.

Conducting the Haggai Institute seminars in Switzerland was a big blunder for several reasons. First, the late sixties was a time of hijacking sprees. Third World leaders from the Orient and the subcontinent did not like the prospect of refueling in Mideastern capitals plagued by terrorists. Second, the climate and cuisine of Switzerland was incompatible with most Third World experiences. I have often seen people, well fed with three wholesome, nutritious meals, who feel as if they had not been fed if they did not have rice during the day.

Third, although the leaders coming for the international training all spoke English, few of them spoke German. If any difficulties with airline connections arose, it would not be easy for the leaders to contact us. Most didn't even know enough German to ask for an English-speaking telephone operator. Fourth, the facility we were using was two-and-a-half hours from the nearest airport, Zurich. Picking people up and returning them became a logistical nightmare. Fifth, when most people think of Switzerland, they think of numbered bank accounts, expensive ski holidays, and high-priced vacations. They don't think of human suffering and need. That made fund raising for a ministry based in Switzerland difficult.

Out of this blunder came a painful conclusion and a complicated transition: a move to Singapore. But in doing that we eliminated the causes for the blunder.

Singapore is just as neutral as Switzerland. It is situated in the heart of the Third World. The climate and cuisine of Singapore relates more compatibly to the lifestyles of the majority of the people in our seminars and Singapore has a good racial mix. Eighty-five percent of the people in Singapore speak English. The entire Republic of Singapore covers only 230 square miles, and so it would be difficult for a person to get lost and not be found.

Singapore is without question the cleanest major city in the world, and its very cleanliness, orderliness, predictability, and noncorrupt, highly sophisticated government are all models for observation by leaders coming from other nations.

Sixth, salvage what you can. Years ago, a company overproduced hundreds of thousands of fly swatters. It could not handle the expensive inventory and storage requirements, and so it engaged one of the world's leading persuaders, Elmer Wheeler. He looked at the fly swatters, noticed that they were square, and suggested the sales line, "These fly swatters are square so you can kill flies in the corners." In a matter of a few weeks all the fly swatters were sold. This company used good judgment. To secure the services of Elmer Wheeler cost it a fortune, but it was a wise expenditure, based on a calculated risk. The problem was salvaged.

Seventh, revise your modus operandi *so that the blunder won't be repeated.* You should be constantly evaluating what you do to see if it can be improved—not just in relation to this one blunder, but in relation to all your activities. This requires constant questioning and study.

Perennial learning insures productive leading. Learn from others. Devour biographies. Read journals relating to your particular field. No matter who you are or where you live, you can probably find in books and periodicals stories of prominent people who serve God in the area of your endeavor. These writings will review their failures and their achievements. My heart becomes heavy when I talk to aspiring Christian leaders who have not learned any Scripture in years, who have not read an average of five books a year for ten years, and who have done nothing to enlarge their knowledge or sharpen their skills.

Continually learn from the experience of others so that you won't reinvent the wheel. In your reading of biographies and in your association with other leaders, write out the application of what you learn to your everyday demands.

My own knowledge of leadership and other subjects has come from many sources. Among many others, I am indebted to John Sung of China and James Chalmers of Scotland; to Han Kyung Chik of Korea and Joseph Parker of London; to Benjamin Moraes of Brazil and John Calvin of Geneva; to Chandu Ray of Pakistan and Roland Payne of Liberia; to John Wesley of England and to Sam Arai of Japan; to John Gladstone of Canada and to Baki Sadaka of Egypt; to Martin Luther of Germany and to Neson Cornelius of India; to Saint Francis Xavier of Spain and France and to Reginald Klimionok of Australia; and to such publications as *Korean Review, Asia Week, Board Room Report, Success,* and *Fortune.* You will notice that my list covers every continent and spans hundreds of years.

Your learning has to be followed by action. Put your revision into practice. In the Haggai Institute program we used to make the error of scheduling sessions too close to the Chinese New Year. This caused great problems in logistics, image, and faculty availability. We admitted the blunder, assumed accountability, evaluated the damage, studied the cause, salvaged the situation, and revised the calendar. Today no scheduling is done near the Chinese New Year.

Eighth, begin to execute the new program immediately. If the blunder is causing your program difficulty, procrastination will only make the situation worse. Begin your correction right away.

As you embark on the new course, maintain a detailed chart of progress so that you will know exactly where you are at every stage of the program. One reason Japan has done so well in productivity allegedly derives from its having consulted a statistical physicist, Dr. Demming, who suggested that managers know by the day and even by the hour where they stand in their productivity compared with previous performances and current goals.

Ninth, use blunders as road signs. Blunders can serve as road signs that mark both where you have been in the past, as well as where you should go in the future. What you learn from the mistakes you make and the obstacles you encounter and overcome will help you to be a better leader in the future.

Charles Haddon Spurgeon of London said that when a leader commits a David-type wickedness which is made public, he should not resume active ministry until his confession and repentance are as notorious as his sin! You must openly acknowledge such blunders in order to learn from them. When you truly repent, God promises to restore the ruins.

The prophet Hosea talked about the healing of backslidings. He said that when the backslider returns to the Lord, God will heal the backsliding and "his beauty shall be like an olive tree." He promised that the restored backslider "shall grow like the lily." When the backslider has truly repented, he may grow in grace with great rapidity, whereas while living in sin he had not grown at all. The beauty of the lily is in its delicate texture and coloring. A touch or blot will mar it, and once marred, it can never be restored. The backslider need not expect to recover the virgin beauty of the lily which he had before sin blurred and bruised him. The scars of sin will remain even after the wound has been healed.

The olive tree, on the other hand, may not be in itself beautiful. It is often gnarled and crooked. Its beauty is chiefly in its fruitfulness. When the tree is full of olives, you forget the unsightliness of its trunk and branches while you gaze at the beauty of its fruit. So the restored backslider, while he mourns the loss of lily beauty, may rejoice in the beauty of olive fruitfulness.

Tenth, remember that obstacles enhance leadership. In overcoming obstacles, you improve your leadership capability by (1) the credibility you develop with others who realize you have experienced what they are experiencing, (2) the conditioning of your own spirit for service, and (3) the opportunity to demonstrate love, humility, and self-control.

The Reverend S. Arnold Mendis, an Anglican priest, returned to Sri Lanka from attending a Haggai Institute seminar and began a series of large meetings in a northern city. Some Buddhist monks openly opposed the preaching. Mendis, realizing that confrontation would neither honor God nor forward His work, stopped preaching and began cultivating the friendship of these monks. He talked with them in love. He did not seek government action to protect his rights as one with a minority status. He employed the weapons of his warfare: love and prayer. Within months he was invited by these same monks to conduct Christian services in the Buddhist temple! Today, several of those monks are committed to the person of Jesus Christ, and a few are studying for the ministry. Under God, Mendis creatively turned what could have been a severe problem into a glorious opportunity.

In 1935, my preacher father was a leader at a boys' camp in Michigan. It was in the middle of the Great Depression, and Dad had to watch every penny. One day he filled the car with gasoline to go to a city fifteen miles away. But before he got there, the car stalled; it was out of gas. A spike had punctured the gas tank. It did not take long to identify the culprit—a ten-year-old boy in the camp. I disliked this rich, spoiled, arrogant boy. I wanted my father to see that the "spoiled brat" was severely disciplined. Instead, I was appalled (and angered) to see Dad sitting on the edge of the dock with his arm around the boy, discussing calmly what had happened. He demonstrated love and compassion, and I have reason to believe the future course of that boy's life was altered for good because my father, under God, creatively turned a serious and expensive problem into an opportunity for witness.

An H.I. alumnus from a Mideast nation (who must remain anonymous) returned from the training in Singapore to be thrown immediately into prison without any charge. When released six months later, he inquired what the charge was. The officials informed him that since he had left an affluent medical practice to become an evangelist, they concluded he must hate Muslims. He smiled and said, "No, it is precisely because I love Muslims that I am spending my time telling them about Jesus Christ, the One of whom the Koran speaks so often and so glowingly. And I want to thank you for throwing me into prison because it gave me the opportunity to tell some criminals about Jesus Christ just before their execution. Had I not been in prison, I would have had no way of talking to them about Jesus."

In 1950, God blessed my wife and me with a son who was brutalized at the point of delivery by a world-famous but intoxicated doctor. Our son, Johnny, lived as an invalid for more than twenty-four years.

I never cease to be amazed by the demonstrable change in attitude and expression of those who find out that I was the father of a son with cerebral palsy. Suddenly, those who felt that I didn't know what problems were, that I lived in a fine house, drove a fine car, saw people at their best, jetted around the world, met with leaders, and wrote books, decided that just maybe I did understand their problems. Those who had considered my messages to be theoretical, although rooted in Scripture, realized that my wife and I understood suffering. Johnny was such a blessing to me personally. What could have been an overwhelming obstacle became a minister of mercy to my own life and ministry.

The leader, under God, will develop the habit of creatively converting obstacles into opportunities. This habit will enhance his leadership by inspiring those who follow him.

I need to give two words of caution. First, a leader neither attempts to shine or whine. When confronting difficulties, he must not complain that he is sacrificing. He is to be characterized by rejoicing rather than railing. Some, however, seem to label any unavoidable difficulty which they must endure as "sacrifice."

A mother can't avoid the care of a sick child. Let her not delude herself that such care is sacrifice. A father can't evade his role as breadwinner just because he'd rather be playing golf. Let him not complain, "How I sacrifice for my family!" That is an outrage! A pastor may not be provided a study by the church. Let him not call "sacrifice" his surrender to the inescapable situation. A young lady may fail to charm the wealthy young bachelor and instead marry a lowly, ill-paid day laborer. It's almost sacrilege for her to refer to her life as a "sacrifice."

Those who demonstrate a true sacrificial spirit *never* complain of sacrifice. Those who bemoan their alleged sacrifices think too much about themselves. They have not grown up.

Second, it's unrealistic and dishonoring to God to treat obstacles as though they don't exist. Nor must we fall into that heretical trap set by well-meaning but ill-advised Christians who say, "If you have enough faith, the obstacles will disappear." Hebrews 11 is the classic chapter on faith in the Bible. Verses 32 through the first part of 35 show the victories of faith, the great deliverances. However, from the last part of verse 35 through verse 40, we read of those who suffered, who experienced no physical deliverance but still had spiritual victory. They were just as much loved by God as those who were delivered physically.

Obstacles *do* exist and God does not promise that He will always deliver us from them. However, He will always help us to turn our blunders into blessing. In His strength, every obstacle can be an opportunity!

SUMMARY

Your greatest opportunities are cleverly disguised as insurmountable problems. The principle of opportunity says that life is a series of obstacles and that these obstacles hold the key to your greatest opportunities if you only discipline yourself to see opportunities everywhere.

Anyone can make a mistake. That takes no genius. You should learn from your blunders. Convert them to unexpected benefits. To put the principle of opportunity into practice, you need to learn how to handle mistakes and how to profit from blunders.

First, admit the blunder the moment you know about it. You can never correct a situation if you don't admit that it exists. And if mistakes are uncorrected, they multiply and grow worse.

Second, assume accountability for the blunder. Unless you assume accountability both for your own mistakes and those of the people in your group, you cannot correct them and profit from them.

Third, evaluate the damage. Ask yourself such questions as: What effects will the blunder have by upsetting deadlines? How will this blunder interfere with the work of others? Will it adversely affect the "big picture"? How will it affect the testimony I have?

Fourth, do an in-depth study of the possible causes of the blunder. Blunders are the result of (1) an error in judgment, (2) poor planning, (3) insufficient information, or (4) defective follow-up. Examine all these areas in depth.

Fifth, immediately eliminate the causes for the blunder. Take action. Write down your plan. Work this into your goals program.

Sixth, salvage what you can. Make the most of the assets you have.

Seventh, revise your modus operandi so that the blunder won't be repeated. Constantly evaluate what you do to see if it can be improved, not just in relation to this one blunder, but in relation to all your activities. This requires constant questioning and study.

Eighth, begin to execute the new program immediately. Procrastination will only make the situation worse. Begin your correction right away.

Ninth, use blunders as road signs that mark both where you have been in the past, as well as where you should go in the future. Learn from your mistakes.

Tenth, remember that obstacles enhance leadership by (1) the credibility you develop with others who realize you have experienced what they are experiencing, (2) the conditioning of your own spirit for service, and (3) the opportunity to demonstrate love, humility, and self-control.

There need to be two words of warning: first, a leader neither attempts to shine or whine. He must not complain that he is sacrificing. Second, it's unrealistic and dishonoring to God to treat obstacles as though they don't exist. They do.

The leader, under God, will develop the habit of creatively converting obstacles into opportunities. This habit will enhance one's leadership by inspiring those who follow him.

10

The Principle of

ENERGY

A leader without energy is like a pianist without hands or a runner without feet or an orator without a voice. The very tool needed to accomplish the purpose is missing. People follow an enthusiastic leader, and it is energy that produces enthusiasm. Some psychologists believe that the only common denominator of all leaders is energy. Not tact, not humor, not organizational ability, not vision, but energy.

Napoleon said that he owed his success to youth, health, and the ability to stand physical strain without limit. He had the "power to sleep at any moment" and a stomach which could "digest anything."

Florence Nightingale, according to her biographer Edward T. Cook, "stood twenty hours at a stretch, apportioning quarters, distributing stores, directing work, or assisting in operations."

John Wesley traveled on horseback the equivalent of ten times around the world's equator. He preached as often as fifteen times a week for fifty years. He authored more publications than any writer in the English language until the contemporary science fiction writer Isaac Asimov. He read books while making his horseback journeys. When he was past eighty, he complained that he could not read and work more than fifteen hours a day!

You can't explain the leadership of Napoleon, Florence Nightingale, or John Wesley if you ignore their tireless energy. The same is true of the late Sir Bruce Small, former chairman of the Haggai Institute (Australia) board of directors. Sir Bruce served simultaneously as a member of Parliament and as the mayor of the Gold Coast in Queensland, while also heading up the largest property development company in Queensland. He is in *The Guinness Book of World Records* as the oldest man ever to run for an elective office and win. He was seventy-six at the time.

Sir Bruce insisted on having his phone number listed. He told me his constituents had a right to get to him when they needed him. His wife, Lady Lillian, told me he hardly ever slept through a night without several emergency telephone calls. His internationally heralded leadership got its thrust from a seemingly limitless energy supply.

A person may be in a position of leadership because of popularity, because of connections with the right people, because of intellectual ability, or just because he was available. But a real leader must exude energy. He must first capture the attention of those he leads. Attention requires movement. Movement demands energy. The effective leader works longer hours, reads more voluminously, wastes less time, and generally lives life optimally. He glows with energy. Energy enables the effective leader to make more contacts, write more letters, travel more miles, study more concentratedly, train more people, and make more phone calls than others. Study any area of human endeavor, and you will find a correlation between the level of energy and the effectiveness of leadership.

Energy is the "vigorous exertion of power" and "the capacity of acting or being active."[30] A leader's energy is communicated to his followers through his physical vitality, his mental alertness, his hard work, his commitment and persistence, and his attention to details. After examining how the principle of energy is demonstrated in leaders, we will also look at how to develop and nurture your own energy level. While it is true that some people seem naturally to possess greater energy than others, it is possible to increase and develop your energy level.

HOW ENERGY IS DEMONSTRATED

A leader's energy is demonstrated through physical vitality. We are all attracted to those people who have physical vitality—those who radiate good health and purposeful activity. Young people, especially, are drawn to those who are characterized by energy demonstrated through physical vitality. We can lament the way they are drawn to rock concerts and music videos while forsaking the church, but until the church starts demonstrating the same physical vitality and energy that the world's music performers do, it will be a natural reaction for young people to be attracted to them.

At the age of sixty-six, Dr. Ernest H. Watson assumed the deanship of Haggai Institute, a herculean responsibility. No one, including myself, has matched the hours he invested in the training sessions. For five weeks, he sat through every single period. In addition to that, he was available for counsel. Immediately after his quiet time in the morning, he would plunge into the Olympic-size swimming pool for fifty laps before men half his age were out of bed. Between seminar sessions, he would be writing, screening applicants, preaching, traveling, and writing extensive reports to the donors who made the program possible.

I remember a man from India coming to me and complaining that the regimen at the Haggai Institute was too demanding. He said, "It's inhuman to expect anyone to start the day at seven in the morning and continue until nine at night for five solid weeks."

I asked his age.

"Thirty-six."

"This year Dr. Watson is twice your age. Have you noticed that he has been at the morning devotions every day, at each meal every day, at each lecture period, at each tea break? He works past eleven at night and then is often awakened by one of the participants who is sick."

After this young man returned to an effective indigenous leadership role, he confessed that it was Dr. Watson's energy that made as great an impact on him as the subject matter itself.

Demonstrating energy through physical vitality lets others know you are in control. It gives your followers a feeling of confidence and well-being. Other people find it attractive because physical vitality is a desirable trait, and people follow those who have characteristics they want to imitate.

When the celebrated clergyman Dr. J. C. Massee was in his nineties, he told me, "John, you can have greater insights at my age than you did when you were thirty. You can have a greater understanding of the really important priorities. You can empathize with people much better than in your younger years. But when you lose your physical vitality, something happens. You lose your leadership power because people will not follow a man whom they perceive to be feeble."

Then he made a strange comment. "I have never seen a man without robust energy who could give an effective public invitation for people to accept Christ. I am not saying that spiritual power is dependent on human energy. But there is some kind of relationship between energy and the ability to give an invitation that God owns and honors."

It is important to emphasize that a leader does not have to have perfect health to draw others to himself by energy demonstrated through physical vitality. Franklin Delano Roosevelt, for instance, was unable to walk because of having polio, but he had boundless energy and physical vitality and is the only person in history to have served more than two terms as president of the United States.

A leader's energy is demonstrated through mental alertness. Claude Brown owns a thriving trucking business in Atlanta, Georgia. He makes decisions faster than anyone I have ever known. One day I asked him about it. He said, "Well, John, the Lord has given me an adequate mind, and I figure if I am right fifty-one percent of the time, the sheer speed with which I make decisions will put me ahead of the competition."

At sixty-seven, Claude Brown exudes more energy than many much younger people. Such mental alertness has made him successful. He's a leader. He has energy, and it is demonstrated through mental alertness.

All leaders are not intellectual giants any more than all leaders are ideal examples of physical health and strength. But all leaders do have a mental alertness as well as a physical vitality. Moreover, intelligence supported by a high energy level and governed by good character guarantees exceptional leadership. The leader who has intelligence will use it for observation, foresight, reflection, and reasoning.

The leader with intelligence will observe trends. He will see big issues and essential details. Observation lays the groundwork for wise action. The best observation constantly questions the meanings, the motives, and the relationships behind the obvious.

When World War II ended, Dr. Han Kyung Chik was teaching school in North Korea. He observed the large number of children orphaned by the war; he recognized the critical need for educational facilities. He grasped the areas of social service required to meet the needs of the people brutalized by war. Out of his keen observation came the leadership philosophy that has governed his work for more than forty years: evangelism, education, social service.

The leader with intelligence will have foresight, which implies preparedness. Foresight makes provision for every possible emergency. When Roald Amundsen made the trip that resulted in the discovery of the South Pole, he took along 97 selected dogs from Alaska. As he proceeded southward over ice barriers, he established supply stations. He marked them so well by signs and flags that when he returned he found them, even though they were hidden in dense fogs or covered by fresh snow. He thoroughly prepared for the expedition and made the 350 miles across an ice-covered plateau 11,000 feet high without difficulty.

Reflection and reasoning reveal intelligence at its highest level. It is through reflection and reasoning that the leader penetrates the heart of the profoundest problem. Reflection and reasoning pierce shams, uncover hidden secrets, command respect. They create leaders by their incisive drive. They climb to the summit of understanding and open the gate to personal achievement.

I have been blessed by the friendship of two men who, on hearing a plan, can lay bare the weakness of it with explosive speed. If you do not have this ability yourself, strengthen your leadership by making yourself vulnerable to the criticism of colleagues whose ability to reason and reflect will spare you some errors costly in time and money.

A leader's energy is demonstrated through hard work. Work is the most common expression of human energy. No sluggard ever excelled as a leader. When John Wanamaker was postmaster general of the United States, he stunned Washington society by going to work at 7:30 every morning, two and half hours earlier than official Washington. In 1920, when he was eighty-two years old, Wanamaker was at his office in Philadelphia from eight in the morning until six in the evening.

Since 1941, I have made it a point to interview men and women whom I consider outstanding leaders. Without exception, when I ask the secret of their success, they include somewhere in their response the words *energy* or *work.*

Horace Mann was a remarkable person. Until he was fifteen he never attended school more than ten weeks in a year. But when he was twenty he prepared himself so that in six months he was admitted to the sophomore class at Brown University where he graduated with highest honors three years later.

Mann practiced law, returned to the University to teach Latin and Greek and serve as librarian, and then took an interest in public affairs. After serving in the Massachusetts legislature, he became secretary of the board of education. His educational program in Massachusetts made that state's system the prototype for the rest of the United States. At fifty-two, Mann became a U.S. Congressman and then became president of Antioch College in Ohio.

His last words to students, delivered in a baccalaureate address just a few weeks before his death, were, "Be ashamed to die until you have won some victory for humanity." Often people asked how he had succeeded in this project or that. His consistent reply was, "In almost every case, it has required constant, hard, conscientious work. I consider there is no permanent success possible without hard and severe work, coupled with the highest and most praiseworthy aims."

I often chuckle at union leaders who put in a sixty and seventy and even eighty-hour week trying to get a thirty-two-hour week for the union members! Could that be why a union leader is a leader and the members are not?

A leader's energy is demonstrated through commitment and persistence. It was Thomas Edison who said that genius is one percent inspiration and ninety-nine percent perspiration. In 1878, Edison predicted that he would be able to light homes and offices with electricity. "When it is known how I have accomplished my object, everyone will wonder why they have never thought of it," he said.[31] The amazing thing about that statement is that Edison had not yet invented the electric light bulb. He had many obstacles to overcome before he accomplished his goal, but he believed he could do it. He had commitment and persistence. It took thousands of experiments, for instance, to find the right material for the filament of the electric light bulb. Platinum, beard-hair, lamp black, and every other substance Edison could think of were tried until he found success with carbonized cotton thread. Edison's commitment and incredible persistence gave the world the electric light bulb which, at the time of its invention, was considered to be the eighth wonder of the world.

Commitment and persistence require a tremendous amount of physical, intellectual, and emotional energy because it means believing in and working toward your goal against all odds. It means doing the tasks no one else will do.

Shortly before his death, Bob Pierce told me, "I honestly believe that God intended another man to do what I finally did." He mentioned the other man's name. "But," he said, "he wouldn't make the kind of total commitment necessary to achieve it. He was too lazy to lead. And so God took me, despite my lesser gifts, education, and personal charm, and used me. I was willing to commit everything to the accomplishment of that goal."

You cannot do much travel in Asia without noticing the large footsteps of this man. To describe Pierce's leadership without mention of energy is impossible. He made his last missionary journey around the world as an advanced cancer victim. He was confined to a wheelchair. To the end, Bob maintained his original commitment to help those in need and do it as a witness for Christ's love and salvation.

It takes energy demonstrated through commitment and persistence for a mother and father to maintain a proper discipline in the home, resist peer pressure in determining their child's activities, and to rear their children "in the nurture and admonition of the Lord." To stand by your convictions when those closest to you—even your own family members—strenuously object takes energy.

Henrik Ibsen said, "The greatest of men is he who most stands alone." And Henry Ford disclosed a similar spirit when he said, "I refuse to recognize any impossibilities."

American President Woodrow Wilson said to his opponents, "You can turn aside from the measure if you like; you can decline to follow me; you can deprive me of office and turn away from me, but you cannot deprive me from power as long as I steadfastly stand for what I believe to be the interests and the legitimate demands of the people themselves." That's leadership. That requires strong character, commitment, and persistence. And that demands energy.

Commitment and persistence will let you overcome opposition and persecution. The apostle Paul tells of the opposition he received:

> . . . In labors more abundant, in stripes above measure, in prisons more frequently, in deaths often. From the Jews five times I received forty stripes minus one. Three times I was beaten with rods; once I was stoned; three times I was shipwrecked; a night and a day I have been in the deep; in journeys often, in perils of waters, in perils of robbers, in perils of my own countrymen, in perils of the Gentiles, in perils in the city, in perils in the wilderness, in perils in the sea, in perils among false brethren; in weariness and toil, in sleeplessness often, in hunger and thirst, in fastings often, in cold and nakedness—besides the other things, what comes upon me daily: my deep concern for all the churches (2 Corinthians 11:23–28).

And yet in spite of the opposition and persecution he received, Paul was able to say, "I have fought the good fight, I have finished the race, I have kept the faith" (2 Timothy 4:7). Endurance impregnated his leadership with vitality. That took energy.

A leader's energy is demonstrated through attention to details. A careless attitude regarding a small matter can be dangerous. One of America's most prominent religious leaders went to Rio de Janeiro for a large evangelistic crusade. The Brazilians, with their usual charm and fiesta attitude, met the evangelist and his wife at the airport and presented his wife with a gorgeous bouquet of flowers.

She thought the flowers were beautiful, but on the way from the airport to the hotel, she found it awkward to handle them along with her carry-on luggage. At the first sight of a trash bin, she had the driver pull over and dropped the flowers into the bin. She did not know that several carloads of the greeters were following and saw her discard the flowers. Understandably, she created hostile feelings among the group without knowing it and without meaning to. A word, a look, an accent may affect the destiny of not only one person but of an entire nation. The little things make or break you. Trifles are important in determining the effectiveness of your leadership. A leader with energy takes the effort to pay attention to details.

How to Raise Your Energy Level

Francis Xavier left wealth and position and set out across the world with the message of redemption through Christ Jesus. It took energy for him to labor twenty-one hours out of twenty-four, to learn to preach in twenty different languages in ten short years, to beg passage on a troop ship and later sail with pirates as he tumbled about the oceans in unsafe vessels. It took energy for him to sleep in tents with the Bedouins, cross the burning deserts and the snowy ranges of Asia. It took energy for Xavier to dare death in every form, shake hands with every ailment and disease, endure the pangs of hunger and the horrors of thirst after a decimating shipwreck and bitter persecution. But no Christian in the history of Japan has made such an impact as Francis Xavier.

We are challenged by the energy demonstrated by Francis Xavier's leadership—or by the energy of Napoleon, Florence Nightingale, John Wesley, or Ernest Watson. Leadership requires a physical vitality, a mental alertness, hard work, commitment, persistence, and an attention to details.

It is true that some people naturally possess greater energy than others. Nevertheless, it is possible to increase your energy level. The leader will want to raise his energy level to the fullest extent he can. You don't have to feel sluggish. You can be more energetic than you are now.

There are many factors that can sap your strength and deplete your energy. Being overweight, lack of exercise, poor sleeping habits, depression, stress, and tension can all make you less effective by reducing the energy you have available for leadership. You can maximize your energy level by eating right, exercising regularly, maintaining a proper mental attitude, eliminating negative emotions, and by walking in fellowship with God.

Eat Right

Your energy level is affected by what you eat. A friend of mine returned from a three-week vacation with her family during which she had eaten mostly in fast food restaurants. She felt sluggish, her joints ached, and she couldn't sleep. Her energy level was very low. By changing her diet, she was able to restore her energy level, feel younger, sleep better, and get rid of her aches.

How do you eat right for maximum energy? I do not pretend to be a nutritionist, and I know there are a number of good diets that I could recommend. Let me mention the diet given in *The Aerobic Program for Total Well Being,* by Dr. Kenneth H. Cooper,[32] the world's leading authority on total wellness. Cooper says that no matter who you are, you can be an energetic person if you will pay attention to your body and its need for right food and good exercise. The secret, says Cooper, is balance—balance in terms of *when* you eat and balance in terms of *what* you eat. In many parts of the world, people eat too much at the last meal of the day. The proper balance is to have 25 percent of one's calorie intake in the morning, 50 percent at noon, and 25 percent in the evening.

In addition, a person should have balance among the three major food types: 50 percent of what one eats should be complex carbohydrates, 20 percent should be protein, and 30 percent should be fats. Complex carbohydrates include fresh fruits, fruit juices, fresh vegetables, pasta, bread made from whole grain flour, cereals, brown rice, and bran. Complex carbohydrates are beneficial because they are high in water content and fiber, and yet their calories are low. Protein-rich foods include fish, poultry, meats (eat only lean cuts), cheese, milk, yogurt, eggs, peanut butter, and dried peas and beans. It is easy to let fats comprise more than 30 percent of one's diet. The best way to keep fat consumption down to the recommended level is to avoid fried foods, sauces, gravies, rich desserts, cold cuts, hot dogs, and excessively large meat portions. Also, limit the quantities of margarine, mayonnaise, and salad dressings. Fats from vegetable sources are much better for you than animal fats.

A similar program of eating is recommended by Nathan Pritikin. He says that eating this way "will enhance the acuity of all your senses, give you boundless new energy, take away that tired feeling, and may even reduce your daily sleep requirement. Some symptoms of aging even disappear."[33]

The Pritikin Program also recommends restricting salt and eliminating alcohol, caffeine beverages such as coffee and tea, and smoking. Salt contributes to hypertension. Alcohol is bad for the liver and for the effective functioning of the brain. It makes arthritis worse, and causes a host of other problems. Caffeine is a drug that increases the rate of heartbeat and contributes to high blood pressure. The danger of cancer from smoking is well known, but smoking also increases the risk of heart disease, stroke, and emphysema.

Eating right is not a matter of going on a diet for a week or two. It is a matter of changing the way one thinks about food—especially if processed foods are available. You have to become constantly aware of what is good for you and what is not because you may eat items that are not good for you without knowing you are doing it. For instance, sugar in one form or another is added to most processed foods and to fast foods as well. So is salt. Caffeine is found not only in coffee and tea, but in many cola drinks (which is why noncaffeinated cola drinks are now available) and also in chocolate.

I am aware that what Kenneth Cooper and Nathan Pritikin suggest is a way of eating that is more like the eating habits of the Third World than that of Western countries such as America. It is a terrible irony that our "advanced" countries have developed foods that are bad for us. But if you develop an eating habit such as I have described, you will not only live longer, be more healthy, and look better, you will feel better and have more energy.

Exercise

A regular program of exercise is essential not only for increased energy, but for a healthy body and a long life. Marie Beynon Rae in her book, *How Never to Be Tired,* says the answer to fatigue is not rest, but work.[34] She insists that boredom produces fatigue and work produces energy. I have found that during those times when my work load has caused me to go without some sleep, I have more energy, not by trying to catch an extra half hour sleep, but by spending that time in exercising.

The best kind of exercise is that which increases your heartbeat and sustains it for at least thirty minutes a day. Walking, running, and swimming are three excellent means of exercise. Isometric exercise—such as weight lifting—may serve a useful purpose in building up muscle tissue, but it does not help your heart and should not be viewed as a substitute for walking, running, or swimming.

The important thing about exercise is to do it regularly. Schedule it into your day. Make it a priority. Your increased health, feeling of well-being, and added energy will make it worthwhile.

Maintain a Proper Mental Attitude

Increased energy comes not just from conditioning your body through proper eating, exercise, and plenty of sleep, but also from conditioning your mind through developing positive attitudes and eliminating negative emotions. Your body provides you with your storehouse of energy. How much is in the storehouse depends on your physical care and development. But it is your attitude that decides how much of that energy should be released.

Do you know people who have a hard time getting up in the morning? Are any of them zealous fishermen? On a work day they would have a hard time getting out of bed by six o'clock or seven o'clock. But if they are going fishing, they know that they are to meet their friends at four-thirty and so they set the alarm for four. A few minutes before four they are wide awake! They hook up the trailer, they pull the boat to the fishing place, they slide down muddy river banks, and they get wet. They exert more energy over the next fifteen hours than during the preceding three weeks in their vocation. If they are successful in catching a lot of fish, they come back feeling better than they have felt in weeks. They seem to be aglow with energy. What makes the difference? Attitude!

If you want to be energetic, act energetic. Energy will come if you are as interested in the people you are leading—and the beneficial changes that will come to them because of your leadership—as you are in your hobbies.

Eliminate Negative Emotions

Nothing will divert your energy from constructive leadership faster than negative emotions. They will direct your energy into nonproductive channels. There are many negative emotions and effective leaders learn how to deal with them in constructive ways so they will not turn their attention from the job of leadership.

Anger is a common emotion often repressed or denied. In itself, anger is not wrong, but unless it is recognized and dealt with, it can become a matter of constant concern. Tensions, ulcers, and high blood pressure may result. Much energy can be spent needlessly by either repressing or nurturing anger. The correct approach to anger is to recognize it, analyze why you are angry, make changes where possible to relieve your anger, and accept the situation if changes cannot be made.

Hatred and bitterness are negative emotions that are wrong. They are mental and physical poison that will destroy you if you let them. Hatred and bitterness can seem to generate a lot of energy. But it is a diversion of energy from constructive to destructive purposes. Usually the harm and destruction do not happen to the person or thing hated, but to the person doing the hating. The only way to overcome hatred and bitterness is with love. Christ said, "You have heard that it was said, 'You shall love your neighbor and hate your enemy.' But I say to you, love your enemies, bless those who curse you, do good to those who hate you, and pray for those who spitefully use you and persecute you" (Matthew 5:43–44). With Christ's help, you can overcome hatred and bitterness.

Anxiety is a general sense of uneasiness or discomfort. It differs from fear in that there is no specific object or situation which is feared. This vagueness makes anxiety difficult to deal with. Focusing one's attention on anxieties leaves little energy for constructive accomplishments—precisely the thing that would help relieve anxiety. Christ warned against anxiety when He said, "Therefore I say to you, do not worry about your life, what you will eat or what you will drink; nor about your body, what you will put on. Is not life more than food and the body more than clothing?" (Matthew 6:25).

Fear can be good or bad, and like all emotions, fear produces energy. If someone approaches you with a stick to kill you, you will experience fear. That fear will give you the energy to turn and run faster than you ever thought possible. Fears that are phobias—exaggerated and irrational fears—also generate energy, but they turn energy away from constructive purposes to destructive ones. The fear of the dark, of heights, of closed places, of speaking before a crowd inhibit your development as a leader. The first step to overcoming your fears is to identify them and study them. Begin slowly to face your fears in the strength of Jesus Christ.

Guilt is a legitimate feeling because we have "all sinned and fall short of the glory of God" (Romans 3:23). But if we are not freed from guilt, it can become a demoralizing emotion, and we will look for reasons to condemn ourselves for things about which we should not feel guilty. Jesus Christ offers the only freedom from guilt. Through His salvation the guilt for our sins is removed and remembered no more. God has forgotten our sins, and we should too.

Worry, doubt, loneliness, jealousy, and depression are some of the other negative emotions that can divert our energy. Eliminating these negative emotions increases our energy available for leadership.

Walk in Fellowship with God

All things being equal, your energy level will be in proportion to the intimacy of your walk with God. When you are in fellowship with God, you walk with God, study the Word of God, spend time in prayer to God, tell other people about God, and relate all your concerns and activities and feelings to the will of God. This eliminates the energy-destroying frustrations, fears, and guilt that come from ignoring Him and walking in your own inadequate strength.

The apostle Paul said, "Be fervent in spirit, serving the Lord." That will produce energy the world cannot give and the world cannot take away, energy that gives the leader a magnetic influence.

The apostle Paul and his companion Silas, languishing in a Philippian jail, prayed and sang hymns of praise to God at midnight. Were they fatigued? Bored? Did they have the blahs? Not those two! They pulsated with the energy that vitalizes true leadership. God was their energy source.

SUMMARY

Energy attracts attention. Energy attracts followers. The leader who demonstrates enthusiasm and energy will gain the acceptance and confidence of others. Energy conveys the ideas of authority, of excitement, of success, and of purposeful activity. The principle of energy says that a real leader must exude energy, "the vigorous exertion of power" and "the capacity of acting or being active."

The leader's energy is demonstrated through physical vitality. Even though he may be older or have a physical handicap, the leader radiates good health and purposeful activity. The leader's energy is demonstrated through mental alertness. He is not necessarily an intellectual giant, but he will use his mind to its fullest for observation, foresight, and reflection and reasoning. The leader's energy is demonstrated through hard work. Work is the most common expression of human energy and the leader will enjoy it and pursue it. The leader's physical, intellectual, and emotional energy is demonstrated through commitment and perseverance as he believes in and works toward his goal against all odds. A leader's energy is demonstrated through attention to details because the little things will make or break you.

It is true that some people naturally possess more energy than others. Nevertheless, it is possible to increase your energy level. You can maximize your energy level by eating right, exercising regularly, maintaining a proper mental attitude, eliminating negative emotions, and by walking in fellowship with God.

11

The Principle of

STAYING POWER

In the late 1960s, I was asked to conduct an evangelistic crusade in Lisbon, Portugal. It was an exciting opportunity because it was the first time in the history of Portugal, which is 99 percent Catholic, that a Protestant minister had been invited to conduct meetings in public buildings.

I was an itinerant evangelist, having been a pastor for several years before that. As a pastor, I had not wanted to travel. Our only child had been victimized by cerebral palsy from birth, and in the pastorate I had repeatedly declined trips that had been offered to me. I didn't feel right being away unless it was absolutely necessary. Johnny needed me; so did my wife, Christine. Only the bedrock conviction that God was pushing me to become an itinerant evangelist led me to take that step. The conviction came when I received 420 unsolicited invitations to conduct meetings—evangelistic crusades, preaching missions, evangelistic Bible teaching seminars—during the last 18 months of my pastorate.

No sooner had the planning for the Lisbon evangelistic crusade begun than a prominent American parachurch organization (which I will call "Gospel Enterprise") sent two executives to meet with our Portuguese committee chairman. They damned our ministry with faint praise. Then the main spokesman of the two said, "I don't think Haggai will make much of a difference. But surely he can't hurt anything. We'll plan to come at a later date for a history-making evangelistic effort. You may just want to wait for us." The Lisbon leadership declined their recommendation.

Next, one of Gospel Enterprise's friends, a missionary to Portugal and a good man, used his influence to stonewall our crusade, even though he had cooperated with us enthusiastically two years earlier. It was tempting to give in to discouragement, but the Lord wanted us to persevere, and so He gave us staying power. The crusade proceeded on schedule. Toward the end, after thousands had made decisions for Christ, the missionary said he wasn't going to resist the obvious work of God any longer. He candidly told us he had been instructed by Gospel Enterprise not to cooperate, but to wait until it came with its programs to Portugal.

The late Bob Pierce flew from Dacca, Bangladesh, specifically to warn me that "Gospel Enterprise is out to stop you." He advised me to be on guard; he didn't want to see the ministry hurt.

This opposition did not surprise me, for just prior to the Portugal crusade, a family friend of one of my associates said he had sat in on an annual board meeting of Gospel Enterprise and had heard one of its executives comment that "Haggai is the only one we haven't been able to sweep under our umbrella." I had known for a number of years that Gospel Enterprise opposed our ministry.

As a pastor, I hadn't wanted to be away from home. And yet I knew God wanted me to be an evangelist. Giving up would have been easy in the face of the opposition from Gospel Enterprise—opposition I didn't understand then and I don't understand now. The opposition in Portugal wasn't an isolated incidence. I had encountered opposition earlier. No sooner had I begun my evangelistic ministry than the leadership of Gospel Enterprise attempted to end it by getting my engagements cancelled. Sometimes they used a direct approach as when they torpedoed a city-wide crusade in Honolulu that the clergy had asked me to consider.

The opposition to my ministry came from the top. Some European friends showed me a letter belittling our ministry which the head of Gospel Enterprise had written to one of the continent's highly placed Christian laymen. The favorite instruction of the head of Gospel Enterprise to his associates, when he faced a sticky situation, was known to be, "Do this. Get it done. Don't tell me how you do it; just do it." And they did it!

The active opposition continued for many years. Gospel Enterprise seemed determined to destroy our ministry. I asked God for the grace to stay true to Him and to the vision He had given me. For 15 years I tried every way possible to get an appointment with the head of Gospel Enterprise. He refused to meet with me. I had supported the organization from my college days. It was in my daily prayers. My son, Johnny, prayed with special fervency for the head of Gospel Enterprise. I never told Johnny the facts because I didn't want him to lose confidence in the people involved. I still pray for this man and the organization.

One night in Florida, a man connected with Gospel Enterprise phoned me. Since I did not know him too well, I was surprised at how determined he was to meet with me. "Fine," I said, "come over to our hotel and have dinner with us at 7 o'clock tonight."

"Oh no, this meeting must be kept in confidence. Let's meet at 11 o'clock tonight. We must not meet at a public place like your hotel or even my home." He then mentioned a remote spot where a street, deserted that time of night, dead ends into the ocean. "Let's meet there."

We met. With tears in his eyes, he said, "If you tell what I'm about to say and name me as the source, it could cost me my position with the organization. I've wrestled over whether to meet with you, but I don't want to see God's work hampered. So I determined to warn you of a vigorous attempt to eliminate your ministry." He then told Christine and me details of the efforts undertaken by Gospel Enterprise to terminate my ministry.

With a puzzled look, he said, "You don't seem surprised."

"No," I said, "I could tell you a few things. For instance, Gospel Enterprise's strategic planner, after volunteering on Wednesday to encourage the Indonesians to cooperate in a Total Evangelism—Plus project we had coming up, flew to Jakarta on Friday where he subtly denigrated the project before the chairmen of the various committees we had set up. They couldn't believe their ears. Later they played a recording of what he had said to my associate, who then went to great lengths to suggest that Gospel Enterprise was a great organization and maybe there was an innocent misunderstanding.

"Two of Gospel Enterprise's top executives went to unimaginable lengths to try to persuade the man who became Haggai Institute's executive vice president and director of worldwide operations not to join us. I could keep you here the rest of the night with documented story after documented story. I think I know every ploy, ruse, innuendo, and tactic they have used."

"And you're not upset?"

"I'm grieved, but not upset," I said. I appreciated the man's efforts to warn me of Gospel Enterprise's intentions. In the early years, I could not bring myself to believe Gospel Enterprise was deliberately obstructing my ministry and working to end it. I was the last to see it. My wife saw it. Members of my family and my friends saw it. Dr. Ernest H.

Watson, our dean, grieved over it. A multinational tycoon friend of mine, who also knew the principals of Gospel Enterprise, was so infuriated by the situation when he learned about it, he said, "I will put up $50,000 to arrange an international press conference in London. We'll blow the whistle on these folks."

"No," I said, "we cannot permit the ministry to be blamed."

"But this is dishonest. It's unjust. It's defamation by innuendo."

"Yes, but I believe they must have reasons they feel valid, although you and I cannot understand them. The Lord will take care of it all."

If we had followed a course of documented exposure and retaliation, we would have created havoc among Christians and great mischief among skeptical unbelievers who are looking for something like this to justify their rebellion against God. They fail to realize that the power of the gospel is verified by the fact that it survives such human frailties.

Gospel Enterprise's unrelenting opposition worked unspeakable hardship on us. In the early days, I went through all my savings, sold my car, and borrowed money to keep the ministry afloat. This was necessary because each time Gospel Enterprise got our meetings cancelled, we would lose all the money we had put into the preparation for the meetings—money that would normally be reimbursed by the crusade finance committee. On four different occasions we were faced with bankruptcy and closure. It could very well be that the leadership of Gospel Enterprise honestly believed we were not qualified to work in the field of evangelism. Yet for more than a decade they plagiarized our materials (one magazine article was almost word for word), and, of course, plagiarism is the most sincere form of flattery.

I rejoice in the great good Gospel Enterprise does. I know it is committed to reaching people for Christ. The fact that it has opposed our ministry can't negate that. Even though it caused us no end of grief and difficulty, God has used Gospel Enterprise to touch thousands of lives. Today, many individuals in Gospel Enterprise not only commend the work of the Haggai Institute, but several support it with their money as well as their prayers.

Whatever the motives of the leaders of Gospel Enterprise, their opposition made me and those who worked with me stronger. We had to have staying power to survive their attacks. And the exercise of staying power produces stronger staying power. God saw us through.

Cecil Day had only one wall picture in his original office. It showed a cat with eyes bulging and front paws desperately grasping a chinning bar. The cat was high above the ground and didn't want to fall. The eyes were just above the bar. The words below read, "Hang in there,

Baby." Cecil Day had staying power. That's why he appreciated the picture.

Difficulties do exist. Let's not kid ourselves into thinking they don't. Every leader has pressures and problems that can make him want to give up. The opposition I received from Gospel Enterprise made me question God's direction and my strength to fulfill the vision He had given me.

Charles Swindoll, senior pastor of the First Evangelical Free Church in Fullerton, California, decided to keep a record of the difficulties he faced in one 36-hour period:

• A mother and dad committed their teenager to a local psychiatric ward.

• A relative of a girl in our church took her own life.

• A fifteen-year marriage went up in smoke as the wife walked out. She is now living with another man.

• A young couple had their first child. It is mongoloid.

• A woman in her twenties is plagued with guilt and confusion because of an incestuous relationship with her father years ago.

• A young woman on a nearby Christian campus was raped and stabbed.

• A former minister is disillusioned. He has left the faith.

• A middle-aged husband and wife cannot communicate without screaming. Separation seems inevitable.

• An employer is embittered because his Christian employee cannot be trusted.

• A missionary wife who has returned to the States has suffered an emotional breakdown.

• Christian parents just discovered their son is a practicing homosexual.[35]

Swindoll then comments, "And then I got in my car after a late meeting last night—and it wouldn't start!"

The leader is guaranteed he will face problems, difficulties, discouragement, opposition, persecution, and betrayal. God has given you a vision, and you have established a goals program to accomplish your mission. At times it will seem as if it is impossible. Something will happen that can make you want to give up. Don't be surprised if this happens. I had to realize that I was doing the work God had given me to do as an evangelist, and the opposition I was facing did not mean I should quit. It only meant I had to exercise staying power. Moreover, God sends us opportunities to exercise staying power so that we will be strengthened to overcome greater problems and difficulties later.

Charles Swindoll lists what he calls "four spiritual flaws" about Christian maturity that show the need for staying power in the Christian's life:[36]

"Flaw 1: *Because you are a Christian, all your problems are solved.*" When I began an evangelistic ministry—one that complemented the work of Gospel Enterprise—I expected that we would work together to spread the gospel of Jesus Christ. But just because I was a Christian doing God's work did not mean all my problems were solved. Let's not promise the unbeliever that becoming a Christian will solve all his problems either.

"Flaw 2: *All the problems you will ever have are addressed in the Bible.*" The fact of the matter is, they are not. God tells us many things in the Bible, but He also requires us to walk by faith, receiving our guidance from the Scriptures, the Holy Spirit, and from the counsel of godly believers.

"Flaw 3: *If you are having problems, you are unspiritual.*" For some reason this is one of the most tenacious lies I know. It won't go away even though it isn't true. In fact, it's probably true that if you *are* spiritual and *are* doing the will of God, you *will* have problems. Job wrestled with this when his friends accused him of suffering because he was unspiritual. Swindoll says, "Some of the most spiritual men and women I have ever known have wrestled with some of the deepest problems life offers." When you have made your peace with God, you've declared open and unrelenting warfare with the devil. You *will* have problems.

"Flaw 4: *Being exposed to sound Bible teaching.automatically solves problems.*" Instruction in the Word of God will help you solve your problems, but it won't solve them for you. If you have stolen some money, the Bible will tell you that you should confess your sin to God and to the person from whom you stole and repay it. But that doesn't solve the problem. You need to be a "doer" of the word and not just a "hearer."

The apostle Paul said, "We are hard pressed on every side, yet not crushed; we are perplexed, but not in despair; persecuted, but not forsaken; struck down, but not destroyed" (2 Corinthians 4:8–9). That's staying power.

The leader will have problems and discouragements, but God wants him to persevere in following his vision. The principle of staying power says that these problems and difficulties can be overcome, but the leader has to hang in there. He has to have staying power.

Mastering other principles of leadership can take study and practice. But you can master this principle of staying power as fast as you can read these words. You don't need education, or charm, or well-connected family ties, or influential friends, or staff, or equipment, or materials, or prestige, or even profound biblical understanding. All you need is will. You don't have to wait until tomorrow; you can begin employing this principle right now. You have no excuse not to. If God wants you to be a leader, He wants you to have staying power. The question is, do you have the determination?

Staying Power Overcomes Illness

A serious and persistent illness can be one of the most discouraging obstacles to face in carrying out your goals program. Sickness will sap your physical and mental strength. And yet staying power can overcome illness.

Charles Haddon Spurgeon of London continued steadfastly with his multifaceted ministry when he was so sick he had to spend most of his time resting in southern France. His wife, who became an invalid after the birth of their twin sons, transcended her physical limitations by staying power. Though paralyzed, she directed from her bed an unprecedented book distribution effort. It is because of her staying power that Spurgeon's books are on the shelves of more people around the world than the books of any other minister.

Dr. John Sung, even when cancer was ravaging his body, continued to preach three times a day for periods of two hours and more. He did this in tropical heat, when there was no air conditioning and not even an oscillating fan. He did it thirty days consecutively and for eleven months out of every year. He did it until he died at the age of forty-four. Because of his staying power, God was able to use him to change the complexion of China and Southeast Asia.

Will Houghton, pastor in Atlanta, Georgia, and later president of Moody Bible Institute, suffered mental torture created by headaches that were so severe they could have made death a welcome relief. And yet most of us who knew Dr. Houghton had no idea of his illness. He did not speak of his great problem. His humor could put at ease all the students who would tense up in his commanding presence. This man, who demonstrated a unique leadership from the time of his spiritual conversion in the early part of the century until his death in 1946, pursued his work with a staying power that continues to challenge me personally.

Staying Power Overcomes Personal Desires

Thirty years ago I read a line that moved me and has stuck with me. "Efficiency is the willingness to sacrifice personal desires to the will to win." In every leader's experience, there are times when it would be easier to abandon a project, give in to the detractors, or take the easy road. A leader will also frequently be faced with the opportunity to satisfy a personal desire that may not be bad in itself but would interfere with the accomplishment of his goals. But efficiency is the willingness to sacrifice personal desire to the will to win. That takes staying power.

William Borden of the famous Borden family in America graduated from Yale University in 1909. While he was a student, cars were just beginning to come on the streets. One day he was looking out the window and admired a car. His roommate said, "Bill, why don't you buy one? You have the money." But Borden had different priorities. He had committed his life and his money to missions. Before he died at the age of twenty-nine, his leadership had made its impact on both sides of the Atlantic. The secret to Borden was total commitment to Christ and a leadership rooted in staying power—staying power that sacrificed personal desires to the will to win.

Staying Power Overcomes Financial Limitations

Many have demonstrated outstanding leadership by practicing staying power in the face of financial limitations. George Muller, who founded homes for orphans in Bristol, England, is a well-known example. He changed the lives of thousands of children and made a positive impact on England by his compassionate care. He did it by faith. Many times he did not have money for the food required for the next meal. He never complained. He never whimpered. He never threatened to discontinue his ministry to the orphans. Instead, he prayed. In answer to his faith, thousands of pounds came in to support the work from all over the world, much of it from people of whom he had never heard. What set George Muller apart was not his prayer life, for thousands of people around the world are faithful in fervent prayer. What made Muller unique was his staying power. His staying power gave validity to the faith undergirding his prayers.

Staying power is built on a deep commitment to the leader's vision. A weakness of many who occupy positions of leadership today but lack the qualities of a true leader is a "bail-out" mentality. When you talk with them intimately, you find out they are already making plans in case they fail. I have even heard clergy say, "If things get rough in the church, I'll move into the field of insurance. I can certainly maintain myself there." Their failure has been programmed and its arrival assured because the so-called leader lacks staying power.

Staying Power Overcomes the Peril of Prosperity

Almost nobody fears prosperity. We fear dishonesty, impurity, gluttony, jealousy, and the various sins of the flesh. But not prosperity. And yet prosperity and easy living constitute the biggest challenge staying power has. Prosperity can be a bigger danger than other difficulties.

Prosperity is also a threat to a close walk with God. The Bible never says that wealth itself is wrong (although it does say in 1 Timothy 6:10 that "the *love* of money is a root of all kinds of evil"). But wealth is the one thing that Christ said would make spirituality difficult. "Assuredly, I say to you that it is hard for a rich man to enter the kingdom of heaven. And again I say to you, it is easier for a camel to go through the eye of a needle, than for a rich man to enter the kingdom of God" (Matthew 19:23–24). And yet most Christians I know are actively pursuing wealth.

If our primary goal in life were a close walk with God, it seems clear that we would stop the pursuit of riches for the sake of amassing wealth because wealth makes such closeness more difficult. Usually, however, we rationalize our pursuit of riches by saying we need to provide financial security for our family. Or we say we want more money so that we can give more to the Lord's work. (Thank God some do give generously to God's work when they become wealthy.) Or we say that others may not be able to handle riches, but we can.

A powerful orator and a good friend of mine said several years ago, "Russia will never bury America. No matter what Khrushchev said, it just isn't so. America will bury America unless America breaks the stranglehold of self-indulgence, wanton waste, and narcissism." That could be said of many countries, not only in the West but even in the East, where preoccupation with things and self-indulgence are robbing the people of character and values of permanence.

Staying Power Overcomes Family Opposition

Fortunate is the person whose family supports the responsibilities of his leadership role. Unfortunately, it is not always so. A leader has a 24-hour, 7-day-a-week job. It requires doing unpleasant tasks as well as enjoyable ones. It is easy for members of a leader's family to feel they are getting second place.

David Livingstone, who opened much of Africa for exploration and missionary work, was not only a missionary himself, but a writer, a cartographer, and an anthropologist. He was a man of many and varied skills and achievements. Livingstone's wife, Mary, gave him such trouble, always complaining and criticizing, that it made Livingstone's work almost impossible.

Let it be said that the demands on Livingstone were great. In that day there were no jet airplanes making it possible for him to visit a city a thousand miles away and be back home the same day. However, as General Dwight D. Eisenhower said in 1945, "There are no victories at bargain prices."

The tension became so great that Livingstone sent his wife home to England for a period of more than twelve years while he suffered and bled and ultimately died in Africa for the Africans.

Staying power overcomes the obstacle of family opposition. The leader fixes his eyes on his mission and does not let opposition even from his own family move him from the path of accomplishing that mission. This is what Jesus meant when He said, "If anyone comes to Me and does not hate his father and mother, wife and children, brothers and sisters, yes and his own life also, he cannot be My disciple" (Luke 14:26). The leader's staying power must overcome family opposition.

Staying Power Overcomes Betrayal and Persecution

Polycarp, the Bishop of Smyrna, exercised enormous leadership. While he was in his eighties, for instance, he undertook a journey to Rome where many were converted to Christ. Shortly after his return home, persecution broke out in Asia. For sport, the Romans abducted eleven Christians, mostly from Philadelphia, and martyred them at a great festival in Smyrna.

The appetite of the mob was inflamed by the spectacle of the martyrdom. A cry was raised, "Let a search be made for Polycarp." Polycarp took refuge at a country farm, but his whereabouts were betrayed. He was arrested and brought back to the city where the proconsul urged him to "revile Christ," promising that if he would deny his faith, he could be set free. To this demand, Polycarp made his memorable answer, "Eighty and six years have I served Him, and He has done me no wrong. How then can I speak evil of my King who saved me?" These words only intensified the fury of the mob, which clamored for a lion to be let loose on him. The request was denied and instead timber and kindling were hastily collected, and Polycarp was placed on a pyre. With calm dignity and unflinching courage, he was martyred by being burned alive.

It wasn't Polycarp's death that accounts for his position of prominence; it was his leadership. And his leadership was characterized by an unswerving staying power. Right up to the time the flames licked his body and he breathed his last, he remained faithful to his calling and to his Lord.

One nation I have frequently visited has laws that require the death penalty for anyone who evangelizes or "converts someone to Christianity." In that country, a government informant went to a secret meeting of believers in 1982 under the guise of interest in Scripture and a desire to accept Jesus Christ as his Savior. Since the informant was to be away from his family for a few weeks and since hospitality is an important part of that culture, he was invited to live at the home of the host of the meeting. While the host, his wife, and family were out, the informant had television cameras hidden in the ceiling. The next worship service was photographed, with a clear shot of each person in attendance. As a result, each of the adult men was thrown in prison.

I have two friends in that country who have the staying power to overcome the obstacles of betrayal and persecution. They walk and work in peril of their lives. Every phone call is bugged. Every letter is censored. Every step they take is hounded. Both of these men have been offered positions of prestige which carry large incomes outside that country. But they have declined. They are leaders in their own country. Staying power keeps them there, even though both of them have been roughed up physically on occasion. Both have suffered government-sanctioned pressure, including the vandalism of their buildings. Staying power keeps them on course.

Betrayal and persecution can take many forms and come from many sources, but the leader with staying power does not deviate from his vision and goals. I mentioned the opposition I experienced from "Gospel Enterprise." Such opposition is most heartbreaking because it comes from those who are fellow believers. It is then that the leader needs staying power the most.

Staying Power Overcomes Misinterpretation of Events

The leader has a clear view of his vision and attempts to communicate it to others. But when others don't understand the vision with the same clarity as the leader, it is possible that the leader's actions will be misinterpreted. Or it is possible that some will not see how the pieces fit together. Or some may want to give in to discouragement.

The leader with staying power properly interprets the events, explains the situation to the people, and despite continued opposition, proceeds in love to insure the success of the enterprise.

When Spurgeon was hardly in his twenties, such large crowds came to the church services he held that the building could not accommodate them. He met with thirty of his leaders and suggested they build an auditorium that would seat more than 5,500 people. Allegedly, he told them that if any of them doubted the possibility of accomplishing this, they should leave. Twenty-three left! A leader without staying power would have had all kinds of doubts, but Spurgeon had the vision. The goals were clearly defined. He had the staying power to see it through. For more than thirty years, crowds packed out the Metropolitan Tabernacle morning and night, and it became the most influential Baptist church in history.

Staying Power Overcomes Impossibilities

What problem are you facing? I have mentioned the problems that can be caused by illness, personal desires, financial limitations, prosperity, family opposition, betrayal and persecution, and misinterpretation of events. But just because I haven't talked about the problem you're facing doesn't mean it can't be overcome. Every problem has its own solution, and although the solutions are different, staying power is the key to each one. If you give up, you have already failed. But if you have staying power, you will find a solution with God's help. Staying power insures success when every circumstance seems to insure failure.

When the Young Nak Church was established in 1946 with twenty-seven North Korean refugees, it met on a mountain in Seoul. All they had was a threadbare tent. One Sunday the weight of the melting snow caused the tent to collapse. All the members of the church were destitute. Not one of them had money. And yet the young pastor, Dr. Han, suggested they needed a church building. That seemed like an impossibility.

But leaders of faith don't confuse problem solving with decision making. They don't counsel their fears. They don't insist that every possible obstacle be overcome before they engage in an enterprise. They determine what needs to be done, they make the decision, and then they seek solutions to the problems. Leaders of faith know that staying power will overcome impossibilities.

One lady in the congregation said she had no money but she would give her wedding ring. Another lady said that other than the clothes she was wearing, her only possession was a quilt which she would give to the church fund. She would sleep when another woman with whom she lived was awake and use her quilt.

A third woman said that all she had was a spoon and a rice bowl. She gave that. She could borrow her friend's spoon and rice bowl.

The money began to come in.

Construction began on a magnificent church edifice. Then in 1950 the Communists came down from the north and pushed the South Koreans nearly into the sea. It was almost four years before the members of Dr. Han's church could get back to Seoul to worship in that building and during the Korean War, the Communists converted the church into an ammunition depot.

Just as the United Nations' forces were pushing the Communists back, an elder of the Young Nak Church went to the building to examine its condition. Communists were hiding in it and said they were going to kill him. Before shooting him, they granted his request for a moment to pray. If you visit the Young Nak Presbyterian Church in Seoul today, you will notice a tombstone just to the right of the front door. It is the burial place of Young Nak's first martyr.

Setbacks, discouragements, martyrdom, oppositions—all sorts of impossibilities—have been faced by the members of the Young Nak Church. And yet their staying power, which comes from their faith in God, kept them going. Today the church is the largest Presbyterian church in the world.

> "Got any rivers you think are uncrossable;
> Got any mountains you can't tunnel through?
> God specializes in things tho't impossible;
> He does the things others cannot do."[37]

Whatever impossibility you are facing, have faith in God, and He will give you the staying power to see it through. We are all faced with a series of great opportunities brilliantly disguised as impossible situations. Staying power lets you see the great opportunity in your own impossible situation.

How to Maintain Your Staying Power

You need staying power to maintain your staying power. Every leader gets discouraged. Most leaders at some time question whether they ought to quit. When those moments hit you, you can renew your staying power. But don't wait for discouragement to come. Begin now to practice strengthening your staying power—

By Remembering Your Vision

Your leadership began with a vision. You had a clear picture of what your group could be or do. You saw how you could move the group toward goals of beneficial permanence that would fulfill the group's real needs. The vision you had was valid when you started and the need was real. The goals were worthy ones. You can maintain your staying power by remembering your vision and renewing your commitment to it. Doing that will put your problems in perspective.

By Focusing on Your Goals

Remembering your vision will give you the motivation to maintain your staying power. You will renew your commitment to the calling God has given you. Yet individual problems are overcome by focusing on your goals. If I were to think only of my personal vision of world evangelization, I would be overwhelmed. There are too many people in the world. There is too much that needs to be done. Where should I start? But focusing on one or two goals is manageable.

Goals are the specific, measurable steps designed to achieve the mission that arises from the vision. Focus on your goals and tackle them one by one. The progress you see in accomplishing them will strengthen your staying power.

By Visualizing Your Goals As Accomplished

I have noticed that leaders frequently talk as if what they want to see accomplished has already been done. A president of a company may tell you of his large chain of retail stores, how much business they do, and where they are located when, in fact, the first store has not yet opened. The president is not lying to you. If he is an effective leader, he has visualized his goals as being accomplished so often that to him his stores *are* a reality. And he is setting new goals as if the stores were fully operational.

The late Max Stoffel of Liechtenstein, whose Stoffel linens are known around the world, practiced visualizing his goals as accomplished. He told me that every morning he would get a cup of coffee, return to bed, prop himself up on some pillows, sip his coffee, and in a state of complete relaxation, he would mentally rehearse his plans for the day. If he had some appointments, he would mentally rehearse the opening words, what the tone of the conversation would be, the expression on the faces. He said, "I attribute my success as much to this as any other one discipline. Actually, when I left my house to go to the office, I was simply replaying the role I had already experienced. It relieved a lot of pressure and dissipated a lot of stress."

By Relaxation

Tension is the enemy of staying power. Most outstanding leaders know how to relax. They understand and practice the habit of solitude. In addition to a quiet time with God, they spend time with their own thoughts, planning, thinking, dreaming.

Interestingly, it is possible to be alone in a crowd. One of my associates used to spend two hours a day commuting by bus to work in New York City and back. Moving to another part of the country reduced his commuting time to less than half an hour by car, but he said he missed the bus ride because it was a time when he could relax, be alone, commune with God, and review his vision and goals.

By Reading Biographies

Biographies of great people will strengthen staying power because they let you see how God worked in the lives of others. Thousands have been inspired by the story of Dwight L. Moody's response to the challenge that "the world has yet to see what God can do with one man totally committed to Him and who doesn't care who gets the credit." Moody said, "By God's grace, I will be that man." His commitment changed thousands of lives through his preaching and through the establishment of Moody Bible Institute and its many ministries. But his commitment has also changed many lives because of the example it has set for those who have read Moody's biography.

By Living in Communion with God

Living in communion with God enhances the leader's staying power by helping the leader to focus his thoughts not on himself but on God, His majesty, His power, His goodness, His mercy, His love. Focusing on God tends to put the leader's own problems and obstacles in an eternal perspective, making them seem smaller and less overwhelming and making the vision God has given the leader more important.

Dr. Han Kyung Chik can be found in church at daybreak, spending time in prayer every morning of the year. During the day, whenever he begins a new task or a new meeting, he quietly bows his head in prayer without obtrusiveness, without awkwardness, without rudeness. If he goes to visit a person, for instance, he will take a moment, just after shaking hands, to silently commit the interview to the Lord. It does not matter if the person is a preacher of the gospel or a head of state. Dr. Han lives in communion with God. And God has given him staying power.

Staying Power Insures Success

Problems and discouragements will face the leader, but he can overcome them with staying power. It seems as if many of the world's famous leaders faced some of the greatest difficulties and discouragements in carrying out their visions.

Christopher Columbus, for instance, concluded from information he acquired from his travels and from studying charts and maps, that the earth was round and that he could reach Asia by sailing west. But he needed a patron to finance such an expedition. He first tried John II, King of Portugal, without success, and then the Count of Medina Celi in Spain. The Count encouraged Columbus for two years, but never actually provided him with the money and supplies he needed. Ferdinand and Isabella, king and queen of Castile in Spain, were then contacted. A review of Columbus' plans by a committee appointed by the queen resulted in the conclusion that his ideas were vain and impractical. But they kept talking.

After the better part of a decade of trying to find a patron, Columbus was in despair, but he didn't stop. He had staying power. He believed in his mission, but he held out for high terms from Ferdinand and Isabella. He asked that the rank of admiral be bestowed on him right away and that he be made viceroy of all that he should discover. In addition, he would receive one-tenth of all the precious metals discovered within his admiralty. His conditions were rejected and negotiations were again interrupted. Columbus left for France. However, the queen had a change of mind and sent for him. In April, 1492, Ferdinand and Isabella agreed to subsidize the expedition on Columbus' terms.

It seemed almost impossible to get crews together even in spite of the indemnity offered to criminals and "broken men" who would serve on the expedition. But Columbus demonstrated once again his staying power and finally three ships, the *Niña,* the *Pinta,* and the *Santa Maria,* set sail 3 August 1492. Three days later, the *Pinta* lost its rudder. They had to quickly and secretly repair the boat because three Portuguese ships were trying to intercept Columbus. The voyage was punctuated with experiences that unsettled the crews and put them on the threshold of mutiny more than once. It wasn't until 12 October 1492 that they landed on North America.

Columbus did not visit the Grand Khan of Cathay as he had hoped. But he did discover two new continents. He was successful because he had staying power.

SUMMARY

Difficulties exist. Every leader has pressures and problems that can make him want to give up. But if God has given you a vision and you have established a goals program to accomplish your mission, you need staying power to overcome these difficulties. The principle of staying power says that problems and difficulties can be overcome, but it takes staying power. The leader has to hang in there. Moreover, God sends us opportunities to exercise staying power so that we will be strengthened to overcome greater problems and difficulties later.

Charles Swindoll warns against the "four spiritual flaws" that show the need for staying power in the Christian's life: (1) "Because you are a Christian, all your problems are solved"; (2) "All the problems you will ever have are addressed in the Bible"; (3) "If you are having problems, you are unspiritual"; (4) "Being exposed to sound Bible teaching automatically solves problems."

The leader does not need education, charm, well-connected family ties, or influential friends, staff, equipment, materials, prestige, or even profound biblical understanding to master the principle of staying power. All you need is determination. You can do it today.

Staying power is essential to overcoming problems. Staying power can overcome illness, personal desires, financial limitations, the perils of prosperity, family opposition, betrayal and persecution, misinterpretation of events, and a host of other impossibilities.

Many leaders at some time question whether or not they ought to quit. When those moments hit, they can strengthen their staying power by remembering their vision, by focusing on their goals, by visualizing their goals as being already accomplished, by relaxation, by reading biographies, and by living in communion with God.

Staying power assures success. Problems and discouragements will face the leader, but he can overcome them with staying power.

12

The Principle of

AUTHORITY

For years I have admired an insurance salesman named Ben Feldman. He has broken every sales record in insurance history, and yet he lives in a small city in Ohio, not in a metropolitan center. He sells more insurance than 70 percent of the insurance companies in the United States.

When I arrived home from the office one evening, my wife, knowing of my fascination with Feldman, said, "Ben Feldman was just on television."

"What does he look like?" I asked, thinking he would have an impressive physique, a compelling voice, and good looks.

"Like a kind, short, somewhat overweight Jewish man. He is not what you would call handsome. He is certainly not imposing. Nor is his speech impressive."

"Then I wonder what the secret of his success is."

"The camera went on his eyes," she said. "When you saw his eyes you could understand his success. There was an authority that is hard to describe. It was indefinable, but it was there."

I have since met Ben Feldman on two occasions. He is gracious and respectful. Although not physically impressive, he has an authority about him that nearly knocks you over. It's not that he has an aggressive personality. He is quiet, subdued, and speaks softly. I believe Ben Feldman could be put down in any place in the world, totally unknown, and would shortly rise to the top. He has that kind of authority. He is a natural leader.

William Golding's novel, *Lord of the Flies,* tells the story of a group of school boys who are stranded on an island after a plane crash. No grown-ups survived—only the children. The boys all meet on a beach, get to know each other, and wonder what they will do and how they will be rescued. One of the first things is to "vote for a chief." A boy named Ralph is elected, although, says Golding, "The most obvious leader was Jack. But there was a stillness about Ralph as he sat there that marked him out."[38] Besides, he had the conch shell, which became the symbol of the leadership of the group. The story of the book centers on the struggle between Ralph and Jack for leadership. Both of them have an air of authority about them to which the other boys respond. Both of them are natural leaders.

Charles G. Finney, a lawyer of great intellect and scholarship, became an evangelist after his conversion and made a greater impact on America than anyone else of his time. He had no entourage, no press corps, no public relations advance team, no public address system. Yet under his preaching, 30,000 people professed faith in Christ each week during one six-week period.

His most vigorous detractors begrudgingly admitted he had an air of authority about him that commanded attention and respect. They told of one time when he walked into a textile mill in New York State. Before he was introduced, before he had said a word, all eyes turned toward him. And even more remarkably, many asked how to get right with God. Nearly the entire work force repented of their sins and professed faith in Christ. He had an authority that captured their attention. He was a natural leader.

It is true that the twelve principles of leadership found in this book will help you understand and practice effective leadership. They are all important. But a natural leader will be a leader without studying any of them. A person with a charisma, an air of authority, a strong force by which he exerts influence over those with whom he comes into contact, will become a leader and will "naturally" practice many of these principles. We say that such a person is a "natural leader." He has internal authority. Ben Feldman has it. The fictional Ralph and Jack had it. Charles Finney had it. Haile Selassie, Achmed Sukarno, Winston Churchill, and Jan Christian Smuts all had it.

"It" is an internal authority that causes a person to command the respect of others and by which the person can exert a powerful influence over others by virtue of his own charisma and personality. It is visible in a person. It's not dependent on his club membership, his social position, his race, or his intellectual ability. This internal authority sets the possessor apart from other people. Internal authority is different from external authority.

External authority causes a person to exert an influence over others by virtue of symbols or position. The conch shell Ralph held gave him external authority. External authority depends on entourage, automobiles, membership in particular clubs, and many other status privileges. External authority can be taken away from a person; internal authority cannot. External authority can impress people, but it will not cause a person to command the respect of others and exert special influence to move a group toward goals of beneficial permanence that fulfill the group's real needs. That comes only from internal authority.

The principle of authority recognizes the distinction between internal and external authority and says that the leader should develop and enhance his internal authority. I am firmly convinced that every person of normal mind, spirit, and body possesses the seeds of internal authority, some in greater measure than others. I am also convinced that it can be developed to the benefit of the people led and, above all, to the glory of God.

INTERNAL AUTHORITY

Internal authority is difficult to define. In this respect it's like life itself, which seems to defy precise scientific and legal definition. But nonetheless, internal authority is the quality that makes a person a leader. Let us examine what internal authority is not, give some examples of it, and identify some characteristics of internal authority.

Internal authority has nothing to do with physical properties or actions. The person with internal authority may be short or tall; he may be fat or thin; he may be handsome or ugly; he may be eloquent or halting in his speech.

Internal authority has little to do with wealth, social position, or status. The person with internal authority may be rich or poor, famous or unknown, socially prominent or an ordinary person. Internal authority may be used to bring riches, fame, and social prominence to a person if those are his goals in life, and I would guess that a higher percentage of rich, famous, and socially prominent people exhibit internal authority than those who are not. But it is important to realize that these things are one *result* of internal authority—not the cause of it.

Internal authority has little to do with success. Like riches, fame, and social prominence, success can be a result of internal authority, and the person with strong internal authority will have a better chance of success than the person without it. But internal authority does not guarantee success.

Internal authority does not mean that you feel you are better than others. Rather, it is a conviction that you can move the people in your group toward goals of beneficial permanence. It is not pride, but it is a belief that your vision, your ideas, and your leadership will benefit your group. At some point, every leader realizes that he is actually able to make a difference. People will act and be different because of what he says and does. That's the realization of internal authority.

Apparently the apostle Paul had this internal authority. Paul was plain looking, without an impressive physique, and not eloquent. But he must have had an internal authority to capture the attention of the world's leaders, as well as people on the extreme opposite sides of the social and economic spectrum.

Of course, Jesus was the ultimate example of a person with internal authority. We are not told that He had a commanding physical presence. He did not have wealth, social prominence, or status. He was not a success by the world's standards. And yet He commanded the respect of others and exerted a powerful influence over others by virtue of His authority. After recording the "Sermon on the Mount," Matthew says that Jesus "taught them as one having authority, and not as the scribes" (Matthew 7:29).

Nicodemus was one of the seventy most important Jewish people in Judea. As a member of the Sanhedrin, he helped rule the nation. Religiously, he was without peer. He knew 400 ceremonial laws by heart. He fasted two days a week and prayed four times a day. In contrast, Jesus had no position, no status. Undoubtedly, Nicodemus was older than Jesus. And yet when the two met, Jesus was the undisputed leader. Nicodemus opened their meeting by addressing Jesus as "Rabbi," meaning "Teacher." Jesus possessed an internal authority that no one, not even His detractors, denied.

When Jesus drove the money-changers out of the Temple, He was confronted by the chief priests and elders precisely on the point of authority. They asked, "By what authority are You doing these things? And who gave You this authority?" (Matthew 21:23). Jesus did not answer their question although His authority came from God. He also had authority over unclean spirits (Mark 1:27) and could convey to His disciples the power over demons and to cure diseases (Luke 9:1).

One ingredient of internal authority is individuality. Internal authority sets the possessor apart from other people. As a result, others regard the possessor as unique, not as one of any group or class or crowd. Others want to be in that person's presence because of the person himself. His individuality is apparent. It is *always* in existence. It is not something he can turn on when people see him.

Another ingredient is a realistic assessment of the leader's own authority and a sense of humility. The person with internal authority is not flattered by people, nor does he feel the need for flattering others unnecessarily. He neither looks up to any person, nor down on any person. While he is receptive and gracious, he is not a flatterer, and he never condescends. The Christlike leader who possesses this internal authority simply lays every compliment, as a tribute, at the feet of Jesus Christ Whom he serves.

The person with internal authority is never a weak, flabby, or jelly-fish type. He may be physically aging and weak, but he exudes an impression of strength.

Most important, the person with internal authority has self-confidence and a strong sense of self-esteem. His awareness of his own personal dignity is wholesome. He is not dependent on outside support to determine who he is, how much he has achieved, or what people think of him. He monitors himself in the most objective terms. He does not need anyone to give him the key to the city to verify his importance. It would never dawn on him to manipulate a testimonial dinner in his honor. He has a sincere belief in himself that is developed through understanding, forgiving, and accepting himself. It is this self-esteem that gives the natural leader his internal authority.

EXTERNAL AUTHORITY

External authority, on the other hand, derives its influence not from personal strength and ability, as internal authority does, but from external signs, symbols, and manipulations. It is an authority that can be taken away from a person, which indicates that the person never really possessed it in the first place. It is an authority immediately recognizable to those who know how to read the signs.

In the army, everyone's relative authority is clearly marked on his sleeve or chest for all to see. The general is more important and can exert more influence over more people than the sergeant, who is more important and can exert more influence over more people than the private. The authority each has comes from his position, which is reflected in his uniform. The general can do certain things because he is the general with external authority, not because he has the ability, strength of character, or intelligence—the internal authority—to do them, although it is hoped that he will.

There are many groups in which one's position of external authority is indicated by clothing. Policemen indicate authority by uniforms. Certain American Indian tribes indicated it by the kind and number of feathers in the warriors' headdress. Medieval knights indicated authority by gold spurs. In theory, signs of external authority are to be given only to those with a strong internal authority. However, it is no secret that people quickly realized that by acquiring the sign or symbol, they could bypass the discipline of developing real authority—the internal authority.

In his book, *Power: How to Get It, How to Use It,* Michael Korda describes the symbols that constitute external authority in the American business world.[39] A limousine is one such symbol. "Rented limousines are less prestigious than ones that are owned, a Rolls Royce carries more prestige than Cadillacs, and nothing equals a Mercedes 600 with the chrome painted black and the rear windows tinted to make the occupant invisible." A telephone in the limousine is a standard symbol of authority, and you can even buy a dummy telephone aerial so that others will think you have a phone in your car, even though it isn't connected to anything.

Telephones themselves are not just a means of communication, but another element of external authority. One telephone may be adequate, but two, three (or more!) phones in a person's office indicates more authority or power. Korda tells of executives who insist on having a telephone brought to their table at a restaurant to indicate how important they are. But for all the phones he may have, a person who is intent on developing external authority should never place a call himself. He has someone else do it for him. "With rare exceptions, power people do not dial telephones, use Xerox machines, add up figures themselves, type, or sharpen pencils. The first sign of a rise to power is often creeping helplessness."

Even shoes can be part of what gives a person external authority. "Powerful people generally wear simple shoes," says Korda. "—Peal & Co., Ltd. five-eyelet shoes from Brooks Brothers for example, and always put the laces in straight, not crisscrossed, and use round, waxed shoelaces. Shoes that have square toes, or high heels, or large brass buckles, or stitching in odd places, or are cut like jodhpur boots, are all definitely not power symbols, and to be avoided."[40]

A key to the executive washroom, a parking place with one's name on it, a certain kind of briefcase, a second secretary, a large salary, and many other symbols are the signs which constitute external authority.

External authority is also developed by manipulating situations and people. Korda says, for instance, that receiving telephone calls does not develop external authority, but placing them does. Therefore, one should do whatever is necessary not to actually take phone calls, but to get phone messages and return calls to people. If you spend enough time making calls, you probably won't be able to receive many anyway.

Upstaging others is another manipulation tactic that I personally find wearisome. No matter what you may say and no matter how innocently, there are some people who will upstage you. If you mention you have been to London, they have been with the queen. If you have visited Houston, they have just declined an invitation to be the first person in their professional group to fly on the next Challenger shuttle. If the waiter is a foreign student, studying at the local university, they must immediately tell you, with every conceivable embellishment, how their children have established new academic records and I.Q. levels.

Acquiring symbols of authority and learning how to manipulate people and situations are the means of developing external authority, an authority that is contrived and artificial. The Christlike leader seeks to develop his internal authority, an authority that is powerful and permanent. But there is a relationship between the two kinds of authority. For instance, the person who exhibits internal authority and as a result becomes head of a division of a company will get a larger office, his own secretary, and other symbols that give him external authority. To the extent that the person with internal authority seeks after and uses the symbols and manipulations of external authority, he denigrates his internal authority. But he should be aware of the symbols and manipulations, although he does not pursue them as an end in themselves.

A friend of mine who was a department head of a large publishing company was made vice president and given the external authority symbols that went with his new position: invitations to high-level meetings, a company car, a new parking place, a new title. He found that those symbols did not just give him greater status, but they were important for everyone who worked for him as well. They were interpreted to mean that the whole department was more important.

The Christlike leader seeks to develop his internal authority and not rely on external authority. However, if he is aware of his leadership (see chapter 13) and develops it by developing his internal authority, he will also be aware of what are considered the symbols and manipulations of external authority in his situation. Although he will subordinate it to his internal authority, he will nevertheless make external authority work for him.

DEVELOPING YOUR INTERNAL AUTHORITY

You have within yourself an internal authority. If through failure to exercise it or through lack of self-esteem you do not exhibit that internal authority, you must take steps to develop it if you are going to be a leader.

First, though, let me mention this: I do not believe that anyone should exercise authority over others until he has first learned to accept authority over himself. Moreover, even when a person is in a position of authority, he must be accountable to others. Perhaps the person in authority is accountable to an individual—as in a company or in churches with an episcopal form of government. Perhaps the person in authority is accountable to a board of directors or to stockholders. In some situations, Christian leaders are becoming part of an accountability group in which the members of the group make themselves accountable to one another and seek spiritual direction from each other. Lack of accountability leaves even the best-intentioned person open to the misuse of his authority. God wants each of His servants to be accountable not only to Him, but to Christian brethren of spiritual maturity as well.

Discover Yourself

Developing your internal authority begins by discovering yourself. You must know who you are, and you must be happy with what you know. Though you are a Christian and realize that you are a sinner who has been saved by grace, you also realize that having been saved, you are superior to the angels.

Do you know yourself? Too often we try to keep our real selves secret even from ourselves. To most people, the possibility of discovering themselves is frightening. They hide behind images they create of themselves or behind a fear of rejection or a fear of failure. Don't try to be somebody else. Your internal authority is yours alone and reflects your personality. To use it effectively, you must first discover yourself.

The only way to discover yourself is to walk closely with God. Commune with Him. Immerse yourself in His Word, the Bible, enough so that you begin to see things as God sees them. Then, regularly spend some time each day reflecting on the things you did and the things you learned during the day. View them not from the standpoint of your own selfish interests, but see them from God's viewpoint. Gradually a pattern will emerge letting you discover yourself.

Develop Self-Confidence

Self-confidence or self-esteem is one of the most important factors contributing to internal authority. Therefore, the development of self-confidence is essential, and one begins developing self-confidence by eliminating the fear of failure. Fear of failure is not usually a fear of the failure itself, but a fear that if one fails, his friends will forsake him, he will be humiliated and ashamed, and he will lose his self-esteem. Fear of failure can be overcome if you realize that the results of failure are not loss of friends and/or humiliation. Your friends will not condemn you for missing the mark, but they will criticize you if you never even try. Good people never abandon the courageous, honest, enterprising loser. They will admire your effort at trying. They will abandon you only when your fear of failure has caused you to abandon yourself. It is far better to attempt to do something great and fail than attempt to do nothing and succeed. In fact, as I have often said, you should attempt something so great for God, it's doomed to failure unless God be in it. The first step to self-confidence is eliminating the fear of failure.

Guilt also stifles self-confidence. Perhaps you have been programmed to feel guilty for having special gifts or power or skills. Those are gifts from God, and you should not feel guilty about them. Perhaps you feel guilty because of your sins and mistakes. If you are a Christian, God has forgiven you. "As far as the east is from the west, so far has He removed our transgressions from us" (Psalm 103:12). God has forgiven and forgotten your sins. Now you need to forgive and forget them too. You must reject guilt caused by sins that God has already forgiven. Affirm His forgiveness. Say it aloud!

God has not only forgiven you, He has accepted you as you are. Have you accepted yourself? Perhaps you are not happy with a habit you have. Perhaps your personal appearance or a physical handicap bother you. If you cannot change these things, accept them. Accept yourself just as you are.

Next, compliment yourself. Thank God for your pluses. If you really accept yourself just as you are, you will find certain things about you that are worthy of gratitude. Each of us has negative things about us, but we all have positive things as well. Recognize those things out loud. Say, "By God's grace I am a generous person" or "God has given me an exceptional mind" or whatever those things are of which you are most proud.

Only after accepting yourself and complimenting yourself for your existing good points should you try to improve yourself. The Christian is first accepted by God just as he is, and *then* God begins a work of sanctification in his life, making the Christian more like Jesus Christ. So, too, you should accept yourself as you are, and *then* begin to improve yourself. Perhaps you should begin a program of vocabulary building or a diet to lose weight or a careful plan of increasing your wealth. Whatever it is, your improvement will mean change for the better. And positive change means hope. Having a vision for a change, planning the change, and seeing the change occur will develop your self-confidence which will strengthen your internal authority.

Believe in the Importance of Your Mission

It has been my observation that people who are completely immersed in the importance of their life work, who with singleness of mind pursue their mission, tend to reveal a greater internal authority than others. The difference is that the person who is totally immersed in his mission knows where he is going. The others, while generalizing what they want to accomplish, seem to be ceaselessly looking for some new fad, some new activity that will get the attention of the public. Moreover, the person who is immersed in his mission has committed himself to people, projects, and causes and has had an opportunity to assume responsibilities. Those responsibilities create self-confidence, for responsibility fulfills the need to be needed.

Remember Your Relationship with Others

In developing internal authority, the leader must be careful in his relationships with others and the impression he leaves.

Don't reveal fatigue. If you are committed to a goal and you are enjoying working toward that goal, you can sometimes overlook your fatigue warnings. Others will notice it, and it tends to dilute your internal authority. When you are tired, get out of the public view. Get your rest. Let people see you only when you are vigorous. You may be the boss, the page-one celebrity, the lauded athlete, but the moment others see you fatigued, they instinctively jump to the conclusion of considering you to be equal with everyone else.

Keep your own counsel. Sharing your joys and woes, your achievements and setbacks, and finding a sympathetic ear all give comfort, but except in rare instances—as between a husband and a wife, or between a person and his mentor—it dilutes internal authority. Benjamin Franklin said, "Let no man know thee thoroughly; men freely ford that see the shallows." This does not mean that you are to be furtive or devious; it simply means that you are your own person. Let your counsel be shared with God, of course, but with few others.

Respect the rights and emotions of others. There are hundreds of guidelines that could be given, but I'll list only a few. Let people know you are aware of them. Be sensitive to their individuality, their achievements, their position. Give "honor to whom honor is due," but don't do it obsequiously. Show regard for the concepts, the intelligence, the abilities of others. You don't tell the carpenter how to do his work, nor the doctor how to diagnose your physical condition. Use good manners, be courteous. Practice the Pauline dictum, "In honor preferring one another." Show as much respect for the person who answers the telephone in an office as you would for the president of the company. Show knowledge of and concern for the culture of another person. When you are in Rome, do as the Romans do, unless doing so would violate your own value system.

Respect the personhood of others, and in so doing, you will be demonstrating the principle of love, for love delivers you from rudeness or criticism or inconsiderateness. And showing love is one of the best ways to develop your internal authority.

Strive for Excellence

In all you do, do the best you can. Excellence brings its own satisfaction, and doing your best will reinforce your internal authority in the eyes of your followers.

Everyone can excel in some area. Look at those areas of strengths you found when you discovered yourself. Those are the areas you should concentrate on in your striving for excellence because those are the places where you can most naturally achieve excellence and where you will enjoy doing so the most.

Believe in Your Own Success

Having committed yourself to the principles set forth in this book, visualize yourself as the exponent and practitioner of them. This develops your internal authority. Visualize yourself as already in possession of the qualities that enhance leadership and honor God. See yourself under His leadership, demonstrating the fruit of the Spirit in every facet of your life.

It is vital that you develop a strong belief in your ability to succeed.

And if you practice the twelve principles of leadership, you will succeed and your internal authority will blossom.

A Portrait of Authority

She systematically shuns all symbols of external authority. She owns only two changes of clothing. When she was given a white Lincoln Continental convertible with red leather seats, she auctioned it off to benefit the poor. Her office contains only a single telephone line, and for a while she was not sure whether even that was necessary. She travels in the third class compartments of trains. Her organization has no public relations officials and keeps a low profile.

Without any of the symbols of external authority that most people think are so necessary, Mother Teresa has founded an order of dedicated nuns and brothers who now work on five continents. She has become an international symbol of goodness and is honored by kings, popes, journalists, and the rich and powerful of this world. In 1979, she received the Nobel Prize for Peace because "the loneliest, the most wretched, and the dying . . . have at her hands received compassion without condescension." The $192,000 she received went to build a leprosarium in India.

Born in Skopje, Yugoslavia, in 1910, the daughter of an Albanian grocer, Agnes Conxha Bojaxhiu (the name given to Mother Teresa at birth) was called to be a nun at the age of twelve. She became one of the Sisters of Loreto and a missionary in eastern India. In 1946, she received a second call, this time to leave the convent and help the poor while living among them.

This tiny lady founded the Missionaries of Charity. One of her first projects was a home for dying destitutes in Calcutta. Here the homeless and forsaken could die in peace, experiencing at the end of their lives love and tenderness. One project led to others: an orphanage for abandoned children, a colony for lepers, a home for the elderly and bewildered, a workshop for the unemployed, and a free lunch program. Today, the Missionaries of Charity minister to the sick, dying, and destitute in thirty-one countries.

Mother Teresa exhibits internal authority that affects people around the world. She is quoted and respected. Malcolm Muggeridge, the British journalist, called his book about her *Something Beautiful for God* and describes her as a person "through whom the light of God shines." That is the key to her internal authority. She radiates the love of Jesus Christ, and when she holds a child, washes a putrefied wound, or feeds a dying mother, she does it as if she were doing it for Christ Himself. Mother Teresa is a person who demonstrates internal authority. She is a leader. And the source of her internal authority is the love of God.

SUMMARY

Internal authority is the charisma, the self-esteem, the personality that causes a person to command the respect of others. It is the element that characterizes all "natural leaders." External authority, on the other hand, is derived from the symbols and manipulations attached to a person's position. The principle of authority recognizes the distinction between internal and external authority and says that the leader should develop and enhance his internal authority.

Internal authority has nothing to do with a person's physical characteristics or actions, with his wealth, social position, or status. Nor is it derived from success. Rather, internal authority is a conviction that you can move the people in your group toward goals of beneficial permanence. The person with internal authority is an individualist with a strong sense of self-esteem.

External authority derives its influence not from personal strength and ability, as internal authority does, but from external signs, symbols, and manipulations. It is an authority that can be taken away from a person. It is an authority that is immediately recognizable to those who know how to read the signs.

You have within yourself an internal authority. If you are going to be a leader, you must take steps to develop this authority. First, though, it must be said that no one should exercise authority over others until he has first learned to accept authority over himself. Internal authority is developed by discovering yourself so that you know who you are and so that you are happy with what you know. It is developed by acquiring self-confidence. It is developed by believing in the importance of your mission. It is developed by not revealing fatigue, by keeping your own counsel, and by respecting the rights and emotions of others. It is developed by striving for excellence. Internal authority is developed by believing in your own success.

All of the principles of leadership are important, but not all are absolutely essential. Cultivating the principle of authority is. It is essential that a leader have and demonstrate to others internal authority and use to his benefit the symbols of external authority that go with his position.

13

The Principle of

AWARENESS

Awareness undergirds excellence. This is true not only of leaders, but of athletes, musicians, orators, businessmen, dancers, and writers— it is true in every area of life. To excel, a person must be aware of the elements that contribute to excellent performance and constantly measure his own performance against the standard of excellence he has set for himself. There are some people who are "natural" leaders or "natural" athletes or "natural" orators. They can do well following their natural talent and instinct. They can heighten their skill through training. But whether they train or not, it is essential that they be aware of their skills.

A musician should make his performance appear effortless so his presence does not interfere with the audience's enjoyment of the music. But although it may seem as if the music is just happening, the musician must constantly be aware of tempo, dynamics, chord progressions, and expression, as well as what the other musicians with whom he is playing are doing.

A writer's goal is to communicate effectively without calling attention to the writing itself. To do that, he must constantly be aware of many elements of writing, such as grammar. Do the verbs and nouns match? Are adjectives and adverbs used correctly? Do pronouns have identifiable antecedents? The excellent writer has made such things second nature to himself. He is constantly aware of them.

A boxer gets into the ring only when his awareness is heightened and prepared. He must be aware of his footwork, his hands, his pacing, his breathing—and that of his opponent. To let down his awareness for only a few seconds can mean the end of the match.

Could a teacher be effective while unaware of teaching principles? Or a physician while unaware of the principles of healing? Or a jurist while unaware of the principles of jurisprudence? Or a mother while unaware of the principles of child care? Of course not. Neither can anyone attain the level of effective leadership who fails to be constantly aware of leadership principles.

The principle of awareness says the leader will be aware of his own leadership, constantly monitoring his performance of the leadership principles against a standard he has set for himself so that he can achieve excellence. Awareness is the keystone in the arch of leadership. Knock out the keystone, and the arch, which consists of leadership principles, comes crashing down.

Awareness of how to be a leader requires sensitivity and exacting self-discipline over a period of time. One isolated experience of a group following a person's suggestions does not mean he is a leader. For example, suppose a fire rages through a building. A young man clearly and commandingly gives directions for those trapped inside. He tells some to go out one door, others out another, and still others down an outside staircase. His lightning-quick response to the crisis and his brilliant command of the situation make it possible for everyone to get to safety.

The young man would seem to have an aptitude for leadership. Nevertheless, that one instance does not assure solid and continuing leadership effectiveness. If he is to be an effective leader, he must be aware of his leadership and, by discipline, develop the principles of leadership.

The importance of awareness lies in the fact that it is the basis of the self-image the leader must have if he is to be effective. The leader cannot mistake weakness for humility, reluctance for waiting on the Lord, willfulness for individuality, excessive socializing with effective sociality. Awareness of his leadership role, of what leadership is, and of how to exercise it will sustain the discipline the leader needs for effectiveness. At times, a leader will experience loneliness that cries out for companionship, weariness that cries out for understanding, and risk-taking responsibilities that sound the sirens of fear. But an awareness of his leadership role will reinforce the leader's commitment. That commitment is essential to sustain the exacting discipline required for effective leadership. His leadership will collapse without both awareness and commitment.

THE LEADER IS AWARE OF HIS OWN LEADERSHIP ROLE

Leaders are aware of their own leadership role. They know they are in charge. They enjoy the privileges and bear the responsibilities that go with giving direction to the group's future. On the one hand, the effective leader will have many people look to him with admiration and loyalty, which puts him in an influential position. He knows that if he suggests to his followers something needs to be done, he can expect it will be done. He knows he will have a significant effect in people's lives for he has a vision, and by exerting special influence he will move the group toward goals of beneficial permanence. He is aware of the impact and influence he has on other people's lives.

On the other hand, leadership brings with it an awesome responsibility, and the leader is constantly aware of this. Ultimately, the leader is responsible for the well-being of the group. If there is a serious threat to the group's welfare, it is the leader who must find a solution. Others can comment, criticize, or have the luxury of merely talking about the problem. But the leader must find a solution. The people in the group expect him to do it.

The leader is part of the group, but he is also set apart; to some extent, he must distance himself from the other members of the group. This contributes to making the leader aware of his leadership role.

The early church leaders held a council in Jerusalem to discuss the divisive issue of whether Gentiles needed to be circumcised before they became Christians. There was much debate. After an appropriate time of interaction, James, the leader of the church, declared, "Therefore, I judge. . . ." He was keenly aware of his leadership role, which allowed him to listen to certain controversial issues, consider God's leading in the matter, and make the decision for the group.

THE LEADER IS AWARE OF THE MEANING OF LEADERSHIP

Leadership is the discipline of deliberately exerting special influence within a group to move it toward goals of beneficial permanence that fulfill the group's real needs.

Reread this definition of leadership. Think about it. Memorize it. Analyze it. Begin by centering your awareness on each of the components. Then think about that component's interaction with every other component. It will take time and effort, but the leadership our changing world demands deserves your best attention.

Leadership is a discipline. It is hard work. It takes effort and concentration. It takes staying power.

Leadership is deliberate. The leader leaves nothing to chance. Daily he's fine-tuning his leadership skills. Having carefully thought out his plan of action, the leader deliberately exerts special influence. His vision is deliberate (even when he receives a divine call, he deliberately responds). His choice of the group is deliberate. His selection of goals is deliberate. His assessment of the real needs of the group is deliberate. The orientation of his leadership to beneficial permanence is deliberate.

Leadership exerts special influence geared to change. When people want an improved lifestyle, they look to a leader for direction. The leader can change the course of history for God and for good. When the infant mortality rate is shockingly high, people look to a leader for an improved change. When thugs terrorize the public so that people are afraid to leave their homes at night, they look to a leader who will give direction.

John Sung, the Chinese scholar-preacher-leader, visited Indonesia for a few months in 1938. He organized five thousand evangelistic teams, each team composed of three young men. So great was his leadership that long after he had left Indonesia, the teams continued their work. Many observers have concluded that the influence and impact of these 15,000 young men, middle-aged by 1965, contributed toward the abortion of the Communist-attempted coup. Change calls for leadership and the leader exerts special influence geared to change.

Leadership sets goals of beneficial permanence. The leader takes his role seriously and sets goals that are continuing, enduring, and lasting, and in harmony with God's will for the group.

Leadership focuses on fulfilling real needs. This means that the leader understands his people well enough to distinguish between what they say they want and what they really need. The leader maintains a sensitivity to and a keen awareness of the people for whom God has given him responsibility.

THE LEADER IS AWARE OF THE PRINCIPLES OF LEADERSHIP

It will be good for us to review what we have discussed as the principles of leadership because leaders are aware not only of their own leadership roles and the meaning of leadership, but they are aware of the principles of leadership. These principles are the essential elements of effective leadership. Just as the writer is constantly aware of rules of good grammar while he is writing, the leader is constantly aware of the guidelines to effective goalsetting or the necessity of exhibiting energy while he is leading.

The Principle of Vision

Leadership begins with a vision. A vision is a clear picture of what the leader sees his group being or doing. A vision could be of health where there is sickness, of knowledge where there is ignorance, of freedom where there is oppression, or of love where there is hatred. The leader is wholeheartedly committed to his vision, which involves beneficial change for the group. The leader is aware of the importance of his vision and makes it the driving force behind his leadership.

The leader also seeks to communicate his vision to his followers. He captures their attention with his optimistic intuition of possible solutions to their needs. He influences them by the dynamism of his faith. He demonstrates confidence that the challenge can be met, the need resolved, the crisis overcome. If his followers grasp the vision, the group will become more cohesive and be able to work together toward a common goal. The significance of a person's leadership depends on the "bigness" of his vision; the effectiveness of a person's leadership depends on how well he moves the group toward the fulfillment of that vision and their needs.

Since the leader's vision is the basis of his leadership and since he is to be wholeheartedly and enthusiastically committed to the vision—that commitment is called the mission—the leader must be constantly aware of his vision. It must be before him always so that he will not grow weary in working toward the vision's fulfillment, nor will he be sidetracked into doing things that do not contribute to the fulfillment of the vision.

A God-given vision is an awesome responsibility. Fulfillment can lead you to heights of tremendous service to God and your fellow humans. Or failure to follow the vision will deprive others of the leadership they need. The leader must constantly be aware of his vision, be aware of whether he is effectively communicating it to the people in his group, and be aware of whether the group is moving toward fulfilling the vision.

The Principle of Goalsetting

Having a vision is not enough. There must be a commitment to act on the vision. That is called a mission. There must also be a set of specific, measurable steps designed to achieve the mission. Those steps are called goals. Goals design the program for achieving the mission and thus fulfilling the vision.

Goals must be S-M-A-R-T: specific, measurable, attainable, realistic, and tangible. The leader must also predicate his goals on his own behavior rather than on hoped-for behavior of others. He should let his mind soar and not limit God when he sets his goals. The leader should write out his goals in detail. He should also state his goals positively, and he should make his goals personal ones.

Because goals need constant review, the leader must constantly be aware of the goalsetting process. Goalsetting is not a one-time exercise. Rather, it is an ongoing discipline. As soon as one goal is accomplished, another goal—which also contributes to fulfilling the vision—takes its place.

Effective goalsetting demands a constant awareness of the leader's goals: goals that have just been accomplished, goals on which the group is now working, and goals that are about to be adopted. An awareness of the goals that have just been accomplished will be a great encouragement to both the leader and the group as they consider other goals.

The Principle of Love

There cannot be leadership without love. *Love* as used here refers to a mindset, an act of the will. It includes unconquerable consideration, charitableness, benevolence. It means no matter what people do by way of humiliation, abuse, or injury, the Christlike leader works toward their highest good. Without this kind of love, leadership fails the ultimate test—permanence.

The exercise of the principle of love demands awareness. Love relates to the real needs of people and the leader must, therefore, know what those real needs are. He must be aware by constantly searching them out because the needs change. What the needs were last month is different from what they are today. Also, the leader cannot show love only when he wants to or when he has the time. The essence of showing love is that it must be done when the other person needs it or wants it. It takes awareness and perceptiveness to determine when those times are.

In chapter 4, ten principles were given of how to express love to our neighbor. Each one demands a high degree of awareness to make it work. For instance, consider, "It takes a conscious effort to nurture an authentic interest in others"; "It will always take time—often a long time—to understand one another"; "Simply be there to care, whether you know exactly what to do or not"; "Emphasize the strengths and virtues of others, not their sins and weaknesses." All these principles demand awareness.

Love sets a true leader apart from a power-holder. If one is a power-holder, he does not have to be aware of his followers if his position is defended securely. But if one leads by love, a high degree of awareness is essential. The goal of a leader, however, is not just to practice love himself, but also to build love into the lives of those who follow him. He should be a role model, showing how love works, demonstrating its development, its practice, and its benefit.

The Principle of Humility

Humility is the lowliness that pervades the leader's consciousness when he contemplates God's holy majesty and superabundant love in contrast to his own unworthiness, guilt, and total helplessness apart from divine grace. The humble person is free from pride or arrogance. He is willing to submit himself to others and is helpful and courteous. The humble person does not consider himself to be self-sufficient, and yet he recognizes his own gifts, resources, and achievements. Both love and humility are characteristic of true leaders.

It is not accurate to say that the leader is aware of any aspect of his humility, for humility has no self-consciousness. There is a sense in which the humble person is *not* aware. He is not aware of wrongs done to him; he is not aware of presumptuous attitudes of others; he is not aware of his own humility. However, the spirit of humility frees the leader to concentrate on the real needs of others. He doesn't dissipate his energies wondering what kind of impression he is making. While the leader is not aware of his own humility, he is watchful of those things in himself that would violate humility.

The Principle of Self-Control

Self-control is a way of life in which, by the power of the Holy Spirit, the Christian is able to be temperate in all things because he does not let his desires master his life. Self-control is usually seen as a restriction. And yet it is impossible to permanently defeat the leader who exercises self-control, for self-control brings freedom, confidence, joy, stability, and a stronger sense of leadership.

Self-control is an essential attitude and characteristic for a leader. Without it, the leader diminishes his effectiveness and will lose the respect of his followers. With it, people will view him as one who has the determination and strength to be in charge.

Awareness is an essential ingredient in the development of self-control. This is because successful leadership requires self-control and yet successful leadership makes it difficult to practice self-control. Therefore, it is only by being constantly aware of the need to practice the steps to self-control that it will happen. Our natural tendency is to revert to a state of a lack of discipline and control. Self-control is developed through dependence on God, through a life of discipline, through making decisions ahead of time, through gratitude for adversity, through ruling your spirit, through controlling your thoughts, and through control by the Holy Spirit.

Self-control is love's mastery. It is something most people rebel at or avoid. But strength and power in leadership come from developing self-control. Awareness can produce self-control, but self-control will also produce in you a greater awareness of yourself and others.

The Principle of Communication

The ability to communicate through speech and writing is possibly the leader's most valuable asset. To develop this ability takes careful attention to the seven rules of communication. To use this ability on a day-to-day basis takes an awareness that makes these rules second nature.

The leader needs to be aware of the importance of effective communication. Each time he speaks or writes, he must be aware of the need to create understanding, not just to repeat words.

The leader must be in the habit of assessing his audience. He must determine its characteristics and attitudes before he starts to speak or write. He must be aware.

The leader must select the right communication goal. The goal is determined by his assessment of the audience and the purpose of his communication. An awareness of the goal will permeate everything he does while he speaks or writes.

The leader must break the preoccupation barrier. He must be aware of the concerns and desires of his audience and what will attract the audience's attention. While he is speaking, the leader should be aware of the audience's reaction so that he can tailor what he says and how he says it to the particular audience.

The leader must refer to the audience's experience. Again, the leader must know his audience. However, his assessment is not static, and he must be aware of changes in the audience. He must be sensitive to the audience becoming hostile, tired, enthusiastic, or agreeable. Awareness is the key.

The leader must use cumulation, restatement, exposition, comparison, general illustration, specific instance, or testimony to support his assertions. The leader must be aware of what will work best in his particular situation.

The leader must motivate action by an appeal to desire. He wants action. He wants to effect change. The most effective way to do that is by an appeal to the dominant desire of the particular audience.

Awareness is the key to effective communication. The leader must be aware of his audience, aware of the communication principles he is using, and aware of the effect they are having on his audience. Communication is a process; it is not static. The leader should constantly evaluate his communication, based on the feedback he receives from his audience, to see if it needs to be changed. That takes constant awareness.

The Principle of Investment

Wise investment demands awareness. A profitable investment is possible without awareness, but it would be the result of happenstance, not planning. The wise investor does not depend on happenstance, but instead he studies industry trends, market conditions, government regulations, and other factors that may have an impact on his investment in order to be in control. He is aware.

The principle of investment for leaders says that if you invest or give something, you will receive it back many times over. If you invest friendship, you will have friends. If you invest love, you will be loved. If you respect others, you will be respected. And if you invest money, you will receive it back many times over. It is possible to benefit from the principle of investment without being aware, but that is the result of haphazard action. The effective leader will want to plan his use of the principle of investment to maximize its benefit to his group.

The effective leader will be aware of and practice the ten commandments for investment:

(1) Recognize that God is the provider.
(2) Keep your mind on the things you want and off the things you don't want as long as these are compatible with the will of God.
(3) Invest what you want.
(4) Invest on the front end.
(5) Be patient.
(6) Do not be deterred by an occasional crop failure.
(7) Put your money where you want your heart to be.
(8) Rejoice.
(9) Expect results.
(10) Give God the glory.

There are two kinds of people in the world: the investors and the takers. The investors, by their nature, practice the principle of investment; the takers try to hoard whatever they have or spend it on themselves. Ultimately the takers lose. They lose disposition, friends, health, and respect. The investors win.

The leader is aware of the principle of investment and the ten commandments for investment. He seeks to master them and to make giving a habit both for himself and for those whom he leads.

The Principle of Opportunity

Your greatest opportunities are cleverly disguised as insurmountable problems. The principle of opportunity says that life is a series of obstacles and these obstacles hold the key to your greatest opportunities if you only discipline yourself to see opportunities everywhere.

Exercising the principle of opportunity, therefore, takes awareness. The effective leader looks for opportunities. Exercising this principle also demands an attitude that knows how to handle mistakes and turn blunders into benefits. Cultivating this attitude will heighten your awareness of opportunities.

In 1970, James Howard was the 42-year-old head of the sixth largest public-relations agency in America. But he felt "out of control." He was unhappy with the way he saw some of his clients doing business and he had a nervous breakdown. He sold the agency, moved to the quiet of Vermont, and began to put himself and his career back together.

It would seem as if James Howard had failed. But out of the obstacle of his nervous breakdown came Howard's greatest opportunity. He took the time to discover himself. He wrote out his vision and mission and a new set of goals. He analyzed four sample brokerage businesses he might want to pursue: farm and timber, solar homes, real estate, and small businesses. From this emerged Country Business Services, America's most successful small-business brokerage firm. James Howard carefully and systematically turned his obstacle into an opportunity.

These are the ten steps to successfully dealing with blunders so that the greatest awareness of available opportunities can emerge:

First, admit the blunder the moment you know about it.

Second, assume accountability for the blunder.

Third, evaluate the damage.

Fourth, do an in-depth study of the possible causes of the blunder.

Fifth, immediately eliminate the causes of the blunder.

Sixth, salvage what you can.

Seventh, revise your *modus operandi* so that the blunder won't be repeated.

Eighth, begin to execute your new program immediately.

Ninth, use blunders as road signs.

Tenth, remember that obstacles enhance leadership.

The Principle of Energy

Energy attracts attention. Energy attracts followers. The leader who demonstrates enthusiasm and energy will gain the acceptance and confidence of others. Most people are drawn to the person with energy because energy conveys the ideas of authority, of excitement, of success, of purposeful activity, and people want to be identified with those things.

The leader's energy is demonstrated through physical vitality. Even though he may be older or have a physical handicap, he radiates good health and purposeful activity. The leader's energy is demonstrated through mental alertness. He is not necessarily an intellectual giant, but he will use his mind to its fullest for observation, foresight and reflection, and reasoning. The leader's energy is demonstrated through hard work. Work is the most common expression of human energy, and the leader will enjoy it and pursue it. The leader's physical, intellectual, and emotional energy is demonstrated through commitment and perseverance as he believes in and works toward his goal against all odds. A leader's energy is demonstrated through attention to details because he knows the little things will make him or break him.

The effective leader is aware of the importance of energy to a person in a position of leadership and consciously tries to build up his own energy level. He does this through eating right, exercising, maintaining a proper attitude, eliminating negative emotions, and walking in fellowship with God.

The leader who understands the principle of energy is aware of the importance of demonstrating energy before his followers. They will not be more enthusiastic or more energetic than the leader himself is. He knows that the organization will not rise above the level he exhibits. He therefore carefully cultivates the principle of energy in himself.

The Principle of Staying Power

Difficulties do exist. The leader will have problems and discouragements. But God wants him to persevere in following the vision He has given. The principle of staying power says that these problems and difficulties can be overcome, but the leader has to hang in there. He has to have staying power.

Every problem has its own solution, and although the solutions are different, staying power is the key to each one. Sometimes God's answer to a problem is that He will not remove the problem from us, as was Job's experience. In those instances, staying power is especially needed. Staying power can overcome illness, personal desires, financial limitations, the perils of prosperity, family opposition, betrayal and persecution, misinterpretation of events, and a host of other impossibilities.

Many leaders at some time question whether they ought to quit. When those moments hit, they can strengthen their staying power by remembering their vision, by focusing on their goals, by visualizing their goals as being already accomplished, by relaxation, by reading biographies, and by living in communion with God. Staying power insures success because it indicates a strong awareness to a commitment.

I believe it was Ho Chi Minh who explained why the North Vietnamese would eventually win the war in Viet Nam. He said that he could lose ten soldiers to every American soldier killed because eventually the Americans would get tired and leave as the French had done. Ho Chi Minh's comment showed a terrible disregard for human life, but he was in part correct. Historians will long discuss the actual factors contributing to the American withdrawal from Viet Nam, but certainly the staying power of the North Vietnamese was one of them.

It seems as if many of the world's greatest leaders found some of the greatest difficulties and discouragements in carrying out their visions. But what made them great was their success that came because of staying power.

The Principle of Authority

Authority demands awareness. A leader cannot exercise the principle of authority without being aware of what he is doing and why.

Consider the biblical story of Joseph. Alert to the prospect of God's prophesied famine, Joseph, during the preceding seven years of prosperity, ordered all the inhabitants of Egypt to surrender their surplus grain. He would save it until the famine, during which time he would ration it. Surely Joseph's order angered many of the Egyptians. But his superior leadership, marked with authority, served the real needs of the people and sustained them throughout the famine. Joseph was aware of the use he was making of his authority and probably used not only his internal authority, but his external authority as well.

Internal authority is that which causes a leader to command the respect of others and by which the leader can exert a powerful influence over others by virtue of his own charisma and personality. Internal authority has nothing to do with a person's physical characteristics or actions, with his wealth, social position, or status. Nor is it derived from success. Rather, internal authority is a conviction that you can move the people in your group toward goals of beneficial permanence.

The person with internal authority is an individualist with a strong sense of self-esteem.

External authority, on the other hand, causes a person to exert an influence over others by virtue of symbols or position. External authority is developed by manipulating situations and people. External authority can be taken away from a person; internal authority cannot.

The principle of authority recognizes the distinction between internal and external authority and says that the leader should develop and enhance his internal authority. Internal authority is developed by discovering yourself so that you know who you are and so that you are happy with what you know. It is developed by acquiring self-confidence. It is developed by believing in the importance of your mission. It is developed by not revealing fatigue, by keeping your own counsel, and by respecting the rights and emotions of others. It is developed by striving for excellence. Internal authority is developed by believing in your own success.

Every normal person possesses the seeds of internal authority, some in greater measure than others. Those seeds can be developed through cultivating awareness of authority to the benefit of the people led and, above all, to the glory of God.

THE LEADER IS AWARE THAT GOD IS HIS RESOURCE

The leader is aware of his own leadership role, he is aware of the meaning of leadership, and he is aware of the principles of leadership. As he lives in the awareness that he is a leader, he may react, "But I feel so unworthy." Of course he feels that way. Any rational, spiritually sensitive person feels unworthy to the task of Christlike leadership.

Paul the apostle said that he was "the least of the apostles." He admitted freely that he was not perfect, but he learned that God's grace was sufficient and that God's strength was made perfect in weakness.

Jeremiah said, "Behold, I cannot speak, for I am a youth." But God told Jeremiah to stop complaining. He said, "For I am with you to deliver you. . . . Behold I have put My words in your mouth. See, I have this day set you over the nations and over the kingdoms to root out and to pull down. To destroy and to throw down. To build and to plant" (Jeremiah 1:8–10).

When nineteen-year-old Charles Haddon Spurgeon was invited to become pastor of the new Park Street Church in London, he honestly believed that there had been a mistake and the invitation was meant for another man by the same name! But Spurgeon became the most influential Baptist pastor in history. He understood that his strength came from the Lord.

A few weeks before writing this, I was in Japan, the guest of a close friend and director of Haggai Institute. Unashamedly, this multinational businessman, who uses his vocation as a conduit for Christlike leadership, said, "Without Christ, I could do nothing."

You must rely on supernatural resources. This presupposes that you live in the awareness of God's presence and power. While you may feel unworthy, you must not despair. Your resources are in God, but you must exercise the faith and discipline to appropriate them.

God is calling leaders. Not power-holders. Not Madison Avenue hype artists. Not mutual congratulation experts. Not influence peddlers. Not crowd-manipulating, exhibitionistic demagogues. God is calling leaders!

Will you respond to this call in dependence on God Himself for your strength?

SUMMARY

Awareness undergirds excellence. This is true in all areas of endeavor. The principle of awareness calls for the leader to be aware of the elements that contribute to excellent performance and constantly measure his own performance against the standards of excellence he has set for himself. Awareness is the keystone in the arch of leadership. Knock out the keystone, and the arch, which consists of leadership principles, comes crashing down.

The leader is aware of his own leadership role. He knows he is in charge. He is aware of the impact and influence he has on other people's lives. He enjoys the privileges and bears the awesome responsibilities that go with giving direction to a group's future.

The leader is aware of the meaning of leadership. Leadership is the discipline of deliberately exerting special influence within a group to move it toward goals of beneficial permanence that fulfill the group's real needs. The leader knows each component of that meaning and how the components interact with each other.

The leader is aware of the principles of leadership:

(1) The principle of vision. Since the leader's vision is the basis of his leadership, he must be constantly aware of his vision, of whether he is effectively communicating it to those in the group, and of whether the group is moving toward fulfilling the vision.

(2) The principle of goalsetting. Because goals need constant review, the leader must constantly be aware of the goalsetting process. Goalsetting is an ongoing discipline.

(3) The principle of love. Love relates to the real needs of people and the leader must, therefore, be aware of what those real needs are.

(4) The principle of humility. The leader is not aware of his own humility, for humility has no self-consciousness. But the leader is watchful of those things in himself that would violate humility.

(5) The principle of self-control. Awareness is an essential ingredient in the development of self-control because successful leadership requires self-control and yet successful leadership makes it difficult to practice self-control.

(6) The principle of communication. Communication is a process that is always occurring. The leader needs to communicate effectively by being constantly aware of the seven rules of communication and making them second nature to himself. Awareness is the key to effective communication.

(7) The principle of investment. It is possible to benefit from the principle of investment without being aware, but that would be the result of haphazard action. The effective leader will want to plan his use of the principle of investment to maximize its benefit to his group.

(8) The principle of opportunity. A person's greatest opportunities are cleverly disguised as insurmountable problems. Through awareness, the leader must discipline himself to see opportunities everywhere.

(9) The principle of energy. The effective leader is aware of the importance of energy to a person in a position of leadership and consciously tries to build up his own energy level.

(10) The principle of staying power. Difficulties do exist. There will be problems. But these difficulties and problems can be overcome (not necessarily eliminated) by staying power.

(11) The principle of authority. A leader cannot exercise the principle of authority without being aware of what he is doing and why. He is aware of both his internal authority as well as his external authority.

(12) The principle of awareness says the leader will be aware of his own leadership, constantly monitoring his performance so that he can achieve excellence.

The leader is also aware that God is his resource. He understands that his strength comes from the Lord.

Recommended Reading List

Adler, Mortimer J. *How to Speak, How to Listen.* New York: Macmillan Publishing Company, Inc., 1983.

Augustine, Saint. *Saint Augustine's Confessions.* New York: Penguin Books, 1961. Published every year or two since 1961.

Bennis, Warren, and Burt Nanus. *Leaders: The Strategies for Taking Charge.* New York: Harper and Row, 1985.

Blamires, Harry. *The Christian Mind: How Should a Christian Think.* Ann Arbor: Servant Books, 1963.

Bogardus, Henry S. *Leaders and Leadership.* New York: Appleton-Century-Crofts, Inc., 1934*.

Bounds, E. M. *Power through Prayer.* Louisville: Pentecostal Publishing Company.

Bready, J. Wesley. *Faith and Freedom.* New York: American Tract Society, 1946.

———. *Freedom Whence.* Winona Lake: Light and Life Press, 1956.

Brion, Marcel. *Attila, Scourge of God.* Translated by Harold Ward. London: Cassell and Company, Ltd., 1929.

Brown, Barbara B. *New Mind, New Body.* New York: Bantam Books, 1974.

Burr, Agnes Rush. *Russell H. Conwell and His Work.* Philadelphia: John C. Winston Company, 1926*.

Butterfield, Fox. *China, Alive in the Bitter Sea.* New York: Bantam Books, 1982.

Chambers, Oswald. *My Utmost for His Highest.* New York: Dodd, Mead & Company, 1935.

Colson, Charles W. *Born Again.* Old Tappan, New Jersey: Chosen Books, distributed by Fleming H. Revell Company, 1976.

———. *Life Sentence.* Lincoln, Virginia: Chosen Books distributed by Word Books, 1979.

———. *Loving God.* Grand Rapids: Zondervan Publishing Company, 1983.

Connelly, Thomas L. *The Marble Man: Robert E. Lee and His Image in American Society.* New York: Alfred Knopf, 1977.

---

* Although these books are out of print, I feel you would find it worthwhile to find copies and read them.

Cooper, Kenneth H. *The Aerobics Program for Total Well Being.* New York: M. Evans and Company, 1982.

Curtis, Richard Kenneth. *They Called Him Mr. Moody.* Garden City, New York: Doubleday and Company, Inc., 1962.

Daniels, Peter J. *How to be Happy Though Rich.* Unley Park, South Australia: The House of Taylor, 1984.

Dasgupta, A. *Some Management Skills.* Delhi: Department of Business Management and Industrial Administration, University of Delhi, 1968.

Dobbins, Gaines S. *Learning to Lead.* Nashville: Broadman Press, 1968.

Drakeford, John W. *Psychology in Search of a Soul.* Nashville: Broadman Press, 1964.

Drucker, Peter F. *The Effective Executive.* New York: Harper Colophon, 1985; New York: Harper Row Publishers, 1966.

Edersheim, Alfred. *The Life and Times of Jesus the Messiah.* Grand Rapids: William B. Eerdmans Publishing Company, 1947.

Egri, Lajos. *The Art of Dramatic Writing: Its Basis in the Creative Interpretation of Human Motives.* New York: Simon and Schuster; A Touchtone Book, 1960.

Eims, Leroy. *Be the Leader You Are Meant to Be.* Wheaton: Victor Books, 1975.

Engel, Peter H. *The Overachievers.* New York: Dial Press, 1976.

Engstrom, Ted W. *The Making of a Christian Leader.* Grand Rapids: Zondervan Publishing Company, 1976.

Erwin, Gayle D. *The Jesus Style.* Palm Springs, California: Ronald N. Haynes Publishers, Inc., 1983. Assigned to Word Books, Publishers, 1985.

Eubank and Auer. *Discussion and Debate.* New York: F. S. Crofts and Company, 1946.

Fitzwater, P. B. *Christian Theology.* Grand Rapids: William B. Eerdmans, 1948*.

Flesch, Rudolf. *How to Write, Speak, and Think More Effectively.* New York: The New American Library of World Literature, Inc., Signet Books, 1960.

Forbes, B. *America's Twelve Master Salesmen.* New York: Forbes and Sons Publishing Company, Inc., 1952.

Forbes, Rosalind. *Corporate Stress.* Garden City, New York: Doubleday and Company, Inc., 1979.

———. *Life Stress.* Garden City, New York: Doubleday and Company, Inc. 1979.

Garfield, Charles A. *Peak Performance.* Boston: Houghton Mifflin Company, 1984.

Garn, Roy. *The Magic Power of Emotional Appeal.* Englewood Cliffs, New Jersey: Prentice Hall, 1960.

Geneen, Harold. *Managing.* Garden City, New York: Doubleday and Company, 1984.

Gillies, John. *Memoirs of Reverend George Whitfield.* Hartford: Edwin Hunt, 1845*.

Greenleaf, Robert K. *Servant Leadership.* New York: Paulist Press, 1977.

Griffin, Emory A. *The Mind Changers, The Art of Christian Persuasion.* Wheaton, Illinois: Tyndale House Publishers; Eastbourne, England: Coverdale House Publishers, Ltd., 1976.

Haggai, John. *How to Win Over Worry.* Grand Rapids: Zondervan Publishing House, 1959.

———. *New Hope for Planet Earth.* Nashville: Thomas Nelson Publishers, 1974.

———. *My Son Johnny.* Wheaton, Illinois: Tyndale House Publishers, Inc., 1978.

———. *How to Win Over Loneliness.* Nashville: Thomas Nelson Publishers, 1979.

———. *The Steward.* Atlanta, Georgia: Haggai Institute, 1983.

Harvey, Paul. *The Rest of the Story. . . .* Compiled by Lynne Harvey. Chicago: Paulynne, Inc., 1969.

Hayes, James L. *Memos for Management: Leadership.* New York: AMACOM, 1983.

Hiebert, Paul G. *Cultural Anthropology.* Grand Rapids: Baker Book House, 1976.

Hopkins, C. Howard. *John R. Mott, 1865-1955, A Biography.* Grand Rapids: William B. Eerdmans Publishing Company, 1979.

Hughes, John. *Indonesian Upheaval.* New York: David McKay Company, Inc., 1967.

Iaccocca, Lee. *Iaccocca, An Autobiography.* New York: Bantam Books, 1984.

Jones, E. Stanley. *A Song of Ascents: A Spiritual Autobiography.* Nashville: Abingdon Press, 1979.

Josey, Alex. *Lee Kuan Yew: The Struggle for Singapore.* London: Angus and Robertson Publishers, 1976.

Kiev, Ari. *A Strategy for Daily Living.* New York: Free Press, a division of Macmillan Publishing Company, Inc., 1973.

Knight, James Allen. *For the Love of Money.* Philadelphia: Lippincott, 1968.

Kriegel, Robert, and Kriegel, Marilyn Harris. *The C Zone, Peak Performance Under Pressure.* Garden City, New York: Anchor Press/Doubleday and Company, 1984.

Laszlo, Ervin, et al. *Goals for Mankind.* New York: E. P. Dutton, 1977.

Lee, Josh. *Public Speaking.* Oklahoma City: Harlow Publishing Corporation, 1936*.

Levinson, Harry. *Executive.* Cambridge: Harvard University Press, 1981.

Liechtenberger, Henri. *The Third Reich,* Translated and edited by Koppel S. Pinson. Freeport, New York: Books for Library Press, 1969.

Lyall, Leslie. *Flame for God: John Soong and Revival in the Far East.* London: Overseas Missionary Fellowship, 1976.

Mackay, John A. *Christian Reality and Appearance.* Richmond: John Knox Press, 1969.

Macmillan, D. *The Life of George Matheson.* London: Hodder and Stoughton, 1908. The story of this blind Scot inspires me as do few biographies.

Marshall, Catherine. *A Man Called Peter, The Story of Peter Marshall.* New York: McGraw Hill Book Company, Inc., 1951.

Marts, Arnaud C. *The Generosity of Americans: Its Source, Its Achievements.* Englewood Cliffs, New Jersey: Prentice Hall, Inc., 1966.

Matthews, Basil. *John R. Mott, World Citizen.* New York: Harper and Brothers, 1934.

McCartney, Clarence E. *The Making of a Minister, Autobiography of Clarence E. McCartney.* Great Neck, New York: Channel Press, Inc., 1961.

McCormack, Mark H. *What They Don't Teach You at Harvard Business School.* New York: Bantam Books, 1984.

McLoughlin, William G., Jr. *Billy Sunday Was His Real Name.* Chicago: University of Chicago Press, 1955*.

Meyer, Paul J. *Dynamics of Goal Setting.* Waco, Texas: Success Motivation Institute, 1977. Lesson manual, cassette tapes and plan of action. I highly recommend all materials produced by Success Motivation Institute, Post Office Box 7614, Waco, Texas 76714–8018.

———. *Dynamics of Personal Motivation.* Third Edition. Waco, Texas: Success Motivation Institute, 1983. A kit consisting of: "Lesson Manual," "Cassette Tapes," and "A Plan of Action"—covering 16 lessons.

Montgomery, Field-Marshal. *Path to Leadership.* New York: G. T. Putnam and Sons, 1961.

Morgan, G. Campbell. *The Crises of the Christ.* Old Tappan, New Jersey: Fleming H. Revell Company, 1903.

Muir, Sir William. *The Life of Mohammed.* Edinburgh: John Grant, 1923.

Mulando, Godfrey. *How Much Shall I Give?* Ndola, Zambia: Copperbelt Christian Publications, 1977.

Naisbitt, John. *Megatrends, Ten New Directions Transforming Our Lives.* New York: Warner Books, 1982.

Nehru, Jawaharlal. *The Discovery of India.* New York: John Day Publishers, 1946.

Nixon, Richard. *Leaders.* New York: Warner Books, Inc., 1982.

Nizer, Louis. *Thinking on Your Feet.* New York: Norton Company (Liveright Publishing Company), 1963.

————. *The Jury Returns.* Garden City, New York: Doubleday and Company, 1966.

Ogilvy, David. *Confessions of an Advertising man.* New York: Dell Publishing Company, 1963.

————. *On Advertising.* New York: Vintage Books (A Division of Random House), 1985.

Ostrander, Sheila; and Schroeder, Lynn; with Ostrander, Nancy. *Super-Learning.* New York: Dell Publishing Company, Inc., 1979.

Otto, Herbert A. *Guide to Developing Your Potential.* New York: Charles Scribners Sons, 1957.

"Paths Toward Personal Progress: Leaders Are Made, Not Born." *Harvard Business Review* (1980).

Peters, Tom, and Austin, Nancy. *A Passion for Excellence.* New York: Random House, 1985.

Phillips, Arthur Edward. *Effective Speaking.* Chicago: The Newton Company, 1922*.

Pierce, Earl V. *The Supreme Beatitude.* Old Tappan, New Jersey: Fleming H. Revell, 1947.

Pollock, John. *The Man Who Shook the World.* Wheaton: Victor Books, 1972.

Reischauer, Edwin O. *The Japanese.* Tokyo: Charles E. Tuttle Company, 1977.

Roeder, O. G. *The Smiling General, President Soeharto of Indonesia.* Jakarta: Gunung Agung Ltd., 1969.

Roman, Kenneth, and Raphaelson, Joel. *Writing That Works.* New York: Harper and Row, 1981.

Rusher, William A. *How to Win Arguments.* Garden City, New York: Doubleday and Company, 1981.

Rutt, Richard. *History of the Korean People.* Seoul: Taewon Publishing Company, 1972.

Ryle, J. C. *Christian Leaders of the Eighteenth Century.* Edinburgh: The Banner of Truth Trust, 1885*.

Sadat, Anwar. *Sadat, An Autobiography.* London: Fontana/Collins, 1978.

Sandburg, Carl. *Abraham Lincoln: The Prairie Years and the War Years.* New York: Harcourt Brace, 1954.

Sangster, W. E. *The Secret of a Radiant Life.* Nashville: Abingdon Press, 1957.

Sarnoff, Dorothy. *Speech Can Change Your Life.* New York: Dell Publishing Company, 1970.

————. *Make the Most of Your Best.* New York: Doubleday, 1981.

Scammell, Michael. *Solzhenitsyn.* New York: W. W. Norton and Company, 1985; London: Hutchinson, 1984.

Schilder, K. *Christ on Trial.* Grand Rapids: William B. Eerdmans Publishing Company, 1945.

————. *Christ In His Suffering.* Grand Rapids: William B. Eerdmans Publishing Company, 1945.

————. *Christ Crucified.* Grand Rapids: William B. Eerdmans Publishing Company, 1945.

Seabury, David. *How to Get Things Done.* Garden City, New York: Halcyn House, 1938.

Seagrave, Sterling. *The Soong Dynasty.* New York: Harper and Row, 1985.

Sharpe, Robert F. *Before You Give Another Dime.* Nashville: Thomas Nelson Publishers, 1979.

Simonton, Carl O.; Simonton, Stephanie Matthews; and Creighton, James L. *Getting Well Again.* New York: Bantam Books, 1978.

Spurgeon, Charles Haddon. *C. H. Spurgeon's Autobiography.* 4 Vols. London: Passmore and Alabaster, 1899–1900.

Swindoll, Charles R. *Hand Me Another Brick.* Nashville: Thomas Nelson Publishers, 1978.

———. *Leadership.* Waco: Word Books, Publisher, 1985.

Taylor, Jeremy. *Taylor's Life of Christ.* London: William Pickering, 1849*.

Taylor, Robert Lewis. *Winston Churchill.* New York: Pocket Books, Inc., 1952.

Templeton, John M. *The Humble Approach: Scientists Discover God.* New York: Seabury Press, 1981.

Torrey, R. A. *The Power of Prayer and the Prayer of Power.* Grand Rapids: Zondervan Publishing House, 1924.

Townsend, Derek. *Gigsaw: the Biography of Johannes Bjelke-Petersen.* Brisbane, Queensland, Australia: Sneyd and Morley, 1983.

Tzu, Sun. *The Art of War.* Translated by Samuel B. Griffith. London: Oxford University Press, 1963.

Villari, Pasquale. *The Life and Times of Girolamo Savonarola.* Translated by Linda Villari. New York: Charles Scribner Sons, 1888*.

Vitz, Paul C. *Psychology As Religion: The Cult of Self-worship.* Grand Rapids: William B. Eerdmans Publishing Company, 1977.

Waitley, Denis. *The Winner's Edge: the Critical Attitude of Success.* New York: Times Books, 1980.

———. *Seeds of Greatness.* Old Tappan, New Jersey: Fleming H. Revell, 1983.

Wallace, Lew. *Ben Hur, A Tale of the Christ.* New York: Harper and Brothers, 1880.

Wall Street Journal Staff. *Here Comes Tomorrow: Living and Working in the Year 2000.* Princeton: Dow Jones Books, 1966.

Weber, Max. *On Charisma and Institution Building.* Chicago and London: The University of Chicago Press, 1968.

Wesley, John. *The Journal of John Wesley.* 8 Vols. London: Epworth Press, 1938.

Williamson, Porter B. *Patton's Principles.* New York: Simon and Schuster, 1979.

Wills, Garry. *Nixon Agonistes, The Crisis of the Self-made Man.* New York: New American Library, 1971.

Wonder, Jacqueline, and Donavan, Priscilla. *Whole-brain Thinking: Working Both Sides of the Brain to Achieve Peak Job Performance.* New York: W. Morrow; Valentine Books, 1984.

Wood, A. Skevington. *The Burning Heart, John Wesley: Evangelist.* Exeter, Great Britain: Paternostra Press, Ltd., 1967.

Youssef, Michael. *Revolt Against Modernity: Muslim Zealots and the West.* Leiden: E. J. Brill, 1985.

———. *The Leadership Style of Jesus.* Wheaton: Victor Books, 1986.

Notes

[1] W. C. H. Prentice, "Understanding Leadership," *Harvard Business Review,* Number 61511, September-October, 1961, quoted in *Paths Toward Personal Progress: Leaders Are Made, Not Born* (Boston: Harvard Business Review, 1980), page 1.

[2] William Pfaff, editorial, *International Herald Tribune,* 26 June 1983.

[3] Quoted in Stephen B. Oates, *Let the Trumpet Sound: The Life of Martin Luther King, Jr.* (New York: Harper & Row, 1982), pages 260–261.

[4] Peter J. Daniels, *How to Be Happy Though Rich* (Unley Park, South Australia: The House of Taylor, 1984), pages 113–123.

[5] Wilbur M. Smith, *Will H. Houghton, A Watchman on the Wall* (Grand Rapids, Michigan: William B. Eerdmans Publishing Company, 1951), page 82.

[6] Edward J. Green, "Management Objectives" in William K. Fallon, editor, *AMA Management Handbook* (New York: AMACOM, 1983), pages 1–32.

[7] Harold Geneen, *Managing* (Garden City, N.Y.: Doubleday, 1984), reprinted in *Best of Business,* volume 6, page 6.

[8] John Naisbitt, *Megatrends* (New York: Warner Books, 1982), page 85.

[9] Ari Kiev, *A Strategy for Daily Living* (New York: Free Press, 1973), pages 2–3, 30.

[10] Carl O. Simonton, Stephanie Matthews Simonton, and James L. Creighton, *Getting Well Again* (New York: Bantam Books, 1978), pages 97, 173–184.

[11] Willam Funk and Norman Lewis, revised by Norman Lewis, *Thirty Days to a More Powerful Vocabulary* (Garden City, New York: Doubleday, 1984).

[12] Geneen, page 14.

[13] Denis Waitley, *Seeds of Greatness* (Old Tappan, N.J.: Fleming H. Revell, 1983), pages 27–28.

[14] Ted W. Engstrom with Robert C. Larson, *The Fine Art of Friendship* (Nashville: Thomas Nelson Publishers, 1985).

[15] *Ibid.,* pages 128–130.

[16] Erich Fromm, *The Art of Loving* (New York: Bantam Books, 1956), pages 90–92.

[17] Peter E. Gillquist, *Love Is Now* (revised edition) (Grand Rapids: Zondervan Publishing House, 1978), page 132.

[18] A. W. Tozer, *The Pursuit of God* (Harrisburg, Pennsylvania: Christian Publications, Inc., n.d.), page 113.

[19] Richard Foster, *Celebration of Discipline* (San Francisco: Harper & Row, 1978), page 5.

[20] James F. Engel, *Contemporary Christian Communications: Its Theory and Practice* (Nashville: Thomas Nelson Publishers, 1979), page 39.

[21] Herschel H. Hobbs, *Who Is This?* (Nashville: Broadman Press, 1952), page 53.

[22] Russell H. Conwell, *Acres of Diamonds* (New York: Harper & Brothers, Publishers, 1943), page 2.

[23] Victor Hugo's lecture on Voltaire, quoted by Arthur Edward Phillips in *Effective Speaking* (Chicago: The Newton Company, 1922), page 178.

[24] *Ibid.,* page 48.

[25] Roy Garn, *The Magic Power of Emotional Appeal* (Englewood Cliffs, N.J.: Prentice Hall, Inc., 1960), pages 20, 37ff.

[26] Alan H. Monroe, *Principles and Types of Speech* (revised edition) (New York: Scott, Foresman and Company, 1939), pages 132–145.

[27] S. Stansfeld Sargent, "Maslow, Abraham H. (1908–1970)," *International Encyclopedia of Psychiatry, Psychology, Psychoanalysis and Neurology,* 1977 ed., Vol. 7.

[28] Thomas J. Peters and Robert H. Waterman, Jr., *In Search of Excellence,* pages 164–165. Copyright © 1982 by Thomas J. Peters and Robert H. Waterman, Jr. by permission of Harper and Row Publishers, Inc.

[29] E. Stanley Jones, *The Way,* 5th edition (London: Hodder and Stoughton, 1963), page 155.

[30] *Webster's Ninth New Collegiate Dictionary* (Springfield, Mass.: Merriam-Webster, Inc., 1983), page 412.

[31] Quoted in Sterling North, *Young Thomas Edison* (Boston: Houghton Mifflin Company, 1958), page 115.

[32] Kenneth H. Cooper, *The Aerobics Program for Total Well Being* (New York: M. Evans and Company, 1982).

[33] Nathan Pritikin with Patrick M. McGrady, Jr., *The Pritikin Program for Diet and Exercise* (New York: Bantam Books, 1980), page xx.

[34] Marie Beynon Rae, *How Never to Be Tired* (New York: Bobbs-Merrill Company, 1954).

[35] Charles Swindoll, *Three Steps Forward, Two Steps Back* (Nashville: Thomas Nelson Publishers, 1980), pages 13–14.

[36] *Ibid.,* pages 18–19.

[37] "Got Any Rivers," copyright 1945. Renewal 1973 by Oscar Eliason. Assigned to Singspiration, Inc.

[38] William Golding, *Lord of the Flies* (New York: Capricorn Books, 1954, 1955), page 19.

[39] Michael Korda, *Power: How to Get It, How to Use It* (New York: Ballantine Books, 1975), page 219.

[40] *Ibid.,* pages 209–210. 209–210.

Index